THE CLASSICS OF WESTERN SPIRITUALITY

SCANDINAVIAN PIETISTS

Spiritual Writings from 19th-Century Norway, Denmark, Sweden, and Finland

Edited and with an Introduction
by Mark A. Granquist

Paulist Press
New York / Mahwah, NJ

Cover image: *Kvikkjokks kyrka*, the church in the Lapland village of Kvikkjokk, Sweden, where revivalist preacher Lars Levi Laestadius (1800–1861) grew up and where his elder half-brother served as pastor. Photograph copyright © by Nancy de Flon.

Permissions to reprint previously published material may be found on p. 281.

Cover design by Cynthia Dunne, www.bluefarmdesign.com
Book design by Sharyn Banks

Library of Congress Cataloging-in-Publication Data

Scandinavian pietists : spiritual writings from 19th-century Norway, Denmark, Sweden, and Finland / edited and with an introduction by Mark A. Granquist.
pages cm. — (The classics of Western spirituality)
Includes bibliographical references and index.
ISBN 978-0-8091-0618-9 (hardcover : alk. paper) — ISBN 978-1-58768-498-2 (ebook)
1. Pietism—Scandinavia—History—19th century. 2. Pietists—Scandinavia—Biography. I. Granquist, Mark Alan, 1957- editor.
BR1652.S34S23 2015
273`.7—dc23

2014045200

ISBN 978-0-8091-0618-9 (hardcover)
ISBN 978-1-58768-498-2 (e-book)

Published by Paulist Press
997 Macarthur Boulevard
Mahwah, New Jersey 07430

www.paulistpress.com

Printed and bound in the
United States of America

Contents

Contributor to This Volume

MARK A. GRANQUIST is Associate Professor of the History of Christianity at Luther Seminary, a position he has held since 2007. Prior to this he taught in the Religion Department at St. Olaf College, Northfield, Minnesota (1992–2000), and at Gustavus Adolphus College, St. Peter, Minnesota (2000–2007).

Granquist has served in parish ministry or Lutheran higher education since his ordination in the Evangelical Lutheran Church of America in 1988. He was pastor of youth and education at Bethel Lutheran Church, Rochester, Minnesota (1988–1992), and has served several times as an interim pastor in local congregations.

A 1979 graduate of St. Olaf College, Granquist received his MDiv from Yale University Divinity School in 1984, and his PhD degree from the University of Chicago Divinity School in 1992.

He serves as associate editor of the Luther Seminary journal *Word & World*, as editor of the *Journal of the Lutheran Historical Conference*, and has been active with the journal *Lutheran Quarterly*.

His prior publications include *Lutherans in America: A New History* (Fortress Press, 2014) and *The Augustana Story: Shaping Lutheran Identity in North America* (Fortress, 2008). He is one of the editors of the *Dictionary of Luther and the Lutheran Traditions* (Baker Academic), which will be published in 2016, and the author of many book chapters, articles, and essays, especially on the history of Lutherans in North America.

Introduction

A remarkable religious awakening took place in the Lutheran countries of northern Europe during the nineteenth century, in which the piety and power of the traditional Lutheran state churches were challenged and revitalized by new religious movements, both from within these countries themselves and from outside, especially from the great Anglo-American religious awakenings that were paralleling them. The Scandinavian world[1] was awash in new social, cultural, religious, and political ideas, and many of these trends can be seen in new and dynamic pieties that enlivened the existence of many people, from church leaders and aristocrats down to the common people. In many cases these new movements of spirituality constituted the initial wave in a profound transformation of Scandinavian countries, as well as among Scandinavian immigrants to the rest of the world, especially to North America. These awakening movements also empowered the common people in their struggle against the rigid forces that had traditionally held them in check, both in their churches and in their social and political lives, although this was not the central aim of the movements themselves. Northern European Lutheranism was both enlivened and challenged by new movements of piety that took their strongest hold among the ordinary laypeople of these countries; in most instances this produced newer forms of traditional Lutheranism, but in some instances these new movements went beyond the boundaries of Lutheranism to form new, non-Lutheran forms of Protestantism in the Scandinavian

1. This volume will use the term *Scandinavia* for the entire Nordic region, including Sweden, Norway, and Denmark, as well as Iceland and Finland. Certainly the contemporary country of Finland is distinct from the rest, both culturally and linguistically, but in the nineteenth century Finland was more closely tied to its traditional colonizer, Sweden, and the religious awakenings in Finland, though with many distinct aspects, were heavily influenced by the countries of Scandinavia.

world. This volume will survey and sample the spirituality of the nineteenth-century Lutheran awakening movements in Scandinavia.

CHRISTIANITY IN NORTHERN EUROPE

Northern Europe was the last portion of the European continent to become Christian, a process that ran roughly from the tenth century to the dawn of the Protestant Reformation in the sixteenth century. Christianity moved into Scandinavia through England and Germany, with missionaries working among the people, especially in Denmark. But the real impetus for the adoption of Christianity in the North came through the decisions and influence of various local kings, such as Olaf in Norway, who encouraged and coerced their populations to adopt the new Christian religion. In Iceland, with its rough proto-democracy, the Allthing (Parliament) decided for Christianity and for the suppression of the older Nordic paganism. It can be said that the official transition to Christianity in the North came by the end of the eleventh century, first in Denmark, Norway, and Iceland, with Sweden lagging a bit behind. The introduction of Christianity in Finland and the eastern Baltic came much later, through the colonizing efforts of Sweden and German states. The Swedish "crusade" to conquer Finland, along with the efforts of the missionary bishop Henry beginning in the middle of the twelfth century, officially established Christianity in Finland, though the penetration of the new religion into this area was slow. The form of Christianity brought to the North was generally the Western form of medieval Christianity under the papacy at Rome, although there were competing elements from Orthodox Christianity in the eastern Baltic regions.

Although official elements of Christianity, in the forms of bishoprics and parishes, were soon in place in the North, the spread of Christianity into the everyday consciousness of the people was slow, especially in remote, rural areas. Many elements of the older, pre-Christian religion remained strong, and ordinary people tended to merge the older religion and the new together into a creative synthesis that was in evidence as late as the Protestant Reformation. This was particularly true in Finland and the eastern Baltic countries, where Christianity was seen as the religion of the Swedish or German conquerors.

The formal elements of medieval Western Christianity, however, were quickly established in Northern Europe. During the twelfth century, three archbishoprics were eventually established in Scandinavia, at Lund, Nidaros (Trondheim), and Uppsala, along with many other institutions of medieval Western Christianity, including defined local parish units with resident priests. Even in far-away Greenland, a bishopric was founded that continued until the collapse of European settlement there in the fifteenth century. Monasteries and convents were also eventually founded, and they did much to enrich and strengthen Christian life and identity at the local level. It can be said that by the beginning of the sixteenth century the countries of Northern Europe were generally Christianized.

THE PROTESTANT REFORMATION

The Protestant Reformation of the Western church came into the North early in the sixteenth century, through Scandinavian students who went to study with Luther at the University of Wittenberg and through German Protestant theologians who made their way north, such as Johannes Bugenhagen, who was influential in the establishment of Lutheranism in Denmark. In Denmark, King Christian II began to move his country toward Lutheranism in the 1520s, and by 1540 the church in Denmark was transformed into an official Lutheran state church, the medieval church establishment having been transformed into an Evangelical Lutheran one. In Sweden, the upstart King Gustav Vasa, eager to consolidate his power and to free his country from the rule of Denmark, was also an early proponent of taking the Swedish church in a Protestant direction. Working with the reformers Olavus and Laurentius Petri, the Swedish king essentially took over the Swedish church establishment in a manner similar to that of King Henry VIII in England, using his control of the church to consolidate his royal power. Lutheran theology and liturgy were gradually introduced to Sweden, and a church assembly in 1544 ratified the switch to Lutheranism. In Swedish-controlled Finland, the reformer Michael Agricola spearheaded the introduction of Lutheranism in that country and translated the New Testament into Finnish. In Norway and Iceland, which were dominated by Denmark, the Reformation followed on the heels of the Danish example, although medieval Catholicism lingered for a time in the rural areas of Norway. By the middle of the sixteenth century, the Christian church structures in Scandinavia were solidly Lutheran, and the churches were working diligently to inculcate this reformed version of Christianity among the people. Despite pressures from the Roman Catholic Counter Reformation, especially in Sweden, Lutheranism took a firm hold in Scandinavia, and these northern countries assumed an important leadership role within European Lutheranism, especially during the difficult period of the Thirty Years' War in Germany (1618–48), when German Lutheranism was in danger of being militarily overrun.

From 1600 to about 1850, Lutheranism was virtually monolithic within the Scandinavian countries, a situation that became legal and official; laws were passed mandating Lutheranism as the only form of Christianity for the residents of these countries (a few Protestant foreigners were allowed limited religious freedom). The official Lutheran state churches were so closely tied to the royal governments as to be almost indistinguishable from them. Local pastors were essential civil servants, and beyond their spiritual role they also frequently functioned in governmental roles, including taking the census, keeping population and taxes rolls, and filling other civil functions. As with Lutheranism in Germany, the seventeenth century in Lutheran Scandinavia was known as the age of Lutheran Orthodoxy, in which the religious emphasis was on the development and definition of correctly orthodox Lutheran theology; correct doctrine was equated with doctrinal purity and correct faith. It was a period of time in which the clergy were religiously dominant, and laypeople were not encouraged to take up independent religious activities. Still, these centuries saw the development of a rich Lutheran spirituality in Scandinavia, especially through reading of approved devotional classics, such as Luther's *Catechisms* and Johan Arndt's *True Christianity*, and through a rich tradition of congregational hymn singing. Although later Lutherans did decry the "spiritual sterility" of the age of Lutheran Orthodoxy, within limits it did have a strong spirituality that would continue to contribute to

Scandinavian Lutheranism for centuries. Although the clergy and theological professors tightly controlled the doctrinal theology, the laity focused on the consolation of the Christian gospel, especially during the frequently hard times in which they found themselves.

PIETISM AND RENEWAL MOVEMENTS

Toward the end of the seventeenth century, a wave of reform and renewal began to move through the European Lutheran world, a part of the general wave of "religions of the heart" that touched most areas of European religion in the eighteenth century. In Lutheranism this aspect of the movement was known as *pietism*, and its beginning is usually dated to the publication in 1675 of a work entitled *Pia Desideria* by the German Lutheran pastor and theologian Philipp Jacob Spener. In this work, Spener lamented the low spiritual state of the Lutheranism of his day, both among pastors and laypeople, which he generally ascribed to the indifference of pastors to their congregations and to the emphasis of the Lutheran Orthodox theologians on true religion as substantially cognitive assent to "correct doctrine." Spener and his followers and successors sought an increased emphasis on conversion, Bible study, and spiritual living among pastors and people, and on a renewed push for elements of sanctification on the part of all.

Sanctification, or holy living, was (and still is) a controversial question among Lutherans. Luther's theology laid a heavy stress on the passive, imputed justification of the sinner, brought about by God through Jesus Christ and the Holy Spirit. One was "saved" apart from any human works or righteousness solely by the grace of God; human beings could not merit salvation on their own, or even cooperate with the divine work of redemption. In the essential phrase, one was "justified by grace through faith, apart from works of the law." However, this left open the question of the repeated biblical divine commands of believers to live a holy life and to strive for holy living, or sanctification. To some Lutheran theologians, especially many of the orthodox, the call to sanctification or "holy living" seemed to endanger the Lutheran stress on divine justification alone. These theologians suspected that talk about sanctification was a subversive way of restoring "works righteousness," or human moral efforts that led toward holy living, to Lutheranism. Other Lutheran theologians, including Martin Luther himself, were less worried about this, but rather worried that without a serious and sustained call to moral reform and holy living among the people, that church and society would decline into immorality.

To Spener and the Lutheran pietist leaders, this latter situation had already arisen among state church European Lutherans, barely 150 years after the Reformation. They saw the stress on faith as cognitive assent to "pure doctrine" as completely ignoring the biblical call to spiritual conversion and the moral amendment of life, which resulted in the poor state of religiosity they saw around them. They also implicitly laid blame for some of this condition on the structure of the state churches themselves; when pastors saw themselves as essentially civil servants and as preaching erudite (but sterile) sermons on fine points of doctrine, then it was inevitable that the people themselves, and their churches and societies, would slip into moral decay.

To reform the Lutheran churches, the pietists sought a renewal of preaching to push the people toward conversion and the moral amendment of their lives. They also sought to empower the laity themselves to work on these things, whether in the congregational worship setting or outside of it, in small-group meetings of morally serious Christians known as *conventicles.* Other Lutherans, especially significant portions of clergy and church leadership, strongly opposed these proposals, partly for the doctrinal concerns enumerated above, and partly because they feared that lay religious activity would veer into heresy, and that they themselves would lose religious control over the people. Within the pietist movement itself there were also divisions, between the "churchly" pietists, who sought to remain within the state church congregations and raise their moral level, and the "separatist" pietists, who felt that they must remove themselves from these "mixed" congregations of true and false believers and organize themselves in separate congregations constituted solely of "true" or converted believers. Although most Lutheran pietists (clergy and lay) did remain within the state churches, this was not always a comfortable existence for them because of the indifference or hostility of other church leaders toward their positions and concerns.

One other factor that directly influenced this eighteenth-century religious renewal in Scandinavia was the Moravians, who were pietistically inclined Protestants under the protection and leadership of Count Nikolas Ludwig von Zinzendorf. The Moravians, an amalgam of different Protestant groups in eastern Germany, were closely linked to the theology and devotional heritage of Lutheranism but were not structurally a part of it; rather, they saw themselves as simple Christians essentially transcending confessional boundaries. They also modeled Zinzendorf's distinctive spirituality and emphasis on mission. Where the Lutheran pietists tended toward an emphasis on moral introspection and penitence for sin, Moravian spirituality was more focused on the joy in the love of Jesus for the believers. Moravian spirituality also had distinctive emphases of contemplation on the wounds and blood of the crucified Christ, and a piety that at times verged on the mystical. Seeing themselves as the agents of Christian renewal and conversion of the world, Moravian missionaries were sent out to all corners of the world, Protestant pioneers in the great missionary expansion of the eighteenth and nineteenth centuries.

All three of these religious movements—Lutheran "churchly" pietism, radical separatist pietism, and Moravianism—moved into Scandinavia early in the eighteenth century and provided a profound influence (as well as controversy) for the Christian renewal movements there in the eighteenth and nineteenth centuries. The main spiritual and theological questions of these movements, including questions of sanctification, conversion, and the nature of church and society, were all present in their activities, as were questions about spirituality and the nature of the Christian life. Directly and indirectly, these renewal and revival movements challenged the established Scandinavian state churches. In Denmark and Norway, pietism moved into the Danish royal circles early in the eighteenth century, though a later reaction sharply limited lay religious activity and the use of conventicles. Prominent church leaders such as Bishop Eric Pontoppidan and the hymn writer Hans Adolf Brorson carefully introduced spiritual elements of churchly pietism into state church congregations. In Sweden and Finland, the official reception of pietism was more hostile, and church and state erected official barriers against it. But popular forms of pietism quickly moved into the country and were given a boost by Swedish prisoners of war who had been strongly influenced in Russian prison camps by the ministry of pietist pastors. Returning to Sweden by 1724, these former prisoners of war added to pietist circles already active in the country. Though the Scandinavian Lutheran church establishment was generally hostile toward pietism, a few officials and a significant number of pastors were influenced by the movement and were generally overlooked as long as their pietistic activities were kept to a modest level.

The spirituality of these three strains of renewal movements were related, but each had its own distinct elements to define it. The Lutheran churchly piety sought to carefully delineate the need for moral renewal and sanctification within the traditional limits of Lutheran theology, attempting to ensure that the theological primacy of justification was preserved. This form of piety stressed conversion and sanctification as a gradual process, worked out through the contrition of the sinner, the sinner's penance, and reliance on the saving work of Christ alone. This process, sometimes referred to as the "order of salvation" (*ordo salutis*), generally envisioned this process taking place within the Word and Sacrament ministry of the church. The radical pietists dispensed with the formal connection and insisted that once the individual was converted (often in a quick and emotional process, in contrast to what was common in the past), that believer would join together with others so transformed to form a pure and sanctified community of faith. This spirituality was often deeply otherworldly and established strict and often eschatological differences between the purified community of believers and the rest of the world (including the state churches), which were seen to be steeped in evil. Moravian piety was characterized by an intricate balance between the joyful acceptance of the saving work of Christ and a deep and often very mystical concentration on the marks of the physical suffering of Christ, especially his wounds and his blood. Moravian hymnody, which was very influential in eighteenth-century Scandinavia, expressed both these elements as well as a deeply felt attachment between Savior and believer that sometimes took on almost erotic overtones. Elements of all three spiritual traditions can be traced in the spirituality of the nineteenth-century awakening movements in Scandinavia. The last influential peace of the puzzle, the Anglo-American evangelical piety of the nineteenth century, would be added later.

By the end of the eighteenth century, these first three forms of piety would be well discernible throughout the Scandinavian lands, although they lived in some significant tension with state-church Lutheranism, which was general very suspicious or hostile to them. Awakened believers attempted to live quietly, not calling too much attention to themselves, and either sought the ministrations of sympathetic Lutheran pietist clergy or organized to meet independently of the church. The latter course of action was dangerous, as both state and church laws were crafted to expressly forbid laypersons from religious preaching, teaching, or even gathering independently of state church pastors. These so-called Conventicle Acts were not always equally enforced, but could at times bring pious believers into great difficulties with the law, and these restrictions remained on the books of most Scandinavian countries until the middle of the nineteenth century. There were outbreaks of radical pietist activity in places, often guided by self-appointed prophets, but civil authorities often dealt harshly with these religious disruptions. The Moravians remained a constant presence, especially in Denmark and southern Sweden, but generally were not harassed unless they provoked some sort of incident. Moravian piety sometimes melded together with Lutheran piety, and Moravian hymns especially were deeply appreciated and widely sung in Scandinavia, though often not in the formal Sunday worship services.

THE 19TH-CENTURY IN SCANDINAVIA

Unlike the previous several centuries, the nineteenth century was a time of great restlessness and change in the Scandinavian countries, change that affected political, social, economic, and cultural aspects of life, as well as the religious and spiritual realms. By the end of the nineteenth century, Scandinavia was transformed in ways that would scarcely have seemed possible to those living at the beginning of the century. Some of this change was occasioned by movements and developments within the North itself, but much of the change was brought about by outside influences streaming into Northern Europe from the rest of the continent and increasingly from North America. The great religious awakenings of the nineteenth century in Scandinavia were in many senses influenced by internal Lutheran developments as well as by traditions of pietism from previous centuries. But in many important ways, the renewal movements were also deeply influenced by Anglo-American Evangelical revivals, with pieties and spiritualities that reflected different and evolving traditions of Protestantism outside of Lutheranism.

Whereas the renewal activity in the eighteenth century had generally occurred inside of the structures of the Lutheran state churches or quietly avoided open confrontation with them, the nineteenth-century Scandinavian renewal movements were increasingly willing to push the established churches publicly or go outside of them when necessary. The first to challenge the authority of the church openly was Norwegian lay preacher Hans Nielsen Hauge (1771–1824). Hauge had a dramatic conversion experience in 1796 and began an itinerant career preaching wherever he could, usually open fields and farm houses, as churches were generally closed to him. Hauge ran afoul of church and civic authorities, and was imprisoned for seven years (1804–11) for violating laws restricting religious activities to clergy. Nevertheless, he ignited a popular (and democratic) religious uprising in Norway, where pious believers bypassed the state church congregations to worship in local "prayer houses" (*Bedehuser*). After Hauge's death in 1824, the movement continued and was supplemented by two further periods of revival, the Johnsonian revival in the 1850s and 1860s, led by Professor Gisle Johnson, and the "western revival" in western Norway, inspired by the writings of Swedish pietist leader Carl Olof Rosenius. These two revival movements challenged the official state church but did not seek to break with it. But later in the nineteenth century, new movements from outside Norway entered the country, bringing about new and separatist Protestantism; Methodist, Baptist, and Pentecostal congregations were formed, enabled by a change of laws in 1845 to allow for the establishment of congregations by "Christian dissenters."

In Denmark, the nineteenth century began with the trauma of being on the wrong side of the Napoleonic wars, which resulted in Denmark's losing control of Norway to Sweden. The older Moravian pietists were especially active in Denmark at the beginning of the century and would continue to be an active force. The older churchly Lutheran piety in Denmark continued into the new century, to be complemented by two new movements led by very different persons. The first movement was led by Danish Lutheran pastor Nicolai F. S. Grundtvig (1783–1872), whose distinctive awakening theology combined Danish nationalism with a stress on the "living word of God," which Grundtvig identified with the historic confession of faith of the Danish church, especially in the form of the Apostles' Creed. Though his theology was complex and at time controversial, he made a large impact in Denmark (as well as Norway) in the 1840s and 1850s. Grundtvig's most lasting contribution was in the writing of hymns, which remain very popular even today. A contemporary of his, Søren Kierkegaard, is well-known today, but in nineteenth-century Denmark he was particularly known as a religious critic and gadfly, and his positive spirituality was not particularly influential.[2] The other major figure of the Danish awakening was Vilhelm Beck (1829–1901), who revived the older Danish Lutheran conventicle movement, which was eventually organized into the "Inner Mission Movement." This movement organized and directed a religious awakening in Denmark that was located in small fellowship groups around the country, as well as social service and outreach programs. As in Norway, dissenting Protestant groups also made inroads in Denmark; the Mormons, who recruited very actively in Scandinavia, made their most converts in Denmark.

The religious awakening in Sweden was continued among different sources: the older churchly pietists, groups of Moravians, and a movement referred to as the "Readers" (*Läsare*), lay groups that met to read devotional materials aloud and to pray. Sometimes in bursts of enthusiasm these groups would come into conflict with

2. This dynamic is one reason that Kierkegaard is not included in this anthology; it was only with the revival of Kierkegaard's works in English translation in the middle of the twentieth century that his positive theological works became widespread.

state and church authorities, but in many places the local parish pastor left them alone unless they challenged his authority. One of the early figures in the awakenings in southern Sweden was the Lutheran pastor Henric Schartau (1757–1825), who represented a continuation of the older, churchly piety of previous generations and whose sermons achieved a wider circulation. Unlike in Norway or Denmark, however, Anglo-American evangelical awakening pushed into Sweden early, in the person of Rev. George Scott, a Methodist pastor sent from England to minister to expatriates in Stockholm during the 1820s. Scott quickly learned Swedish and began to preach a Methodist brand of revivalism in that country. Though Scott was eventually forced to leave Sweden in 1842, his young Swedish assistant, Carl Olof Rosenius (1816–68), took over the growing revival movement and became its leader. As a layperson, Rosenius's impact came, not through his preaching, as with Hauge, but through his devotional and literary efforts, and through his founding of a national religious organization to further the renewal, the National Evangelical Foundation (*Evangeliska Fosterlandsstiftelsen*). Rosenius sought a broadly conceived revival in Sweden and remained within Lutheranism and the state church of Sweden. However, his successor, Paul Peter Waldenström (1838–1917), came into doctrinal conflict with Lutheran authorities, and his followers soon left the Lutheran congregations to form their own independent ones, which led to the Swedish Mission Covenant. As in Norway, the Baptists and Methodists made sizable inroads into Sweden, and later a rather sizable Swedish Pentecostal movement formed. Many of these newer Anglo-American religious movements reached Scandinavia by means of emigrants who left for America, were converted to these new movements, and brought them back to Scandinavia. A constant interchange took place between the revival movements in Scandinavia and among the Scandinavian-American denominations, Lutheran or otherwise.

The revival movements in Finland are a complicated mixture of Swedish and Finnish influences. For over seven hundred years Finland was a part of Sweden, and there is still a sizable Swedish-speaking minority in Finland today, mainly in the western part. But linguistically and culturally most Finns remained distinct from Sweden, and after the Napoleonic wars Finland was taken from

Sweden and given to the Russians, which ruled it as a semiautonomous grand duchy within the Russian Empire. During the nineteenth century a revival of Finnish culture and nationalism took place that led to an independent Finland in the twentieth century. Religiously the Finns remain mostly Lutheran, with an Orthodox minority in the East, and eighteenth-century Finland had its awakening movements akin to those in Sweden. One of the first leaders of the Finnish awakening was Paavo Ruotsalainen (1777–1852), a Finnish-speaking peasant with a very limited education (he could read but not write), who improbably became a fervent and dynamic lay preacher and traveled widely in Finland. His followers demonstrated a deep piety combined with a nascent Finnish national identity. Another leader of the awakening in Finland and northern Sweden was Lars Levi Laestadius (1800–1861), a Swedish pastor in the north among the Sami (or Lapp) peoples. After a serious illness and conversion in the early 1840s, Laestadius began a powerful awakening movement there. His lasting influence is felt among his Finnish followers, whose Laestadian or "Apostolic" movement is noted by several distinct practices, including lay confession and absolution and lay preaching. The third Finnish awakening movement was headed by Fredrik Gabriel Hedberg (1811–93), who was born in west-central Finland. Like Laestadius, Hedberg was an ordained Lutheran pastor who was deeply dissatisfied with the level of piety within the Church of Finland. At first he was influenced by the awakened followers of Ruotsalainen's revivals, but broke with them on matters of theology and church structure and became the head of the Evangelical movement in Finland. These three strains of piety would remain fairly distinct within Finland.

The nineteenth century was also a time of great movement in Scandinavia, and millions of Scandinavians—eventually over a million from Norway and 1.2 million from Sweden—headed to North America in search of economic opportunities denied them back home. By the time this emigration became a mass movement, in the 1850s and 1860s, the official persecution of dissenters by the church and state had abated, so relatively few Scandinavians were departing because of overt religious persecution, though many who left were less than thrilled with the official state churches. But relatively few state church pastors were willing or interested in following the migrants to North America, and the few that did were generally oriented toward the awakening movements. These immigrants formed a number of linguistic-specific religious denominations among their compatriots in North America; these denominations were much more akin to the revival movements in Scandinavia than to the state churches and replicated the spirituality of their respective awakening movements. In Scandinavia, many of these movements remained nominally within the Lutheran state churches, but without the "umbrella" structure of the state church, these Scandinavian-American denominations often fragmented along the lines of their different nationalities and pieties. As we have seen, a sizable number left Lutheranism behind, forming separate Methodist, Baptist, Pentecostal, and Covenant denominations. A significant trans-Atlantic communication went on between renewal groups among Scandinavian-Americans and their compatriots in Europe, which lasted until the linguistic transition of the North American groups to the English language in the 1920s and 1930s. The spirituality of the nineteenth-century Scandinavian awakenings was also very important in North America.

Having briefly sketched the history and progress of these awakening movements, it is now important to examine in some detail the theology and spirituality of its various leaders as they are represented in this volume. This introduction will look at the various leaders of the awakening movements, by country, beginning with Norway.

NORWAY

The most important and influential leader of the Norwegian awakenings was Hans Nielsen Hauge (1771–1824). At first glance it might seem improbable that Hauge should become such an influential figure; he was a peasant farmer with a limited education, a wandering lay preacher and evangelist who was constantly harassed by the authorities, and his lengthy imprisonment (1804–11) resulted in his broken health and subsequent restrictions on his ability to preach. His actual activity as an itinerant lay preacher spanned only about eight years, from his conversion experience in 1796 to his imprisonment in 1804, yet without a doubt he was the single most important leader in the Norwegian awakening of the nineteenth century. He wrote a number of books and other literary efforts, but perhaps it was the narrative of his life and preaching that was ultimately the most influential.

At the beginning of the nineteenth century, the Lutheran Church of Norway was divided between the older orthodox and pietist movements and the newer religious rationalism of the Enlightenment coming out of Germany. Hauge himself found some comfort in older pieties, especially Johan Arndt's *True Christianity* and the devotional works of Bishop Eric Pontoppidan, but he found most of the Lutheran congregations of his day to be seriously deficient in spiritual emphasis. From all accounts Hauge was, as a young person, religiously serious and deeply concerned about the state of his soul. After a long period of self-examination, he experienced a religious breakthrough (or conversion) in 1796; while out plowing and singing an old spiritual hymn, he found himself overwhelmed by the experience of God's presence. He would later recall feeling that he had received a new light of understanding and that he was born anew of God's Holy Spirit and was put on the path to moral sanctification. This expresses the core of Hauge's spiritual understanding, one that the example of his life and experience modeled for his followers. Conversion or new birth was the vital key, but it was achieved only after a prolonged and serious examination of one's soul in preparation for the work of the Holy Spirit. Hauge was deeply skeptical of quick or easy conversions, finding them shallow and unconvincing. Equally as important as such a conversion, however, was the moral amendment of life that must necessarily flow from this experience and lead toward the sanctification of the believer. This was a strict and disciplined Christian life—which he constantly referred to as a "living faith"—that constantly wrestled with moral temptations and the inroads of the devil. Though his piety was rather austere in its rejection of moral temptations (drinking, dancing, gambling, and so forth), personally he was, by many accounts, a joyful and generous man, with a warm spirit. The later reputation of the Haugean movement as being joyless is probably due more to the influence of some of his later followers than it is to Hauge himself. Conversion did free the believer from the condemnation of God's law, but the believer was still obliged to follow the moral law as a means of showing and deepening this living faith.

Though he did experience a deep and profound conversion, Hauge was no mystic, and found himself at odds with the Moravians over their distinctive piety. Nor was Hauge a fanatic or separatist, although he was harshly opposed by many leaders of the state church, and he rejected any suggestion that he or his followers leave the Lutheran congregations. The Haugeans did establish their own network of separate prayer houses (*Bedehuser*) in which they gathered for regular prayer and worship, but they also generally attended the regular Lutheran worship and partook of the Lord's Supper there, which remained an important aspect of their spirituality.

Another important aspect of Hauge's life and ministry was his deep and practical concern for the spiritual, social, and economic improvement of the lives of the Norwegian people, especially the peasant class, of which he was a part. Himself industrious, hard-working, and inventive, he sponsored many pragmatic activities among the peasantry for their own economic advancement. And although Hauge himself was not politically active, the Haugean movement symbolized a new wave of Norwegian nationalism and of the self-determination of the Norwegian peasantry. Since the Middle Ages, Norway had been politically, religiously, and culturally dominated by Denmark and, in general, persons with deep attachments to Denmark had predominated among the ruling classes in Norway. At the beginning of the nineteenth century, Norwegian nationalism and self-determination were on the rise, and this resulted in the promulgation of the Norwegian constitution on May 17, 1814. In this light, the resentment of many of Hauge's followers over his treatment by religious officials can be interpreted as a rejection of the Dano-Norwegian ruling class and the longing for a religious movement that genuinely addressed the spirituality and religious desires of the Norwegian peasantry.

After Hauge's death in 1824, the movement he started was continued through his writings and example, as well as through a network of prayer houses and leaders throughout the country; some local pastors were sympathetic to this movement and cooperated with it, but much of the official church was still hostile to it. During the 1830s and 1840s the renewal movement of N. F. S. Grundtvig from Denmark made considerable inroads in Norway among the Lutheran clergy and church officials, but it did not have much in the way of popular support and soon faded. But there were also problems within the awakening movements at this time; though Hauge had urged his followers to remain in the Lutheran congregations, Baptist theology and rejection of infant baptisms made strong inroads among them. The cultural and religious division between church leaders and those in the awakening movements threatened to worsen this division. The man who managed to overcome these problems and continue the awakening in Norway was Gisle Johnson (1822–94).

Johnson was a striking contrast to Hauge. Johnson's family was solidly middle class, and he had a number of ancestors who were Lutheran pastors. Johnson studied for the ministry at the newly established University of Oslo, which was dominated by religious rationalism, and he also pursued further theological study in Germany. Johnson eventually accepted a position as a theological professor at Oslo, in which he continued the rest of his life. But in his student years he was also deeply influenced and guided by awakened pastors such as W. A. Wexsels and G. A. Lammers, who assisted him through a crisis of faith and toward a spiritual renewal. Johnson's experience was not as sudden or dramatic as that of Hauge, but it was deeply held and influential, nevertheless.

Johnson's primary influence on the religious life of Norway was felt through the life and service of generations of Norwegian Lutheran pastors who were trained and inspired by his personal witness of faith. Johnson himself did have a direct influence as a preacher in the great national awakening movement in Norway in the 1850s; he traveled and spoke widely during the so-called Johnsonian revivals at this time, but after about 1860 his health no longer permitted these activities. In the 1860s and 1870s, however, he was instrumental in two important tasks: first, guiding the elements of the awakening movement away from separatism and toward continuing affiliation with Lutheranism; and second, developing institutional means to structure and continue the awakening movements. He developed a theological rationale for lay preaching (the "emergency principle") whereby renewal preaching could be maintained in those parishes whose resident pastor was hostile toward the awakening, and he was also influential in developing the Norwegian institutions for mission, both at home and around the world. The latter, especially, came to be a distinctive element of the Norwegian awakening.

Johnson was deeply committed to traditional Lutheran theology, and his own theology and spirituality were very important in modeling how such an awakening movement could be accomplished within the formal boundaries of that theology. He continued many of Hauge's themes, especially the need for conversion, sanctification, and a "living faith," but with his formal theological background, he was able to demonstrate how these ideas could be integrated into the confessional theology of Lutheranism. In doing so he made it possible for many pastors and church leaders to join the lay awakening by overcoming their worries about aspects of the earlier lay awakening movements. His theological explanations of the doctrine of sanctification were especially important; from the beginnings of Lutheran pietism this had been an area of concern, and he was able to define and defend the idea of sanctification within the bounds of Lutheran confessional theology. The call to "holy living," so integral to Hauge's preaching, was continued and deepened in Johnson's preaching and writing.

Hauge ignited the awakenings among the people early in the century, while Johnson solidified its place within the clergy and Lutheran congregations. The third figure of the awakening in Norway was Nils J. J. Laache (1831–92), whose literary and devotional efforts brought the theology and spirituality of the revivals into countless Norwegian homes. He was educated for the ministry, but served as the secretary of the Oslo Inner Mission society until 1864; he was a parish pastor from then until 1884, and after that bishop of Trondheim. The symbolism of this latter appointment is striking: a prominent leader of the awakening movement appointed to one of the premier positions of formal authority within the Church of Norway, something that would have been unthinkable generations before.

Laache was primarily known, however, as author and compiler of devotional materials for use in the home; his *Devotions for the Home* was so widely distributed in Norway (and in English translation in North America) that it went through eight different editions between 1883 and 1922. Laache was also important for translating and popularizing the devotional writings of Swedish awakening leader Carl Olof Rosenius in Norway. Rosenius represented a newer form of awakening spirituality, one that was influenced by Anglo-American models, especially Methodism. His understanding of conversion and awakening did not necessitate the dark and prolonged period of struggle that Hauge had envisioned; rather Rosenius saw conversion as a joyful breakthrough and reception of God's grace. It was through the efforts of Laache that such a spirituality of awakening was introduced widely within the homes of Norway.

DENMARK

The situation of the spiritual movements in nineteenth-century Denmark was in some respects close to that of Norway, but because of the influence of rather unique individual leaders and thinkers, the movements for spiritual awakening in Denmark developed along some very distinctive and original paths. Denmark's spiritual progression was much like that of the other Scandinavian countries, with pietist and Moravian movements entering the Church of Denmark in the eighteenth century; the Moravians were particularly influential in this country. Yet even by objective standards, church life in Denmark at the beginning of the nineteenth century was at a relatively low ebb. Enlightenment rationalism from Germany was particularly influential among the bishops and clergy, while levels of church attendance and standards of personal morality were low. This picture (as with the other countries) is sometimes exaggerated by the leaders of the spiritual renewal movements, but there are a number of contemporary accounts that corroborate it. As well, the Danish psyche was thrown into upheaval by the loss of Norway in 1815 (given to Sweden to punish the Danes for being on the losing side of the Napoleonic wars) and later by the loss of Schleswig-Holstein to Prussia after a short war in 1864. Not only the Danish church but many other levels of society needed to be renewed.

One of the major figures in the early nineteenth-century Church of Denmark was Jakob Peter Mynster (1775–1854), a Danish theological professor and bishop. Mynster saw the problems with religious rationalism and sought (with some success) to bring about the revitalization of Danish Lutheranism, although he himself was no pietist and was strongly opposed to conventicles and lay preaching. Mynster strongly represented the view of the official state church, the so-called *Centrum* party in Denmark. It was this close linkage to the official church and the Danish state that caused Søren Kierkegaard (1813–55), Mynster's one-time confirmand, eventually to attack him as the symbol of everything in official Christianity that was counterfeit and false. Kierkegaard's attack on official Danish Christianity caused a great controversy in Denmark in the 1850s, but his positive theological views had little contemporary impact—nothing compared to his impact in the twentieth century.

The first major leader of spiritual renewal in nineteenth-century Denmark was another distinctive theologian and church leader, Nikolai Frederik Servein Grundtvig (1783–1872). In an age of many original theological minds, Grundtvig must be numbered as one of the most unusual of them all. Born into an orthodox Lutheran pastoral household, Grundtvig studied theology at the University in Copenhagen in 1803. Educated in the prevailing theological rationalism of the day, Grundtvig decided early on in his studies that this form of Christian theology was inadequate at best, but he was not sure with what he could replace rationalism. For a while Grundtvig explored the new movement of Romanticism, as had Mynster, but both eventually rejected this approach (although there may well be traces of this in Grundtvig's theology). After a stinging attack on the official state church in a trial sermon in 1810 entitled "Why Has the Word of the Lord Disappeared from His House," Grundtvig found it very difficult to find a parish position or even a place to preach. He developed a literary career instead and even continued these activities after finally getting a parish position in 1821. Though he had been formulating elements of his positive theology ever since his break with Romanticism, his maturing theology—his "church doctrine" from the middle of the 1820s—began to have an impact in Denmark (and later in Norway).

Grundtvig came to the realization of his "matchless discovery," a theological transformation in his understanding of faith and the nature of the church, and began to work out its implications. Grundtvig was such a creative and nuanced theologian that any attempt to summarize his work is bound to be inadequate, but in short, this discovery came about through a new way of examining the "living word" of faith, the living Word of God. Following Martin Luther's understanding of the Word of God as any part of the Christian proclamation that "pushes Christ," Grundtvig came to believe that the ultimate locus of the living Word of God was not in the Scriptures themselves (though these were important). Rather, the Word of God was located in the historic confession of faith by the church; for Grundtvig this was essentially located in the baptismal profession of faith, the Apostle's Creed, which contained the essence of God's Word, faithfully proclaimed by the church through the centuries. In some respects this was raising the sacramental proclamation of the gospel in baptism and the Lord's Supper above the written Word of God in the Scriptures, which was both innovative and controversial. Coming out of all this is his second main idea, the notion of the church as a folk church, a church of the people. In this sense then, the Spirit of God is to be found in the midst of the faithful people, the Danes, as they gather for worship and praise. In Grundtvig's understanding, then, to build up the Danish people was to build up the church of God. Eventually he became a strong advocate of social, cultural, and educational efforts to build up the state of the Danish people, including educational institutions known as folk high schools.

Grundtvig's spirituality was, then, strongly invested in this understanding of the living Word of God and its embodiment in the worship life of the Danish folk church. Unlike the other awakening movements, Grundtvig was not an advocate of a discernible conversion experience or of a moral denial of certain cultural elements. At its best, Grundtviganism is a joyful affirmation of all that is best in human life and in the worship of the Christian community. The basis of his piety might be said to be "organic," growing out of the perhaps innate goodness in the people, a goodness given by the Creator to his creations, and a goodness it is the duty of the church to inculcate and grow in the lives of the believers.

This theology came to have a strong impact on various elements of Danish society in the nineteenth century. This is, in part, by means of his preaching and devotional writings, but perhaps above all else it is in his poetry and hymnody that Grundtvig has had his most profound impact. In hymns such as "O Day Full of Grace," "Built on a Rock," and "God's Word Is Our Great Heritage," among hundreds of others, Grundtvig came to influence almost all areas of Danish society and religion. Grundtvig was, however, not a supporter of the traditional pietist movements in Denmark; he objected to their separate conventicles and lay preaching, and they deeply distrusted his views on the Word of God and found his lack of emphasis on conversion inadequate. Though he was very influential, his positions came to define only one section of the Danish church; the officially oriented *Centrum* occupied one end of the spectrum, while the pietists came to define the other. It is ironic that in trying to emphasize the faith of the whole of the Danish people, he ended up defining a faction within it.

The man who would come to lead and define the pietist Inner Mission section of the Danish awakening was Vilhelm Beck (1829–1901). The son of a Danish Lutheran pastor, Beck was raised in an atmosphere of religious rationalism, a stance that he inherited both at home and at the University in Copenhagen. Though he studied theology, he did not initially intend to enter the ministry; during his studies he became disenchanted with the prevailing rationalism but was unsure which way to turn. Reading Kierkegaard's *The Present Moment* in 1855 further unsettled him, though he realized he could never be the kind of ideal Christian that Kierkegaard presented. Reluctantly he was ordained in 1855 so as to assist his father, but his religious confusion continued; he was moving ever closer to conversion, but like Augustine the closer he got to this point the more anxious he became. Finally by 1859, he came to his conversion experience, and it changed him as a man and as a pastor, a transformation that was visible to his parishioners and friends. Beck followed in the classic pietist pattern of shunning worldly amusements while preaching powerful awakening sermons that gathered a wide audience, and brought some of his friends to their own conversions.

Beck was called to a succession of larger parishes and eventually became the leading voice of the awakening movement in nineteenth-century Denmark. Much like the similar movement in Norway, some Danish Christians established their own Inner Mission society in 1853; Beck became associated with this movement in 1861 and soon became its acknowledged and widely revered leader. The Danish Inner Mission sought to raise up lay preachers and colporteurs (traveling persons who distributed Bibles and religious tracts), to encourage small group conventicles, and eventually to form their own folk schools, parallel to those of the Grundtvigians. The Inner Mission also gradually began work among the unchurched in the cities and among sailors. Beck also directed the groups' publications, and volumes of his sermons and devotional materials were collected in books; toward the end of his life he published his *Memoirs*, which had a large circulation.

Much like Hauge in Norway, Beck's strongest influence in Denmark came through his own preaching, personal influence, and leadership of the Inner Mission; his writings show a heartfelt Christianity, but they were not his primary forms of influence. Unlike his Danish contemporaries Grundtvig and Kierkegaard, whose theology and spirituality were startlingly original, Beck's theology and spirituality were not noticeably distinctive. Beck demonstrated the best of the spiritual aspects of a classical pietist awakening and was a powerful influence during his years, so it is probably understandable that his *Memoirs*, the story of his life and his conversion, have achieved the most lasting influence. Under Beck, the pietist wing of the Danish Lutheran church was renewed and strengthened and became an important spiritual force in nineteenth-century Denmark.

SWEDEN

The spiritual revival in nineteenth-century Sweden developed along lines similar to those already seen in Norway and Denmark, but as it progressed it took on new features not seen in those countries, including a formal division within the movements between those who would retain a formal adherence to Lutheranism and those who went in a free-church direction, a fairly sizable group of Mission Friends, Methodist, Baptists, and Pentecostal Christians. The majority of those in the awakening movements still remained within the Lutheran Church of Sweden, but a growing influence in Sweden of Anglo-American Protestant movements was discernible as the century went along.

Eighteenth-century Sweden was marked with the influence of three groups of Christian revival movements: the churchly pietists within the state church, scattered groups of radical or separatist pietists, and the Moravians. The influence of the Moravians faded during the century, however, and the separatists were scattered and oppressed by officials from both church and state. Pietism within the Church of Sweden was maintained in scattered parishes by sympathetic clergy, but they too often fell into disfavor with the authorities. Though religious rationalism was not a widespread phenomenon, by most accounts the spiritual condition in Sweden toward the beginning of the nineteenth century was fairly dire. Immorality was rampant, fueled by widespread abuse of alcohol, some of which was brewed and distilled by state church pastors.

The first major figure of the Swedish awakenings in the nineteenth century was really a transitional figure between the older and new centuries. Henric Schartau (1757–1825) was a state church pastor from southern Sweden, whose influence was largely felt in his home territory of southern Sweden around Lund and Malmö and eventually into the southwest, in the vicinity of Göteborg (Gothenburg). Schartau's parents died when he was young, and he was raised by middle-class relatives in an atmosphere that was religiously relaxed and rationalistic. Schartau attended the University at Lund to study theology, but was himself religiously confused and searching until he was twenty, when a conversion experience during a communion service gave him a spiritual way forward. He became a pastor in the Church of Sweden, eventually settling into a permanent position at Lund, from which he had a growing influence on the pastors and parishes around him in southern Sweden. Schartau's major influence was as a preacher and teacher in Lund; though he did not hold an academic position, his catechetical classes were well attended by many people, including theological students. The movement he inspired, which became known as the Schartauan revivals, was driven by many of these theological students who became pastors in Lutheran parishes in southern and southwestern Sweden. This revival was sometimes strongly opposed by other church officials, especially the bishop of Göteborg, who constantly harassed the Schartauan pastors. But the revivals lasted into the twentieth century and had a long-lasting effect on these areas of Sweden.

Early in his ministry, Schartau was influenced by the subjective and emotional piety of the Moravians; eventually he moved away from them, although his spirituality continued their stress on a close and personal relationship with Christ, to which he added a pietist understanding of sanctification and the Christian moral life. Following the path of the older churchly pietism, Schartau described conversion and rebirth as a process, the order of salvation (*ordo salutis*), the way in which God gradually enlightens the mind of the believer through confidence in his Word and leads the believer to the new life. Though this process does have a cognitive or intellectual bent to it, this was only an initial step; ultimately the believer had to come through this to a full acceptance of the living power of God in his or her life. This generally orderly process moves gradually from one state to another to achieve the end result. Schartau's sermons embody this spiritual approach, although the limitations of reading a printed sermon do belie the obvious power and influence that his delivery was said to have had.

Other revivals began in the north of Sweden, especially among the pietists known as Readers (*Läsare*). Some state church pastors were sympathetic to this movement, notably Pehr Brandell (1781–1841), who influenced future awakening leaders such as Lars Levi Laestadius and Carl Olof Rosenius (1816–68). Rosenius became perhaps the best-known figure of the Swedish awakening and had a profound influence not just in Sweden but throughout Scandinavia. He grew up as the son of a pastor in northern Sweden, in the area where the Readers were active. Active from a young age as a lay preacher, he began to study for the ministry at the University at Uppsala, but financial pressures, poor health, and discouragement at the low state of Christianity among the students caused him to discontinue his studies. Eventually Rosenius went to Stockholm, where he came under the influence of English Methodist preacher George Scott, who had his own ministry in the Swedish capital. Rosenius became Scott's assistant, and when Scott was forced to leave Sweden, he took over that ministry. Deciding that he would not become an ordained pastor, Rosenius continued his preaching and built his influence through literary and publishing efforts as well. Gradually the initially hostile public reception toward this midcentury awakening movement softened, and many in the capital and the nation were affected by his message. His powerful hymns became an important part of this awakening in partnership with other hymn writers and composers, including Oscar Ahnfeldt and Carolina Sandell-Berg. Rosenius structured the awakening into a national phenomenon through the establishment of the National Evangelical Foundation (*Evangeliska Fosterlandsstiftelsen*), through his influential publication *The Pietist* (*Pietisten*), and through his devotion writings. Though he could be critical of the state church, he remained a staunch Lutheran and urged his followers to stay in the church and work to revive it from within.

Rosenius's spirituality combines elements of the older Lutheran pietism of the Readers with the new Anglo-American evangelicalism that he had learned from Scott. From Lutheran pietism Rosenius took the bedrock confidence in the justification of the believer solely through the grace of God, the corresponding need for a new birth of the believer in Christ, and the urge for the moral amendment of life (sanctification). The Anglo-American influence on Rosenius is seen most profoundly in his understanding of the nature of the new birth and transformation that come to the believer. Older forms of Lutheran piety, such as that of Schartau, saw the process of rebirth as a lengthy and often sober process of self-examination in which the believer comes to a full realization of God's saving work. But Rosenius saw the process of transformation as quicker and more joyous than perhaps the earlier pietists did; the transformation of the believer could well be a short process whereby he or she could come to faith and an amendment of life. Faith, as trust in God, was the core of this new life, which could be strengthened through the sacraments of baptism and the Lord's Supper, through devotion and prayer, and by means of the moral transformation of the believer. Though his own personal spiritual life was at times beset by doubts and difficulties, he was generally able to maintain a joyful trust in the grace of God, and this attitude is prevalent in his preaching and writings.

The third and final major figure in the nineteenth-century Swedish awakening is Paul Peter Waldenström (1838–1917), a Lutheran pastor who served as Rosenius's successor as editor of *Pietisten* and as a leader in the awakening circles. Born in the north, he came to a gradual conversion in the south, at Kalmar, influenced by pietism along the lines of Schartau. Waldenström initially followed the lines of a Rosenian spirituality, but he was increasingly critical of the established church and aspects of Lutheran theology, as seen in his early satirical work *Squire Adamsson* (1862). Increasingly, he represented one wing of the National Evangelical Foundation, one that was distancing itself from the Church of Sweden and moving toward separation from it, something that Rosenius would never have allowed. Waldenström came into theological conflict with Lutheranism in the 1870s, rejecting Lutheran theological understandings of the atonement and justification, moving away from Lutheran creeds and confessions, and toward an Evangelical biblicism. This wing eventually did form a separate organization, the Swedish Mission Covenant (1878), along these lines; though Waldenström and most of the members of the Covenant did retain nominal ties to the Church of Sweden, they were essentially a new and separate denomination within Sweden. Not all the Covenant followed his new understanding of the atonement, but they came to reject the creeds and Lutheran confessional writings as normative; their cry, "Where is it written?" points toward a sole reliance on the Bible in spiritual and doctrinal matters.

Waldenström's spirituality continues some of the themes of Rosenius, especially in the joy of the believer in the new life in Christ and the traditional themes of the amendment of life and sanctification. Moving away from the traditional forensic (legal) understanding of Christ's sacrifice on the cross that satisfied God's judgment, he instead emphasized the crucifixion as a demonstration to the believer of the love of God and of God's salvation. Similarly, he discarded the Lutheran interpretation of the Pauline doctrine of justification as an alien (outside the believer) work of God; rather, the true justification was brought out of the human person as a part of their new life in Christ. Interestingly, though he was a highly educated pastor, Waldenström's spirituality reflects a deepening hostility to "the world," a sharp criticism of the organized church, and a strong confidence in the ability of the lightly educated laity to come to the truths about God and faith through direct study of the Bible. It is an interesting contrast to view the parallel work of Waldenström and his contemporary Gisle Johnson in Norway; Johnson found a way to structure the revivals in such a way that they remained theologically within Lutheranism, whereas Waldenström did not chose to do so.

FINLAND

The nineteenth century in Finland was a time of trouble and renewal. Though the country had been a part of Sweden, it was ceded to Russia after the Napoleonic wars. Finland had some autonomy within the Russian Empire, but the century saw the rise of Finnish nationalism in which Finland attempted to assert its own cultural independence from both Sweden and Russia. There had been pietist awakenings in the second half of the eighteenth century, mainly among the laypeople of the country, which intensified into the nineteenth. The newfound cultural and religious freedom inspired the quest for conversion and religious activity, but the awakening in nineteenth-century Finland was also marked by factionalism as well as by spiritual and theological disputes among the groups. The revival movement in nineteenth-century Finland had at least four major groups, associated with four different leaders: Paavo Ruotsalainen, Lars Levi Laestadius, Henrik Renqvist, and Fredrik Hedberg, as well as numerous internal divisions and other groupings. Though these groups contributed to the spiritual vitality of Finland, they also often quarreled with one another. The official Lutheran Church of Finland was also renewed by these religious movements but was also often in conflict with them.

Perhaps the most influential figure in the awakening movement was the most unusual of all of them. Paavo Ruotsalainen (1777–1852) was a poor farmer and lay preacher from central Finland whose education was so limited that although he could read, he never learned to write; what we have of his literary productions are letters that he dictated to others to record. Born into a poor farming family, he never achieved much in the way of economic stability. Participating in the local awakening movements, he was deeply troubled about the state of his soul until, with the help of older and wiser pious lay leaders, he achieved a breakthrough, and the assurance of faith that he had sought. Ruotsalainen was active in the lay awakening movement, and after some conflicts with other leaders, he eventually gained a following of his own and became one of the key leaders of the awakening. From accounts he seems to have been an especially effective speaker, and he traveled throughout his region of Finland to preach and counsel the believers. He maintained a status as the spiritual leader of this movement until his death.

Ruotsalainen's own spirituality is, like the rest of his life, distinctly his own and at times difficult to characterize. In differing from some of the other elements of the awakening, which sought immediate release and powerful emotions of joy from their conversion, Ruotsalainen emphasized that the point of conversion was the knowledge of salvation rather than the feeling occasioned by the event. He saw conversion as the beginning of the Christian life, but he also saw that this life would continue to be one of spiritual struggle and occasional periods of darkness. What he emphasized most of all was, in his most celebrated phrase, the need for an "inward knowledge of Christ" to sustain the believer through life and the struggles of faith. In conflict with some of the other groups, Ruotsalainen laid an increased stress on the necessity of continuing personal struggle toward holiness and sanctification throughout the life of the believer, a stance that caused some others in the awakening movements to charge him with legalism. Though a layperson working in a movement that was largely lay led, and although at times some officials of the Church of Finland actively opposed the renewal, Ruotsalainen was not alienated from the Lutheran church and urged his followers to participate in the sacraments of the official church.

The second major figure of the Finnish religious revival was Lar Levi Laestadius (1800–1861), whose ministry was located in the far north of Scandinavia, where Finland, Sweden, and Norway come together. Initially, Laestadius exercised his ministry mainly among the indigenous Sami (Lapp) people, but his influence soon spread into areas of northern Finland, and the Laestadian (or Apostolic Lutheran) movement became predominantly Finnish. Even though he was a university-trained pastor and scientist (he was a renowned botanist), his powerful preaching and spiritual example ignited a lay-awakening movement in the north, a movement that is known for its distinctive religious practices, including lay confession and absolution.

Born in the far northern part of Sweden, Laestadius was religiously influenced at an early age by the Reader movement through his mother. After attending the University at Uppsala, he returned to take a parish in the north, a region where alcoholism and general immorality was rampant. By all accounts he was a serious and dutiful pastor, but it was only after about fifteen years in the parish that he came to his conversion experience, as a result of an illness. His preaching and influence spread throughout the north through collections of his sermons and through a short-lived publication, *The Voice of One Crying in the Wilderness.* Collections of his sermons are still actively used among contemporary Laestadians, both in Scandinavia and in North America. As a powerful promoter of temperance and abstention from the use of alcohol, he had a major influence in this movement in Scandinavia. Though the religious authorities received constant complaints about him, they generally supported his work among the people. In later years of his life, he struggled to keep his movement from splintering; this powerful movement and its lay-preacher leaders had a tendency to go in divergent directions.

As seen in his sermons and writing, Laestadius was a powerful and, at times, intimidating presence whose sharp and unvarnished message of repentance, confession, and absolution, delivered directly to his listeners, sometimes overwhelmed them. He was a prophet, confronting his hearers directly with their need to change their lives and come to the new birth in Christ. For the Laestadians this entailed more than just listening to sermons and reading the Bible and devotional materials; instead it centered around confession, forgiveness of sins, and absolution. These actions were often taken one on one, with lay believers pronouncing the absolution for each other without the need of clergy, and were vital in the continuing struggle to maintain faith and holiness. Laestadius taught that the awakened believer must constantly fight against the loss of faith with prayer, study of Scripture, confession, and the living of a moral life. A quick, emotional conversion was not deep enough to maintain faith over the long run.

The third of the major Finnish leaders was another pastor, Fredrik Gabriel Hedberg (1811–93), whose ministry was located in west-central Finland and who is known as the "father" of the Evangelical movement in that country. He studied for the ministry and was ordained as a Lutheran pastor, but doubts nagged him about the state of his soul and his worthiness for the office of ministry. Eventually he came to his own experience of renewal, but when he started preaching this rebirth in his parishes, he ran into trouble with church authorities, who attempted to hinder his work. Though his initial religious experience was with the awakening leaders such as Ruotsalainen, eventually Hedberg came into conflict with some of their theological emphases and his path diverged from them. Hedberg became close to the Swedish revival leader Rosenius, and their evangelistic approach was quite similar; in 1873 Hedberg helped establish the Lutheran Evangelical Association in Finland along the lines of the NEF in Sweden. He remained active in parish ministry until the end of his long life.

Hedberg's differences with the awakening movement in Finland highlight the aspects of his own distinctive spirituality. He believed that the emphasis by Ruotsalainen and others in the awakening movement on continuing the struggle of faith and the need of an amendment of life was actually undercutting the proclamation and reception of the grace of God as it was proclaimed in the gospel. Hedberg believed that personal certainty in one's salvation came through the objective declaration of grace and justification from God, a declaration that one found in the Word of God and the sacraments. One did not come to this through an emotional reaction of contrition and sorrow, but through the justification that was promised by God through Christ's sacrifice on the cross. Hedberg was wary of forms of legalism and works righteousness that he feared were creeping into the renewal movements in both Finland and Sweden, and instead he stressed the joy that the assurance of grace and justification brought to the believer.

The various renewal movements in Finland were a great boost to the religious life of the country and added to the nationalistic fervor that was awakened in the nineteenth century. Certainly this wave of religiosity affected many areas of the country, and both the Lutheran state church in Finland and Finnish-American denominations were greatly strengthened. Unlike Sweden, Finland did not suffer large losses to the new, non-Lutheran denominations, but the awakening movements in Finland were greatly fragmented internally, more so than in the other three countries. All the awakening groups, but especially the Apostolics (Laestadians), divided into a number of different and competing factions, albeit still within Lutheranism.

HYMNODY AND THE SCANDINAVIAN AWAKENING

One of the perennial and central aspects of Lutheran spirituality is its tradition of hymn writing and hymn singing, which for many Lutherans is the core of their personal faith. As a way to encourage active lay participation in worship, Martin Luther dramatically increased the opportunities for the congregation to take part musically by generally making music and hymnody a central part of worship, having the congregation participate in the service music, and translating old hymns and writing new ones. This change brought about a great expansion of Lutheran hymnody in the sixteenth and seventeenth centuries and produced many hymns that continue to be sung into the present. During the difficult period of the early seventeenth century, these troubles inspired some of the greatest Lutheran hymns ever produced.

Scandinavians are sometimes known (even notorious) for their emotional reticence, but it is often in their hymns that they can give full expression to their religious feelings and aspirations. A rich tradition of Lutheran hymnody in Scandinavia exists from the Reformation onward, and it came to express the people's deepest spirituality, both individually and as nations. As a result of the stress on literacy in the Lutheran Reformation, increasing numbers of people could read, and besides the Bible and devotional literature, most households and many individuals eventually owned *Psalmbooks* (hymnals), which were used for corporate and individual devotions. Changing hymnals and introducing new ones, which was always fraught with peril, at times occasioned fervent national debate. The circumstances of Hans Nielsen Hauge's conversion illustrate the spiritual role of hymns in this culture; while out plowing a field, he was singing an old spiritual hymn (from memory) and experienced his religious breakthrough.

Though many of the older Scandinavian Lutheran hymns were originally meant for use in public worship, they quickly became a part of the individual piety of many groups and individuals. These older hymns are sometimes categorized as more "objective" and corporate, speaking of what God has done for human persons, and the response of the community of believers. In many parts of Scandinavia weather and distance often made it impossible for people to get to the Sunday worship in their parish churches, and the more pious gathered in homes to read the Bible and devotional literature, and to sing hymns. This also happened with groups like the Readers, who were disaffected from their local parishes due to spiritual differences with the local pastor.

When pietism and Moravianism reached eighteenth-century Scandinavia, they brought with them a new kind of hymnody that was generally a more emotionally expressive and subjective appeal to the faith of the individual believer. These hymns concentrated on the spiritual aspects of the individual believer, their journeys of faith, and their relations with God. The new Moravian hymnody, with its devotional stress on contemplating the blood and wounds of Christ, and its mystical (almost erotic) sense of oneness with God, represented a major transformation from the older objective hymns of corporate devotion. Though many church leaders and hymnal editors attempted to keep the two strains of hymnody separate (hymns for public worship and hymns for personal devotion), this was often an artificial distinction, and a division that was usually impossible to maintain.

During the nineteenth century Protestantism witnessed an explosion of new hymns and hymn writers, especially in the Anglo-American world. The revival movements in Scandinavia mirrored this trend and were strongly influenced by the new forms of hymnody and song that came from English and North American sources. Methodist, Baptist, and Pentecostal hymns, especially those by the Wesleys, Ira Sankey, and Fanny Crosby, became well known in Scandinavia alongside their own hymn traditions. The mass immigration of Scandinavians to North America furthered the entry of this music into Scandinavia; Scandinavian Americans translated many of these new hymns into their own languages and sent them back over the Atlantic to their home countries.

Though influences from the past and from sources outside of Scandinavia were important to nineteenth-century Scandinavian hymnody, this movement was, in the end, an independent development, building on these influences and adapting them for their own new hymns. Hundreds of different Scandinavian hymn writers and composers collaborated to produce thousands of new hymns, many of which deeply expressed and represented the new renewal movements in their countries. Many new hymnals and hymn collections were published to supplement (or replace?) the official state church *Psalmbooks*, and the newspapers and journals of the awakening movements often published new revival hymns in their pages. The hymns of the new revival movements became a key element, if not *the* key element, in the dissemination of their message. The hymns and spiritual songs obviously reflected the moods and the spirituality of their various writers; they include the folk church emphases in the hymns of N. F. S. Grundtvig, the joyful gospel hymns of Carl Olof Rosenius and Carolina Sandell-Berg, the deep personal introspection of hymns by Wilhelmi Malmivaara and Lars Oftedal, and the celebrations of God's creation in hymns by Carl Boberg and Valdimir Briem. Some of these hymns have become a part of standard Christian hymnody, especially Carl Boberg's "O Mighty God" (eventually translated as "How Great Thou Art"), the hymns of Grundtvig such as "O Day Full of Grace" and "Built on a Rock," and the hymns of Carolina Sandell-Berg, especially "Children of the Heavenly Father" and "Day by Day."

One important aspect of the nineteenth-century Scandinavian awakening was the way in which it democratized the religious expressions of the people. No longer was piety and spirituality the sole possession of male clergy and church leaders, but much of the life and vitality of these movements came through the expression of the laypeople and, increasingly, women. Nowhere was this more evident than in the hymnody of the Scandinavian revivals, where laymen and women could express their own religious experiences and spirituality in the words and music of deeply personal and heartfelt songs. For women especially, who constituted perhaps a majority of the participants in the revivals, but who generally were not given a leading role in developing the movements, hymnody was one area of expression in which they could take charge. The greatest single example of this was the Swedish hymn writer Carolina Sandell-Berg, who personally wrote hundreds of hymns and is generally recognized as one of the greatest hymn writers in Scandinavia in the nineteenth century; her influence is perhaps only matched by Grundtvig. But there were dozens of other women who made a lasting contribution through their hymns, including Berthe Aarflot and Marie Wexelsen in Norway, and Betty Ehrenborg-Posse in Sweden. Another woman connected to this movement, and who greatly popularized it, was the Swedish singer Jenny Lind, whose musical performances gained her an international reputation.

CONCLUSION

By almost any measure, the revivals and awakening in nineteenth-century Scandinavia were an important spiritual influence, not only in that region but in places around the world. The writings and hymns of the people in this volume are still read and appreciated by many people and groups today, and it is hoped that these representative selections from these authors will continue and broaden their influence. Some of their piety and spirituality is, of course, specific to their times and places and to their own concerns. But many of their expressions of religious life and spirituality are timeless, and give voices to experiences of God and salvation and creation shared by many others. I hope that this volume can be a continuing source of inspiration to readers, some of whom are familiar with these names, and to those for whom they are new.

1

NORWAY

HANS NIELSEN HAUGE (1771–1824)

Religious Experiences

Hauge's importance to the nineteenth-century awakening in Norway cannot be overstated. Though he was an extremely effective preacher and writer, perhaps his most effective influence was through the example of his own life, during which he was constantly harassed by the authorities and even imprisoned for ten years. This autobiographical account of his life was a spiritual example for generations of Norwegians struggling to live out their callings in the world.

From early youth until my twenty-fifth year, I, Hans Nielsen Hauge, was of an outwardly quiet temperament. I had no desire to fight and little inclination to join in the merriment of my companions. Rather I became depressed when I went to parties and saw and heard the noisy gaiety. I was especially grieved when people started quarreling. My father had warned me against cursing and misusing the name of God; so from childhood I had a deeply instilled dislike for such things. I never danced, cared little for games or music, and would not go to taverns. But when somebody told stories or talked about religious or spiritual things, I was deeply interested....

These remarks apply especially to the period of my life from age nine to twelve. During this time I heard some people talking with my father about various religions. This awakened a new anxiety within me, a doubt as to whether our religion was the right one. For even though my parents and others said it was, I was still in doubt when I heard how pious some of the adherents of other religious faiths were.

I also read about their great zeal and how much some of them had suffered because they confessed the name of the Lord and labored faithfully for the salvation of their fellowmen. On this account they were mocked, persecuted, and made to suffer harsh, even cruel, punishment. I concluded from such reflections that we did not live as they did, but were indifferent in our worship of God and evidently were not able to endure the suffering they had endured. This placed me in even greater anxiety and I believed that I would not be saved....

When I prayed God for grace and desisted from impious thoughts, I found not only comfort but often also joy. On the other hand, when I found my mind turning to earthly, unprofitable things during my own devotional reading or as I listened to my father read the morning and evening prayers, these thoughts weighed heavily upon me: "An evil spirit is snatching God's Word from my heart; oh, the devil has me in his power and I shall be lost!" This in turn drove me again to pray for grace for Christ's sake....

I still remember my confirmation day. It was the custom on this day to dress with particular care. But since up to this time I had not wanted to be like the vain and the gay, I had not intended to be any different on this day than I usually was. But one of my sisters took it upon herself to fix me up a little. On the way to church one of the other confirmands said to me and the others who were in the group, "Today even Hans Nielsen has combed his hair!"

"Yes," I answered, "and if we have improved the outward appearance of our bodies today, it is to be hoped that we have not forgotten our immortal souls, but have reflected upon the great promise that we are to make today, namely this: to renounce the devil and all his works and all his ways, and to believe on God the Father, Son, and Holy Spirit." I can still remember the very spot on the road where this conversation took place.

Even though I was kept from gross, open vices by the remembrance of the reaffirmation of my baptismal promise and through the reading of godly books, still love of the world and other sins were not overcome. Just as I grew older as time passed, so too I become more conformed to the world.

It is true I acknowledged my sins when I communed, but my worldly carelessness, instability, and disobedience to my parents disturbed my conscience. Often after remorse over sin and a renewal of good intentions to walk the way of the blessed, I was well satisfied, found my pleasure in God, sang spiritual songs, and so forth....

The older I grew, the more I lost my capacity for noble feeling. Various anxieties began to weigh heavily upon me as on different occasions I met with adversity and experienced fear. Terror overwhelmed me when I was in the dark, just as if evil spirits were after me. Such things troubled me until I was twenty-five years old.

At this time I wanted to try to improve my personal fortunes, so I went to a suburb of Fredrikstad. Here I was exposed to many temptations by evil-minded companions. Up to this time I had abhorred drunkenness. But sometimes for lack of food, and other occasions presenting themselves, I soon took a liking to liquor. So much so that I think I could soon have fallen into the vice of drunkenness. But as I realized that this would lead to the destruction of both my body and soul, I prayed God that he would preserve me. Thereupon I received an aversion to this vice and by the grace of God was preserved from this temptation, so that I have not been drunk more than once in my life. And that occurred while I was in the above-mentioned city.

Finally, by prayerful reading of the Bible and other Christian books, I began to get more knowledge of God's will as well as the desire to do his will with my whole heart. Now I developed an aversion for all sins and talked about what I believed to others so that different ones began to make fun of me and call me "holy." Some people said that if I continued to devote so such time to reading, I would lose my mind. That was what had happened to many others who had read too much, they averred. I answered that I could not believe that those who meditated upon God's Word would lose their minds but would rather gain wisdom to practice those things that are pleasing to God.

God also gave me grace to meditate more upon his will. I thought about his omnipotence and how much he has created for the good of us human beings. I reflected upon his immeasurable greatness and goodness. I sensed how wonderful it would be to be his child and believed that I could become this if I only had a true desire to do so. "Alas," I thought, "many seek to win honor and respect in the world. Some are proud because they are of a high social class or have parents that are rich in the things of this world. Of what help are these things in death! But to have God as Father, to be his child, surpasses anything the mind can comprehend." I cannot describe how exalted and happy I felt during such moments of contemplation.

But I know that I fell far short of truly being a child of God, especially in this: loving him above all things and being humble of heart. I prayed a great deal for grace to practice these virtues and to learn to know his will, both what to do and what not to do. "If thou, my Father, wilt give me power, create thy love in my heart and preserve me in humility, then I will serve thee with all my strength. I will sacrifice everything, even my own life, as did the early martyrs, rather than depart from thy commandments." These and similar feelings filled my heart when I was alone, away from all human associations.

The desire to please God grew more and more. In prayer to him, I would kneel in heartfelt unworthiness of the great goodness he had shown me, ashamed because I had not served the Lord as I ought. Sometimes I fell on my knees and prayed almighty God for the sake of his Son to establish me on the spiritual rock, Christ Jesus. For I believed that then even the gates of hell would be powerless against me. I called upon the God of my salvation to reveal his Son's love in me and grant his Holy Spirit to expose my wretchedness and impotence and teach me the way I should walk in order to follow in the footsteps of Christ.

One day while I was working outside under the open sky, I sang from memory the hymn "Jesus, I Long for Thy Blessed Communion." I had just sung the second verse:

Mightily strengthen my spirit within me,
That I may learn what Thy Spirit can do;
Oh, take Thou captive each passion and win me,
Lead Thou and guide me my whole journey through!
All that I am and possess I surrender,
If Thou alone in my spirit mayest dwell,
Everything yield Thee, O Savior most tender,
Thou, only Thou, canst my sadness dispel.

At this point my mind became so exalted that I was not myself aware of, nor can I express, what took place in my soul. For I was beside myself. As soon as I came to my senses, I was filled with regret that I had not served this loving transcendently good God. Now it seemed to me that nothing in this world was worthy of any regard. That my soul experienced something supernatural, divine, and blessed; that there was a glory that no tongue can utter—that I remember as clearly as if it had happened only a few days ago. And it is now nearly twenty years since the love of God visited me so abundantly.

Nor can anyone argue this away from me. For I know all the good that followed in my spirit from that hour, especially a deep, burning love to God and my neighbor. I know that I received an entirely changed mind, a sorrow for sin and a desire that other people should become partakers with me of the same grace. I know that I was given a special desire to read the Holy Scriptures, especially Jesus' own teachings. At the same time I received new light to understand the Word and to bring together the teachings of all men of God to one focal point: that Christ has come for our salvation, that we should by his Spirit be born again, repent, and be sanctified more and more in accord with God's attributes to serve the triune God alone, in order that our souls may be refined and prepared for eternal blessedness.

It was as if I saw the whole world submerged in evil. I grieved much over this and prayed God that he would withhold punishment so that some might repent. Now I wanted very much to serve God. I asked him to reveal to me what I should do. The answer echoed in my heart, "You shall confess my name before the people; exhort them to repent and seek me while I may be found and call upon me while I am near; and touch their hearts that they may turn from darkness to light."

I spoke first to my own brothers and sisters, with the result that two of them were converted the same day. One of them continued, as far as man can judge, to serve the living God until his death four years later. During this period he exerted a good influence upon many people by his pious disposition. He was a particularly charitable and helpful person, who carefully weighed God's Word and was a real help to me as a young Christian. The second one is also serving the Lord. Eventually the other five members of my family, too, became of the same mind.

At every opportunity I sought to confess God's name and spoke to people about God's grace and his loving desire for their soul's salvation. More and more people became aroused. A few who did not understand what was happening, or who perhaps were resisting the truth, said that they would go mad if I spoke to them anymore.

Others were grieved because they had not served God, and with me sought guidance in God's Word. Because of their despondent spirit and their great concern in spiritual matters, they were regarded by the unbelievers as mental cases. For the unrepentant did not know that godly sorrow produces a repentance that leads to salvation and that those who seek the Lord in his Word and are obedient to the Spirit's correction, receive the greatest, the best, and most enduring wisdom....

I myself was a young Christian, suffering much doubt, anxiety, inner distress, and outward strife because of the many things that happened to me. Many people wanted to talk to me, some even in order to tempt me and lead me astray. These men were often more learned than I was and they attempted in part to distort the Holy Scriptures. Among other verses, I remember they used Solomon's words from Ecclesiastes 7:16–17: "Be not righteous overmuch, neither make thyself over-wise." They showed me a middle way and advised me to follow it.

"Where," I asked, "does this middle way lead? For it is foolish to follow a road if one does not know where it goes."

They were unable to give an answer, so I replied, "There is only one narrow way to life, and one broad way that goes to damnation (Matt 7:13–14). In temporal things there may be a middle way. But if anyone takes a middle way in spiritual things, then I do not doubt it runs along the broad way to hell. Maybe Solomon means that the over-righteous are hypocrites. For the Apostle Peter says that we shall be holy as God is holy."

Others said that not all those could be condemned who were not like I was. This put me in doubt and I sought to rid myself of the feeling, faith, and fire that burned in my soul. For I did not wish to believe that all the others would be condemned. So I went to God in prayer and asked him to show me what was right in this matter. Within me came the answer, "Heaven and earth shall pass away, but my words shall never pass away." I saw that I was not to look at others but to hold fast to his Word and my faith in it as it had been revealed to me. It was not my business to judge other people.

After I had come to this understanding, I was strengthened anew and used every opportunity, whether I was in town on business or someone was visiting me, to speak to people about the way of salvation. If I met anyone on the road, I spoke to him about eternal life and how important it is to work out our salvation. Some accepted what I said, others mocked and contradicted me. But I refuted those who argued against me. Many rumors about me spread in the parish, most of them false....

When people mocked and despised God's Word, persisted in sin, and would not repent, I wept. For cursing, misuse of God's name, foolish and useless talk, quarreling, drunkenness, lies, deception, and other sins wounded me deeply. On the other hand, I was especially happy when others came to the knowledge of the truth and amended their lives. I was reminded of the words of Jesus, "There shall be joy in heaven over one sinner that repents." I felt such great joy at this grace that in comparison with it no temporal thing seemed to be of value....

The many tears that a few fellow believers know I shed in Bergen during the year 1804 will testify to the truth of this statement. For I feared that men would exchange a godly mind for love of the world. I saw some go off to one extreme and some to another while only a few followed the right road. This made the outlook for the future of the church of Christ seem very dark to me. This year was especially a year of tribulation, both inwardly and outwardly, although few people realized it.

In the fall of the same year, 1804, I was arrested and arraigned before a royal commission. I was charged with seeking my own advantage, leading many away from their work, and diverting for my personal gain the greatest part of the rightful wages of the simple-minded. Then too, it was said that I taught doctrines harmful to the common welfare and therefore deserved punishment.

Even though my own conscience acquitted me of such charges, since the feelings of my heart and the intent of my actions had been the exact opposite, still I was tempted with doubt. I was afraid that among the many with whom I had been associated there would be found some who would misinterpret my motives and misconstrue my simple manner of conducting business to conform with the accusations leveled against me, all the more so since some of my trusted friends had now turned against me. Still, what happened? Conscience drove them to tell the truth, yes, even to lament their defection from me and to deplore these false rumors about an innocent person....

For it was a bitter experience to stand before the court and be asked whether this or that person had given me anything. And if such charges were to receive the appearance of truth, then it seemed to me that I had committed the greatest sin. For if I, who had urged such strict denial of love to the world, avarice, and so forth, and who had made known my views to others by tongue and pen on long trips in both kingdoms; if I who had sacrificed everything, even myself, should be revealed as a hypocrite and a deceiver, O eternal misery! Then no witness to God's Word could any longer be trusted.

These thoughts troubled me to the point of bitter anxiety. But after I had considered everything more carefully and had prayed earnestly to God, who can move men's hearts and turn aside the assaults of evil, I became glad instead of distressed. I believed that truth would win the victory and that falsehood would be defeated.

It is remarkable what an excellent opportunity a man who is alone, as I was in this prison, has to clarify his thinking regarding many things and to profit by his mistakes. But many temptations also harass one at such times. Such temptations plagued me also, now from within, now from without.

Inwardly, I was troubled with evil thoughts and doubts regarding the Christian faith. Outwardly, it bothered me that I was in captivity to strangers. It was a bitter experience to see a brother or a friend without being able to speak a confidential word with him. Besides, time passed slowly at first. But little by little, it went faster, partly because I occupied myself with knitting mittens and other things, and partly because I secured books to read. Some of these books I borrowed and some I bought with what I had earned by knitting.

I found few books that agreed with my point of view. Still, I read all I was able to secure in order to become informed in various fields. I read ethical, philosophical, and juridical books, as well as plays, and in time learned something from them all. In fact, the more I read the more interested I became. The letters of Voltaire and others of the same mind held the least interest for me.

The books that did me most harm were those that perverted the truth of the Bible, explaining the miracles of Jesus according to natural laws and denying his divine nature, his ascension, and other doctrines. Even though I did not believe such teachings, the devil found opportunity through them to tempt me. I must admit that by reading this material hostile to religion I was finally led so far astray that I found less interest in the simple Christian writings, the catechism, and the Bible. For even though I desired to live according to these canonical writings, my mind became so puffed up that it seemed to me that I had heard it all before. Consequently, I took little interest in them.

But God in his goodness did not leave me. By his Spirit, he reminded me that all was not well with my soul. Therefore I sought to return to my former simplicity of faith and to regain a desire to search the Holy Scriptures as before. But it was a slow process to get back to my previous attitude of obedience to God's Word and my former love to him. For even though I occasionally spoke about God's Word to others, I missed the light of the Lord's Spirit and Word in my soul and the power that I had sensed earlier.

Two years passed. The Lord was good to me and by his grace, Spirit, and Word worked in my heart. After I had for some time diligently considered the Holy Scriptures and other godly writings and laid hold of God in prayer, certain Bible passages came to mind that more and more quickened my soul.

Once as I was reading to several others I began to weep excessively, to pray, and call upon God. At that moment I experienced a renewal of my spirit and felt a fresh obedience of heart to God's Spirit and Word. I also received the power to speak to other people more earnestly about God's saving grace. I told them that this grace is revealed by the Word and that the Spirit of God is present in the Word to chasten and cleanse us from all sin and to teach us to be diligent in all good works.

Since then my feelings have at times known their former glow and have even burst into flame as before. We all experience from time to time that our spiritual fire burns low, partly due to the distractions of the world and partly due to the sensuality and sinful desires of our nature, which fight against the Spirit (Gal 5). I must confess that I am a poor sinner lacking much and that I am unworthy of the great grace God has shown me. I am far from having anything to glory of in myself when my conscience is reminded of, and chastened by, this acknowledgment of the truth.

On the other hand, I cannot deny that God has faithfully led me on my way through life, this being especially the case the past twenty-one years. Therefore I pray God with a sincere heart that he will preserve me in his truth to the end of my life.

It is true I have learned more and more to respect knowledge and learning in every field. But I abhor the teachings of those who have become wise in their own estimation, despising the Word of God, especially those wretched people who seek to pervert the right way of the Lord, and who not only transgress but also corrupt the Lord's commandments. I pity those who are so puffed up in their own conceit that they despise the foolishness of the message of the cross (1 Cor 1:18).

By the grace of God, nothing shall ever draw me away from the truth of the Holy Scriptures. After many trials, I have found that Scripture alone is able to give true peace, blessed joy, power to conquer sin, comfort in death, and a constant hope of eternal life. In this life it furnishes the mind with all Christian virtue.

I feel a renewed desire to study the Holy Scriptures increasingly, especially the Gospels. I find the teachings of Christ are like a bright sun shining into my soul. The more I meditate upon them, the more fully I grasp the depths of meaning in these pertinent words. I believe that anyone who rightly heeds this doctrine with a believing heart will discover and understand that it is from God; that whoever drinks from this well, from his life there will flow streams of living water.

God grant me, with all others who seek him, this grace to the end that we may be and remain his chosen children, believing on him, loving him, and walking according to his gracious will. Then in his own time he will call us home from this pilgrimage to his eternal rest. Amen.

Religious Convictions

Hans Nielsen Hauge's account of his religious convictions is contained in his autobiographical writing My Travels *(1816). It is the third part of his postprison account of his previous activities; he describes this section as "a short summary or main content of my own conceptions of religion and what I have sought to deliver to my fellow men on that subject."*[1] *Hauge wants to give a description of the true Christian life, and of the faith that brings this about through the regeneration of the believer.*

As far as my reason has taken me I have, as I have been persuaded in my heart, with all my strength endeavored to follow the teachings of Christ and his apostles as it is written in the New Testament and in accordance with the canonical writings of the Old Testament, together with the symbolical teachings of the Evangelical Lutheran Church in this country. When I thus explain to my readers what I, from the convictions in my heart, consider to be the gist of the teachings of Christ, the purpose of his errand in the world, and the rightful interpretation of what we learned as children, everyone must from my explanation understand both what I myself believe and try to conform to and what I wish to instill into my fellow men. That which I myself have believed is the only way to obtain true happiness both here and yonder is what I have, to the best of my ability, sought after, and I most heartily want to advise others to do likewise, so that in truth I can say that "as I have believed, so have I spoken...."

6. This was the glad message, the Gospel for which he was anointed by his Father's hand and sent to preach to the poor: when we feel poor in spirit and have turned away from the world, when our heart is broken and we feel imprisoned in the chains of vices, when we feel our spiritual eyes are blinded and we cannot see our own distress or God's salvation, then he will open our eyes that we may see the former as well as the latter. By his grace he not only proclaims to us his mercy and forgiveness, but he also gives us the strength to conquer our love of sin so it shall have no dominion over us (Rom 6:14). Thus those who were formerly plagued by sin are set free, because the Son makes them free, and they are free indeed, having been promised that they shall continue in the Father's house forever (John 8:35–36).

1. Quoted in Joseph M. Shaw, *Pulpit in the Sky: A Life of Hans Nielsen Hauge* (Minneapolis: Augsburg Publishing House, 1955), 159.

7. Teachers who write about faith and elevate it as the main point in Christian doctrine (with no or only a few words about the highly important change that must precede true faith, or the new obedience, which in every true Christian is a certain result of living faith) are blind teachers who make the way to heaven broad and lazy. They are deceiving souls by comforting the people in the midst of despair, preaching peace and judging souls to life who shall not live (Ezek 13).

It is good and well to believe that there is an almighty God who has created and brought forth all things and still sustains them, and that he by his Son will reconcile fallen humanity to himself and by his Holy Spirit strengthen every obedient man in a righteous life, as we learned as children from the symbolical confessions. A man must have these beliefs before he can come to any conversion or change of disposition because "they cannot believe in one of whom they have not heard nor call upon one in whom they have not believed" (Rom 10:14). One must "believe, when coming to God, that he is and will be the rewarder of them who seek him" (Heb 11:6). But this faith is still not more than science and head knowledge. It has neither power to change my heart nor can it give me victory over sin and the world. On the contrary, it leads many thousands to security, while they are only comforting themselves with this confessional head knowledge, blessing themselves in their hearts, saying, "It will be well with us," even if they are walking in the hardness of their hearts (Deut 29:19). For such people to cry out, "Lord, Lord," avails nothing (Matt 7:21; 25:11). But those who through such a belief declare people saved only lead them astray, and those who are pronounced saved will be devoured (Isa 9:16).

8. It is quite different when one comes to the faith that is given in regeneration. This gift of God, which comprehends Christ, and in him the righteousness by grace alone (Eph 2:7–8), changes and cleanses our hearts (Acts 15:9). It works in the heart new hatred of evil and new love to God and his will; it gives victory over sin (Rom 6:14), it conquers the world (1 John 5:4), by it we can possess Christ as our own, as the one who was made righteousness, sanctification, and redemption by God for us (1 Cor 1:30), in whom we become, when we believe, sealed with the promise of the Holy Spirit, which is the guarantee of our inheritance (Eph 1:13–14), the Spirit that testifies

with our spirit that we are the children of God, and are made righteous by faith and shall live by faith (John 3:36; Rom 1:17), if we show living fruits of this faith (of which I shall speak later) and continue in it steadfastly until death. "If anyone shrinks back, my soul has no pleasure in him," God says in the Scriptures (Heb 10:38), but "he who endures to the end shall be saved" (Matt 24:13).

9. This faith is my most important possession and has been my best comfort in all my trials, because it brings the peace that Christ promised his own (John 14:27; 16:33), not peace as the world gives. The world's peace is peace and freedom to sin. But faith in Christ and the peace of Christ shields our hearts from the allurements of the world, comforts us against its persecution, frees us from the dominion of sin, the curse of the law, and its punishment. But notice, never from obedience to the law. "I have not come to abolish the law and the prophets, but to fulfill them" (Matt 5:17). "Do we then overthrow the law by this faith? By no means. On the contrary, we uphold the law" (Rom 3:31).

10. This is, in brief, the content of my simple comprehension of true and saving faith. The other teachings in Scripture, insofar as they do not deal with the same theme, contain instructions about the Christian life as the earmark and fruit of true faith. Throughout the Scriptures it is proved that these fruits or good works must have a connection with faith, unless in the spirit of antichrist we reject this teaching or wrest one word from another. To do this is madness, evil, and shame. Jeremiah 8:9, "They have rejected the word of the Lord; and what manner of wisdom is in them?" Over such a terrible judgment is pronounced in Revelation 22:18–19.

But when we in simple faith and by the enlightenment of the Holy Spirit seek to know the Word in its totality and context, and especially the true meaning of Christ's teachings, we will always find that he praises faith as that whereby we are assured of salvation, as I have shown here. But we will also see that he just as often, in fact, more often tells people to prove their faith by deeds: "Sin no more"; "Go and do likewise"; "Do that, and you shall live," and several other such sentences.

But he was not satisfied with external good deeds alone. He stresses purity and uprightness of heart, from which flow, as from a spring, good works and deeds to the glory of God and to the blessing of our neighbor. Numerous indications of this we find in the Sermon on the Mount, where he not only urges pure teaching and good works, but also sincerity of the heart. We come to understand the spiritual meaning of the law: that with God the intention is as important as the deed; that the one who looks at a woman with lust has already committed adultery with her in his heart; that hate directed against our brother is murder; and that for angry words we are condemned to hellfire. On the day of judgment, we will have to account for every unnecessary word we have spoken. Our speech should be yes and no, without swearing and cursing. There is to be no taking of vengeance, but on the contrary, we shall love our enemies and pray for those who persecute us. We should be ready for reconciliation with our brother, here and now on our earthly journey. We should give and be merciful to our fellow men, and thus be like our heavenly Father, whose children we should be.

But we should not do this or any other good deed to be seen of men, not even our worship of God. Nor should we gather treasures on earth and forget the eternal, wavering in our faith and serving both God and the earthly. Neither let our hearts become overwhelmed by worries for this life, but let our chief concern be for God's kingdom, that it may come among us and in us. Let us not judge our brother or look sternly at the mote in his eye or at his fault, forgetting ourselves. Rather let us correct our own faults and then the faults of others, with mildness. We should not unthinkingly throw God's Word out among its despisers, but rather have faith and trust in God, and worship him in faith. Finally, Christ tells us that the way to life is narrow, and urges us to try to enter in through the narrow gate. He warns us against false teachers and gives us the characteristics of the false and the true, namely, their fruits, or the way they live. This convinces us that a good confession or "Abba, Father" does not help us when we do not with all our heart and might do the will of God.

Christ finishes his Sermon on the Mount with a parable about a wise and an unwise man who built houses. The first man dug deep until he found a rock to place the foundation of the house upon. The other was satisfied with building on sand, and when the storm and rain came, his house fell, while the first man's house withstood every gale. Those who hear his words, keep them, and act accordingly are likened to the wise man. The ones who do not listen to the Word he likens to the unwise man, in spite of how often they have heard it.

With this Christ ends his Sermon on the Mount, but several places in the Gospels he has given us the same remarkable teachings, though sometimes in different words. Especially are we to take to heart the many parables that, though different, are told with the same goal. See Matthew, chapters 13, 18, 20, 21, 22, and 25; Luke, chapters 13, 14, 15, 16, and 18; and John, chapters 3, 4, 5, 6, 10, 12, 14, 15, 16, and 17, where much instruction is contained that is the power of God to salvation for everyone who believes them and follows them, but also judgment unto death for everyone who despises his grace (2 Cor 2:16).

11. As we now take the aforementioned Scripture passages and teachings of Christ up for closer consideration, we will find that our soul is an eternal spirit, created to live in fellowship and communion with God, its Creator, and given wonderful possibilities for reaching this goal. But by the fall these qualities were so weakened and depraved *(fordærvede)* that there is no righteous inclination in man toward good (Gen 8:21). On the other hand, man is depraved from his youth up, and as a consequence we have lost all the glory for which we were created and also the right to enter into God's kingdom. Instead, a terrible desire to sin has come into the heart, which breaks forth in evil fruits, whose wages are only everlasting judgment from which no redemption can be expected, if a restoration does not take place here in this life.

12. This restoration and reestablishment of the image of God in man's soul has taken place, or it has been made possible for it to take place, by the redemption that came through Jesus Christ. The good tidings are proclaimed through the Gospel about faith in him, of which I spoke earlier. But it is proclaimed to men on certain conditions and in a certain order, which is called "the order of salvation!" To understand this rightly and to use it rightly is the main concern of our religion. That it is not grasped by more than a small group is the sad testimony of Scripture and daily experience. Nor can the merciful God in any wise be responsible. It is rather a result of men's wrong conceptions and perverted minds.

Even if we are born and raised in a Christian country, baptized in infancy, instructed in the outward letter-knowledge of the way of life through Jesus Christ, confirmed in the covenant of our baptism, and use his sacraments and keep the usual ceremonies of the church; even so, the word of Jesus shows us that nothing of all this helps us unless we submit to God's will so that his Spirit may gain control to regenerate us, and plant the true living faith in our hearts. This is the only thing that can recreate and shape our heart's desire and disposition, and thereby restore the lost image of God in the soul, from which there flows a living love to God and to our neighbor. We love God because we experience his grace in our hearts, his indescribable and unmerited love, who loved us so much that he sent his own Son to the world for our sakes, to be our Savior, so that we should not perish, but have everlasting life in him. We love God, therefore, and sense the urge in our soul to love our neighbor. The Lord does not need our services, nor does our good reach him (Ps 16:2–3), but our neighbor needs our service and to that end God has arranged it so that the one man needs the other, and the one has always been given temporal and spiritual gifts that the other needs. Thus mutually, as children of a common Father, they should love, serve, and help each other.

13. Nature and reason together with the whole work of creation also teach us that it is not good for man to be alone; that to be friends and benefactors and to do good is, next to God, the greatest good and the greatest pleasure we can have in the world. When we do not have love to others and show no willingness to serve them, we have no right to ask service and help of our fellow men. This impulse expresses itself in a much higher degree in the regenerate person. With him it is a matter of course, because of his life of faith and his love of God, who loved him first, that he in turn may love his fellow men without expecting a reward. This new obedience breaks forth as a wonderful fruit from the root of faith, whereby it can be proven that God is his Father and he is God's child.

14. This love reaches out to men as far as we are able to reach, with a heartfelt desire and wish that the same good that has been given to us may become theirs, too. We have sorrow over those who do not know the salvation of the Lord, and we are happy for those who receive grace, loving them from the heart (John 13:34–35; 15:17).

We do not worship God with our lips only or with mere external customs, but we worship and serve him with our whole heart in spirit and in truth. When we realize that we, with the shame of our past sins, now possess the blessed joy of newly given grace, we worship God our Father by the Holy Spirit in Jesus Christ, and praise and honor the triune God and exalt his holy name. It is not through reason or by means of "book knowledge," but we do know that God the Father has created us and the world for our sakes, and that we and our race have been placed here to be made ready for an everlasting life. Therefore we do not live for this life, but for the life beyond....

24. Never have I considered learning or science as harmful, and especially not when it is subordinated to faith and love (otherwise, it makes one too proud). On the contrary, I have considered it useful and necessary, for our faith is strengthened by the enlightenment of knowledge, and the usefulness for this life is not inconsiderable. I know, and can substantiate with many witnesses, that I never have advised against being obedient in the fear of the Lord to the ordinances of men, and that older people who have much understanding should be respected doubly, particularly those who labor in the Word and teaching (1 Tim 5:17). We should share every good with those who teach us. Outside of that, we are to give everyone what we owe him: "Custom to whom custom is due, fear to those who should be feared, and honor to whom honor is due."

25. The Apostle James says, "Let not many become teachers," which Luther has translated, "Let not every man think he is a teacher" (Jas 3:1). By this the apostle sets forth a wise and sensible idea: that not everyone, nor too many should be teachers, but everything should be handled decently and in good order. However, I cannot understand that this or any other passage of Scripture forbids anyone to preach and remind of the way of the Lord to his fellowmen, whether it be done by a layman or a learned person. We have often experienced that God used the foolish things of the world, as Paul says in 1 Corinthians 1. When it is ascertained that the country's teaching profession is not obstructed in its work; when the laymen righteously follow Christ's Word, they will not hinder but promote the fear of the Lord and the desire to hear and learn it, they themselves preaching it in season and out (2 Tim 4:2). With Paul they rejoice that Christ is preached (Phil 1:18).

Where there are those whose insights are more sanctified and full, whose understanding is better in how to uphold the faith after the pattern of knowledge as well as in the form of churchly traditions (weak men have often lost their feeling for religion), they should be looked upon as leaders and watchmen in the Christian congregation, and one may expect of every righteous teacher that if anyone should stray from the truth or be overcome by temptation, the teacher would help such a one in a spirit of meekness (Gal 6:1), and never play the Lord over the Lord's inheritance, but continue as examples to the flock (1 Pet 5:3), to "admonish the idle, encourage the faint-hearted, help the weak, and be patient with them all" (1 Thess 5:14).

My confession of faith, in short, is this: Jesus Christ is the way of life and truth unto salvation. He is the Savior of those who let him into their hearts, or, in other words, open their hearts to the Holy Spirit, consider the words of Jesus, and turn their mind, heart, and desire to the Ten Commandments, having as their only wish to please God and thereby give God's Spirit room in their hearts to work living faith within. This faith is recognized by a warm love to God and to the believing brethren, and in a love stretched out to all men, seeking for them the same grace. Both outwardly and inwardly the true believer has genuine humility. A believer's dealings are upright. He loathes sin, loves all virtues, strives after holiness and peace with all, especially those who call upon the Lord out of a pure heart. He feels the promptings of the Spirit of God, has daily battles against the temptations of the enemy and the evil desires of the flesh, and complains with Paul that he cannot do the good he wished to do, but that the evil is too much in his thoughts. He may also stumble by a sinful deed, which hurts all the more. But by stumbling this way, the true believer learns to be careful. He is driven to watch and pray that he can hold fast to Jesus his Savior, and by his love defeat his sinful inclinations, deny himself, and sacrifice himself in the service of his heavenly Father. To do his will and to live according to his commands is the desire of his heart.

The true believer who is full of the teachings of Jesus does not exclude any of what Jesus has taught and commanded, but believes in him as Savior and is convinced in his heart that he has freed him from his sin. But this faith does not lead to security. If it is genuine, it leads to an awareness of the evil that hangs on and tempts us as long as we are in this life. Far from depending on faith and despising God's law, he knows that not one iota of it will perish, and the power of Christ will perfect the moral law in us. Therefore a man will keep the Lord's commandments out of love. First, his Christian example is a light shining before his fellow men in love, humility, chastity, abstinence, and justice. Secondly, he shows charity and service to all, especially his brethren in the faith. Thirdly, he confesses God's name, encourages, admonishes, rebukes, and convinces with patience and wisdom, honoring the Word of God and esteeming it highly, hearing it willingly of others, and teaching it to others. A true believer does not become proud, looking with disdain at others or thinking that he alone has the right to preach or confess the name of God and showing intolerance toward those who think differently. But he is glad for everyone who is sowing the true seed and rejoices where it is received.

Living in this way, he has the hope and assurance that the God of love and peace is leading him closer to his great goal: to be gathered with the elect in the eternal life. Amen!

Testament to His Friends

This extended letter was written in 1821, at a point in time when Hauge felt that his life was nearing an end. He did recover from this serious illness and produced several books from this point until his death in 1824. This letter was not published until after his death. His main concern in this document is that his followers would hold to the essence of his movement, and that they would continue to hold these convictions in the midst of a Norwegian church and society that was generally hostile to them.

Bredtvedt, March 7th, 1821.

As it may happen soon that my hourglass runs empty, especially may this be expected because I am so very weakened from the great exertions and many sufferings, mainly physical:

Therefore I have decided, in the name of God the Father, Son, and Holy Ghost, with prayer for his enlightenment and leadership, to set forth here my last will, which you friends with the friendship, confidence, and love you have reciprocated, herewith earnestly are asked and admonished to execute after my death.

1) That spirit of grace and holiness, which has rested upon me, and which you have received, may that spirit still rest upon you and upon all those who hereafter receive him and believe God's holy Word.
2) The holy God's Word: Jesus' teachings first, then the writings of the apostles and the prophets, inasmuch as they concern the soul's entity, faith, and morale, be for you the most holy treasure above all other things in this world.
3) All other writings that have knitted together the contents of the Holy Scripture, also your catechism and the many you have tested and accepted as good, these you read with an open and believing heart; other untested writings you read with certain reserve, so you don't set your heart's confidence in them before you accurately have tested them. This test shouldn't be done with rumination, nor by imagination, but by prayer to God for the enlightenment of the Holy Ghost, also by concord with all of the Sacred Scripture, especially in these points: About those who teach the true belief in Jesus Christ, which redeems from sin, death, and the kingdom of Satan, so that they who believe do not live in the kingdom of sin and Satan, but serve God righteously, innocently, and blessed. They are not, then, their own, but are his people, and who from their love for him are very assiduous to good deeds. Also that they in the instruction do not overlook, but teach about the Father and the Holy Ghost and also about the Son, so that none of the triune entity is left out or one put higher than the other, for all three are one. Go in for the true doctrine and acknowledge deeply our sin; also about conversion or regeneration, about to love God and your

neighbor as yourself (to salvation), so that one renounces oneself to follow in Jesus' footsteps.

Finally, instruct them like Jesus about the narrow gate and the straight road, about temptations and patience to suffer always, as long as we are living here; stay awake, pray, and have a degree of fear of falling; if we learned, we stand up, that we work for our salvation with fear and trembling. Never to imagine we have grasped it perfectly, but always hasten forward on the pilgrimage through life, that we shall use violence upon the kingdom of God, and those who use violence, take it by force. Safety and halfheartedness are regarded as big sins. Also that it is the duty of every Christian to confess the name of God in words and deeds, according to each one's talent and vigor, so that all endeavor to gather to God's congregation.

These books that have the above-mentioned points united with the many God's Word, and do not strive against the order of God in the realm of nature, but instruct correctly to use the spiritual and physical gift with thanksgiving, guard against the scruples of reason, which destroy the spiritual—and for conceited mystery, which will instruct about spiritual things, which they themselves do not understand, or let their teaching rise above the light they are given from God, therefore it gets dark for them and indistinct.

4) None among you yourselves write and have printed your own or anyone else's writings, nor recommend any new or unknown books, before they are tested in the congregation by the elders. Should any of our fellow confessionists act against this, then the elders join with the younger who have received the light of God; test the published books; if you find them beneficial, then talk to the one who has published it, and ask why he does not take council with you, and you do not recommend them and otherwise do not help him to profit thereby; however, use the good God's Word to the enlightenment of others. On the other hand, if you find

the published books bad, then not only talk to the publisher about it, but inform also those who might have obtained the books, about their bad teachings, also write to others that they do not have anything to do with it.

5) You know, friends, that to this day we have absolutely held to the evangelical in accordance with the legitimate Augsburg Confession or the state's religion; that some have called us a separate denomination, which they absolutely do not have any occasion for, but that we should be called sect, for we have loathed the vices with which many have dishonored the Christian church, and on the other hand applied ourselves to all good virtues in accordance with the Word of God. If we should be called a sect, then let us show in our lives that we ought to be called the virtuous sect or indeed the godly sect, and show in spiritual and temporal acts that these are like the virtues of Jesus. Therefore it is my last will that you hereafter as hitherto fully hold yourselves to our state religion, so that you receive from the official teachers all that pertain to their office. You will then attend church, receive the sacraments, be married by the minister, and at funerals let them officiate in conformity with good order.

6) I am specifically mindful of two things that I have feared, a fear that will rest heavy upon me to my last day, namely if lukewarmness, confidence, and discord should sneak in among the faithful. Therefore it is my fervent admonition that you above all things will guard against these dangerous enemies, so they do not gain access, as they have their roots in other sins. Feeling of confidence stems from pride and imagination of being perfect. Lukewarmness is nourished partly by the unstable mind that gets tired from the pure Word of God, which does not appeal to the senses; partly that oneself does not receive enough of esteem and honor; partly from their lazy nature, the world, or the love of the flesh, which does not like to do the will of God.

Discord is mainly nourished by pride, that one will not admit one's sin, but rule over one's fellow men;—secondly, in jealousy against those who are better; thirdly, from a singular hate against men, and partly because one demands much from others and little or nothing from oneself, beholdest the mote that is in thy brother's eye, but perceivest not the beam that is in one's own eye.

You must therefore always keep watch over yourselves and keep an eye on others, so the enemies of your salvation shall not break in. Bear in mind that where two become divided, there the one pulls to his part, and very soon can destroy the glory with which the rays of God's grace now adorn you. If you notice any discord or estrangement against each other, which most often comes out in an unreasonable and groundless blame, aspersion, and slander in a greater or lesser degree, then sacrifice everything in order to get hold of these yourself or with the help of others, whom you think better qualified than yourself to do so. Point out to those who dispute the big evil they commit against God and their neighbor as well as themselves, investigate if they both are equally guilty, then punish both equally without distinction. If one has more guilt, then punish him harder and admonish to agreement, but enjoin on the less guilty or (which seldom happens) the innocent, that he forgives,—and employ all means to harmony; for of the one who is the better of them, one demands most also here, and yet the truth must not suffer by the liar. Will the one or both not listen to your admonition and appeal, then regard them both as infidels or like those whom you regard as not being of your own faith, and don't want any association with, all in accordance with the word of Jesus in Matthew 18:7; also you make efforts to awaken the lukewarm and let those who feel safe confess their sins.

You know, fellow believers, that occasional discords no doubt have appeared during these twenty-five years.

But, by the grace of God, they have been quelled, and most of them adjusted; at least they have never led to parties who have left the path and voice Jesus has let us hear. For either the guilty one has admitted and regretted his sin, or he has fallen to vices and then left us. But many have feared with me that when I with this tool of mine—my tongue, pen, and deed—leave you, then indeed discords might appear, so the one will go hither, the other thither. Guard against this; for nothing is more important than unity.

7) We have never had any ordered church discipline among us, just as we have never kept any record, so neither I nor any of you know how many there really are who profess the faith, the disposition, and mutual friendship, although we through communications and those who visit each other can know about both the places where there are few or many, and also know personally the names of many, especially of those who are outstanding in godly practice. You also know that we have absolutely no signs or ceremonies mutually; for only through conversations, actions, partly also through recommendations, do we become intimate with each other.

Those things we ought not to concern ourselves in especially hereafter either; but we have had one by many unnoticed church discipline; for all those who have practiced any vice and not soon repented and mended their ways, they are reduced in our esteem and confidence; if their vices have prevailed with them for a longer time, we have had nothing to do with them, but they themselves have felt they are separated from us and have partly avoided us. Such church discipline will we also keep up hereafter, though in such a way that when the fallen ones repent their sins and will hear the Word of God, then receive them according to their circumstances.

8) In the Apostle Paul's parting with the Ephesians, we read in Acts 20:29–30, "For I know this, that after my

departing shall grievous wolves enter in among you, not sparing the flock. Also of your own selves shall men arise, speaking perverse things." Although I hope better at this time, I will anyway warn you with the thirty-first verse: Watch! For I have known some among us who have made several remarks that are not in accordance with the teaching of Jesus, and have had their own aspirations and ideas. Still worse, there might arise either false ones, who indeed might have great intellect, but use it with wiliness to lead astray the wretched ones, so they impel the control over the Lord's inheritance; that is to say, they pursue their own honor and advantage and dominance; they want to be loved without loving God and in him their fellow men; such people will lead you to obedience to them through technicalities of wisdom and instruction that do not give nourishment to your soul. Others step forward in conceit, will affect importance by their spirituality, talk about their feelings; these practice speaking of their inward condition mingled with imagination and qualms of reason, so they in the first affect experience, but soon one can perceive that their words are empty sounds; they have not life and presence of the spirit, they daze but do not shine, for they pursue higher things than are given them, or they have once walked on truth's path, but have gone off it; still they can speak of what they at that time experienced and now falsely make their own. Some go brokenhearted by hypocrisy, speak with broken voice; others are cheerful. Both borrow from the Scripture words that they, according to their knowledge and gift of nature, teach others without paying attention to their own hearts, and without having made any conversion themselves. For they are recognized by the fruits and by their inexperience in spiritual things, also that they do not unite all the Words of God in their teaching. Be on your guard against all such people.

I have reason to hope that as long as you eldest or true children of God live, that you won't let debauchers have free command, but that you convince them and punish them and also warn the simpleminded people against their debauchment. You know, the blind cannot lead the blind, for then they both fall in the ditch; therefore you must advise everyone, especially those who will instruct others, that they themselves must in their hearts first be converted. I will also utter my heartfelt admonition in the name of the Lord that you true fellow believers, especially the oldest and most gifted in each place, keep a sharp eye on those who will edify others; for it behooves those people to demonstrate in a superior way their faith in a godly life and good deeds, and that he has a firm knowledge of the Word of God, so that it may be understood that he is strengthened by the Spirit of the Lord Jesus to lead a life of a sound and clean doctrine. If you should be informed to the contrary, then admonish him in private; if that is of no avail, then let two more listen to it; if the deviating person will not correct himself, then tell him of his aberration in the presence of as many with whom he gathers. If you yourselves have not strength enough to do this in the place where he is, then ask for help from others who are more strengthened in Christ, or who have received more gifts than you. If he leaves you, then find out where he went, write thither or try to visit those others in order to stop the one who deceives the hearts of the simpleminded, who are not wicked, but neither have received enough strength from God to stop the deceivers. The person who shall teach or instruct others, especially one who travels on such errands, ought not to have become a believer just recently himself, yet this might be done under the watchfulness of the eldest; but none ought to instruct others unless it is proved that he himself is indeed converted, and has shown in his life the worthy fruits of the conversion, and still he is subjected to the eldest's supervision and close test, that he daily descends into himself so he feels deeply not only his sins but also his own impotence, that he is also tried in temptations and considerable distress, has good foundation and explanation in the Word of God, so nothing contradictory comes up.

Where several are together of those who have received talents to edify others, then after agreement or according to the eldest's decision, only two or three of them, one after the other, speak, and that so no offense happens. If someone goes astray, or it is something to censure in some person's speech or behavior, convince them as you have been told before about those who will edify others and not walk the straight and narrow path themselves. If he does not correct himself, tell it to the congregation and call him an unbeliever, according to Jesus' word, Matthew 18.

The eldest must not shut their eyes to the vices of their fellow eldest in any kind of vice, but punish them properly, as well as everyone who has acquired the respect of the faithful and wants to be good Christians; you ought to watch closely such persons, don't let them get used to flattery and softness, but endure even sharp admonition or solid food.

A person once converted from darkness to light, who later on has been attracted to darkness and done wrong to someone and by injustice comes about other people's property, if such person later has come to repentance and will return to the faithful, but doesn't right his wrongdoings, then he ought not to be accepted among the faithful or given your heart's confidence; much less allow him to confess the name of God, speak at edification for others, before he has fully amended and indemnified the injured part....

10) Those with whom you have no acquaintance, or those who have conceived other ideas about religion than you, you should bear with and judge as lenient as the verity according to the manifest Word of God permits. For many may have been brought up in an austere, perfunctory concept, and also been charmed by an incorrect exhortation of the Word of God, yet believe and

> seek for truth, as God can have many whom you don't know who love him. Bear in mind the Lord's answer to Elijah and this one's opinion. Therefore deal you kindly with every person; demonstrate willingness to serve and hospitality according to your ability, or just so God's truth doesn't suffer in so doing.

You fellow believers, take these points into consideration, and also those that the daily experience teaches you. Then you shall see by the gracious assistance of God, the wicked and insincere, like the self-deceived people, can do nothing against you, but you, through the power of God, our Savior, obtain through your word and example many souls to his Kingdom, to the multiplication of the fruits of your own faith and glorified gladness, and in common to praise the triune God.

This is my wish, my prayer and only desire, that you will aspire to so infinitely glorious grace, which I feel assured that God our Father through his Son Jesus Christ by his Holy Spirit will bestow upon us, who remain faithful to the end, the supreme good, finally, at the end of time to gather in the eternal happiness. Amen.

GISLE JOHNSON (1822–1894)

Gisle Johnson was one of the most significant Norwegian theologians of the nineteenth century. As a member of the theological faculty at the University of Kristiania for over a generation, he had considerable influence on the future ministers being trained there. By nature a scholarly and quiet person, beginning in 1851 Johnson personally ignited a decade of religious revivals in Norway with his evangelistic preaching. While he was very concerned that this revival remain theologically Lutheran, he wanted to structure this theology in a way that allowed for the revival and regeneration of the believer, something with which Lutheranism has not always been comfortable. This selection is a part of his theological lectures, which had a profound impact on a generation of Lutheran pastors in Norway.[1]

An Outline of Systematic Theology

THE QUICKENING OF THE SINNER

As one justified by God, the believer knows himself essentially also to be quickened or made alive by him. The objective redemption given in justification is inseparably and indissolubly linked to a subjective redemption in which the sinner's longing for liberation from the miserable state that is the necessary result of his unrighteousness has been satisfied. This is a restitution of man's original, normal personal existence, which, as the abolition of that "death" that is the "wages of sin," essentially consists of the quickening of the one who has died, in the gift of a new life. This quickening finds its necessary prerequisite in justification. Just as God can only give the sinner the gracious gift of new life when he has graciously accepted him in justification, and removed the wall of partition that the guilt of sin

1. Originally published in Gisle Johnson, *Grundrids af Den Systematiske Theologi*, part 2: *Den Christelige Dogmatik* (Kristiana, Norway: Jacob Dybwads Forlag, 1897), 88–117.

raises between them, so the sinner, too, on his part, can only begin the new life in love toward God when he in faith has received the grace of God and overcome the slavish fear that excludes such love. But at the same time justification also finds its necessary sequel in this quickening. If the guilt of sin has been removed, then also its punishment must be canceled. God cannot forgive sin without thereby at the same time saving from death; he cannot declare the sinner to be righteous without thereby equally bestowing upon him that life that belongs to the righteous. And thus, neither can the sinner on his part in faith appropriate to himself God's grace, without thereby at the same time loving that God in return who first loved him. This new life that God in this way communicates to the justified believer finds its beginnings and its resultant amplification and organic development as a life existing under the conditions of temporal existence. We must therefore also in the quickening of the sinner distinguish between its beginning and its continuance: between the "regeneration" of the sinner and the regenerated sinner's "renewal."

The Regeneration of the Sinner

The necessary and immediate result of justification is quickening of the justified sinner, in the form of the communication of a new life principle. The believer receives a new power of life in an act of creation: as such, a momentary act of saving grace, by which the fruitful seed of a new existence becomes planted in the organism of sinful man controlled by death. In this way man's organism is renewed in principle, and thus the ideal of human life is once more realized in principle. It is this fundamental quickening of the sinner—this fundamental communication of a new life—that is most particularly designated *regeneration.* This concept of the working of grace as a quickening of one who was dead basically describes a fundamental change in man's subjective existence: an absolute turning point in his life, by which his earlier development is interrupted, and a new life development is set in motion. Certainly, this cannot be thought of as a re-creation of man's substantial being. That which is in principle abolished in man's immediate reality is only his death. The attributes that God himself has introduced into man's reality by his creation, he cannot by his regenerating action destroy. He can only liberate, renew, and glorify. The natural traits and powers received by the individual in creation are purified by regenerating grace and liberated from the corrupting influence of sin—and thereby also glorified, energized, and permeated by the fertilizing power of the new life. The direct, natural gift therefore becomes a gift of God's grace. On the other hand, however, regeneration can nevertheless neither be thought of as the liberation of an already present life from the inhibiting influence of a hostile power. Regeneration consists in the communication by God to the sinner of a life that he does not have, thereby in principle liberating him from the power of death. In this way, God again places the sinner in the normal life situation that he had forfeited through sin, and to that extent "renews" him, creates in him a "new man" in his image, and thus to this extent making him a "new creation": a new "man of God." As a fundamental quickening of the one who is dead, regeneration is more particularly a spiritual rebirth. Just as the sinner's death first and foremost appears as spiritual death reigning in the heart, the central point of the organism, so also must his quickening begin with the regeneration of the heart, by the communication of a new, spiritual life. The "new man," the new life principle, which is communicated to him in regeneration, essentially consists of a new "spirit," which includes within itself the power to permeate the whole organism with its life. The regenerated believer is essentially a new "spiritual" man.

The new spiritual life that thus is the fruit of regeneration is a personal existence in which spiritual death is abolished in principle in the form of its antithesis. That is, it is a state in which man is freed in principle not only from sin, but also from the state of spiritual blindness—the inner lack of peace and joy in which the death-bringing power of sin reveals itself in the areas of understanding and the emotions. Thus, the regenerated life is first and foremost a life in love toward God. In this love a new moral impulse has been planted in the heart, directing the will proceeding from the heart in accordance with God's holy will. There is a heartfelt desire and longing to obey and serve him, in which the power is given for a life of good works. Such willing obedience appears as a "new obedience," in opposition, not only to the old disobedience of natural man, but equally also to the old obedience forced upon him by slavish fear. The holy law of

God itself is written upon man's heart, his holy will has become man's will, and thus also has man's will become a holy and as such truly free will, expressed in a righteous life. The regenerated believer as such is freed from the slavery of sin, purified from the contamination of sin, yes, dead to sin, to the extent that he essentially cannot sin. The regeneration of the sinner is from this point of view in principle his sanctification. But at the same time it also includes as an equally essential factor a new spiritual enlightenment. Its essential fruit in the area of intellectual life is the fundamental abolition of natural man's spiritual blindness and ignorance with the advent of a new understanding of the truth that in its extent, clarity, and certainty enables the regenerated believer to prove all things and judge all things. And in addition to this, there is a third essential factor in the regenerated believer's new spiritual life, in a blessed feeling of inner harmony and a direct experience of inner well-being. Natural man's lack of peace and joy is in principle abolished as peace, joy, and boldness enters his heart. From this point of view it can be said that the believer in regeneration in principle becomes blessed.

Regeneration as a communication of such spiritual life, like justification, finds its source in the grace of God through Christ. The new life is a gift of God's grace. Regeneration is a work of God's saving grace, in which the sinner plays a passive role. Essentially, that life that was forfeited through sin and again communicated to the sinner in regeneration is God's own eternal life. Just as the sinner's spiritual death is the result of his exclusion from the source of life in fellowship with God, therefore, so can the one dead in sin only be quickened as God once more takes him into a life fellowship with him, gives him of the fullness of his own life, and thus makes him his "child" in the subjective sense of the word. And just as this life is a spiritual life, so also is its communication first and foremost a work of the Spirit of God, depending on God's gift of his Spirit to the sinner. By taking up residence in the heart of the sinner and uniting with his spirit, by sinking down into the inner, central point of the sinner's personal existence as a living, inviolable seed, the Holy Spirit makes him a new spiritual man. But this whole activity that brings God's Spirit and life appears at this point to the believer's consciousness as mediated through Christ. At the same time as Christ has achieved for us the righteousness that is imputed to us in justification, he has also achieved for us that life that is bestowed upon us at regeneration. That which he has achieved for us no one else can communicate to us. Just as our justification is founded upon what he has done and continues to do for us, so also is our quickening dependent upon his activity within us and our life fellowship with him. Eternal life is for us only given in Christ, so that the sinner can only share in such life, as Christ gives him his Spirit and through him takes up residence in his heart, bestows his life upon him, and thereby makes alive that which was dead. As a communication of new life, regeneration thus in reality takes place in such a way that God, at the same moment as he in his heart justifies the sinner for Christ's sake, also in and through Christ allows the Spirit of Christ, who is also his Spirit, to enter into the heart of the justified sinner, and thus receives him into spiritual life fellowship with Christ, and in Christ, with himself. In this way, God also makes the sinner to share in Christ's spiritual life, which is his own eternal life. Regeneration thus appears from this point of view essentially as the subjective correlative of justification. Just as the latter is the objective restoration of the fellowship with God that had been disturbed by sin, so is regeneration its subjective restoration. The new life finds its essential basis and prerequisite in the sinner's life fellowship with Christ and in him with God. As such, it is a "mystical union" between God and man, which comes into being as God not only gives man his gifts through Christ in the Spirit that both share, but himself essentially and personally takes up residence in the heart of the regenerated believer. From this, the organic central point of the personality, God permeates man with the power of eternal life and transforms him into likeness with himself.

As the communication of the new spiritual life thus is mediated on God's part by the gift of the Spirit of Christ, it is also on man's part mediated through faith in Christ. Like justification, the quickening that depends on justification therefore also finds its necessary subjective precondition in faith. The gracious gift of the Holy Spirit, too, can only be given by God to the one who is willing to accept it, and this in reality is only he who realizes his sin and death, and in faith in the grace of God revealed in Christ flees to the God of grace, beseeching him for mercy. Faith in Christ is not only the necessary subjective instrument for receiving the Holy Spirit, however. It is also the necessary subjective medium for the activity in and by the Spirit that is the foundation of the new life. Such life is, for the life of man who in himself is sinful, only possible as a life of faith in Christ. Only through his heartfelt, trusting, personal appropriation of God's grace as revealed in Christ can the sinner come to that love of God, that realization of the truth, that peace, joy, and boldness that characterizes the new life. The believing heart is thus the fertile soil into which the Spirit of Christ is sown as a heavenly, quickening seal, and from which he also brings forth as a sprouting seedling a new spiritual life, which according to its innermost being is a human and individual reproduction of Christ's life: God's own eternal life. Since the activity of faith before the communication of the Spirit essentially consists of receptivity, his activity as the indwelling source of the new life must essentially be to influence the activity of faith. He must transform its receptivity into a productivity from which the new life can proceed. He causes this "faith in Christ" to appear as a faith that works in and through a new love. But thereby also he reveals his power in a new realization of truth, and a new peace of mind. This renewed influence of faith on the heart will always depend upon the believing appropriation of grace in Christ. It thus cannot make itself completely felt until the sinner has come to full assurance of his state of grace. To that extent, then, it is also essential for the Spirit in his activity as the "Spirit of life" to appear as the "Spirit of adoption," who "seals" the justified sinner by assuring him of his justification and state of grace.

This faith in Christ that in this way mediates the communication of the Spirit of Christ and the new life is not something that the Spirit finds to be immediately existing in natural man. Even though it is an act of man's own free and personal decision, faith is nevertheless not a product of man's natural development. Rather, like the new life, it is itself a divine gift of grace: a product of the creative intervention of saving grace in man's immediate reality, by the Holy Spirit. By its own power, the heart of natural man is in its spiritual death just as little able to accept God's grace in faith as it is able to fulfill the law of God. Since the heart is closed in itself to the gift of grace, it cannot accept it until it becomes opened to it by grace itself. The sinner cannot "come to Christ" in faith until he has been "drawn" to him by God. The free, personal decision that makes itself felt in the sinner's faith in God's grace is dependent upon a prompting and determining intervention of God, through the gospel concerning this grace. The sinner receives by this intervention the power he lacks in himself to accept the message of grace in faith, to turn to the God of grace, and to lay hold of his grace. Faith's birth in the heart of the sinner is thus a divine work of grace, just as much as the communication of the Spirit, to which man can make no contribution whatsoever, but solely play a purely passive role. Before he can in the Holy Spirit enter the heart, and give it his life, God must himself open it and make it fit for the reception of the gracious gift of life. However, it is only in the abstract concept that the activity of the Holy Spirit in creating faith can be said to precede his giving of life. In the reality of life, the creation of faith completely coincides in time with the communication of the Holy Spirit. In the same moment that the Spirit has generated the required subjective receptivity for himself and his gift, he must also communicate himself to the heart that has been opened in this way, and fill it with his life. Therefore must also faith's birth in the heart, and thus also the sinner's conversion to God, be said to form part of the regeneration of the sinner. Regeneration, then, in this further sense of the word, becomes that gracious act of God whereby he by his Spirit creates faith in Christ in the sinner's heart, and, in the same moment in which he thus has opened it for his gift of grace, also in the Spirit takes residence in the heart and bestows upon it of the fullness of his life. Regeneration thus becomes a union of two factors, of which the one (the gift of faith) is the necessary prerequisite for justification, and the other (the gift of the Holy Spirit) its necessary sequel.

Despite the fact that the creation of faith thus is exclusively a work of God's grace, it is nevertheless impossible without a certain communication between divine grace and human freedom. No one can be forced into faith against his will.

Converting grace cannot be any "irresistible grace"—it cannot work with any power that man cannot withstand. Within the concept of human freedom of will there lies the possibility of an opposition to grace by which its action can be hindered. But that which thus is included in freedom as a possibility appears because of the power of sin over natural man as a reality—indeed, as a physical necessity. Man, controlled by sin and in enmity to God as he is, when left to himself cannot but oppose anything that could lead to a change in his situation. The necessary prerequisite for the true occurrence of conversion, therefore, is a cancellation of the heart's natural opposition to converting grace. The heart must be made fit to be influenced by such grace through a preparation for conversion. Such working of grace must be subjectively made possible, and this preparation, just as much as conversion, can only be a work of God's saving grace. The goal of this prevenient grace, more particularly, can only be to liberate the sinner's will from the natural necessity of this opposition, enable him to freely choose between opposition and nonopposition, and thus make it subjectively possible for him to allow himself to be directed by converting grace. This goal cannot be said to be achieved until the heart has received from the gospel's testimony concerning Christ that impression of its truth that is the necessary subjective prerequisite for faith in him. With the possibility of believing the gospel there lies also in this impression the possibility of giving up the heart's natural opposition to it. The reception of this impression depends on the one hand on the sinner's fitness to receive it, and on the other on his possession of that knowledge and concept of Christ that can produce such an impression. None of these conditions are present in natural man. As such, he knows nothing of Christ, and that which he can learn of him through the testimony of the gospel will in any case make no deeper impression upon his heart, so long as it has not been crushed by conviction of sin. The essential task of prevenient grace must therefore be to bring about both these conditions. Its activity must first and foremost be to "awaken" the sinner from his slumber in sin and bring him to reflection on his situation and conviction of sin. Thus, the state of "contrition" is produced, in which state alone the heart is fit to receive the impression of the truth of the gospel that is under consideration here. However, if its awakening and crushing activity is not to lead to despair and perdition, it must be immediately accompanied by another effect on the sinner that can bring the contrite heart to seek the healing it needs where it can be found, that is, "draw it to Christ." As prevenient grace prepares the soil in the sinner's heart for the seed of the gospel, it must also bring him this seed, communicate to him the necessary knowledge about Christ and God's revealed grace in Christ, and thereby enable him to gain a true understanding of the content of this gospel, and finally through this to give his heart the intended impression of its truth. Both in "crushing" and "drawing to Christ," prevenient grace thus appears as grace "illuminating" the sinner. In both functions it turns first and foremost to man's consciousness in order that through this it might influence the heart. The goal of its activity is to bring the sinner to a realization of sin and of grace that can grip the heart and thereby enable it to make its choice. This means, therefore, that the preparation of the sinner for conversion generally does not appear as a momentary operation of grace; rather it is characterized by a successive development. An additional contribution to this development is the limiting influence that the opposition of the heart to grace can and usually does exercise upon the activity of prevenient grace. At each and every point in this development man has the power both to evade the illumination of grace and to hinder its influence on the heart. Even the impression that the heart can have received from the truth of the gospel, although it is completely involuntary, and to that extent also inevitable, is nevertheless in no way irresistible. The will of the heart is thereby enabled only to give up its opposition. It still has the power to evade the impression it has received, and by this opposition, which is no longer merely natural yet freely chosen, and therefore redoubled, to hinder the birth of faith. In cases where such opposition is not total, but only partial, there often begins at this point a longer period of time during which the individual is drawn to Christ by prevenient grace in regret over sin and a longing for grace. To that extent he can be said to be "on the way to conversion," but he has nevertheless not yet given up his opposition to the attraction of grace, and thus is neither converted nor fit to be converted.

This same grace according to its subjective effect thus must be described as an illuminating and, by its illumination, a crushing grace that draws to Christ. According to its objective mode of action, on the other hand, this grace appears as calling grace. The enlightenment concerning sin and grace, which is the only means by which prevenient grace can reach its goal, cannot be communicated to the sinner except by an objective notification of the truth of which he is ignorant. God can only bring him to the requisite conviction of sin by notifying him of his law, and through this to present his holy will for man and his righteous judgment of the sinner. Similarly, God can only bring the sinner to a realization of grace and salvation in Christ by announcing his gospel, and through this to hold up before him his willingness to make sinners blessed. But in this notification of the truth there is also an urging to submit to it and to give it room in the heart. In particular, this refers to that factor that is our chief concern, to which the other factor is only an additional, subservient point. God cannot present his grace to the sinner in the gospel without at the same time offering it to him, encouraging him to accept the righteousness and life that he has prepared for the whole world in Christ, and inviting him to come to Christ and allow himself to be saved by him. In other words, God through the gospel calls the sinner to that fellowship with Christ in which state alone salvation is to be found for him, and to that conversion by which he can alone share in that salvation. This call of God is thus more closely an expression of the activity of prevenient grace as it "draws to Christ." It is an act of God's grace through Christ by which it presents and offers itself to the sinner. However, even though it thus first and foremost works by the testimony of the gospel as that which alone is able to draw to Christ, it does also make use of the law or "schoolmaster to Christ." Thus, prevenient grace in reality embraces all the sinner's preparation for conversion, and therefore it finds its completion in conversion itself. To answer the call is to be converted to God, and to be "called," in the subjective sense of the word, is to be converted or regenerated. That offer of grace and salvation that goes out to the sinner in God's call of grace, as an expression of his will to grace, is seriously meant, and therefore also objectively efficacious! Just as it proceeds from God with the definite goal of bringing the sinner to whom it goes out to repentance, so also does it include within itself the power to effect its task and achieve its goal. It is an offer or oblation of grace, which wherever it is not rejected becomes by its own inherent power true communication of grace. As an expression of God's universal will to grace, his readiness to allow sinners a share in the redemption that he in Christ has prepared for the whole world, the call of grace itself must be universal. It must go out to the whole world reconciled with God in Christ, even though there may be among the many to whom it is given only relatively few who actually answer it. This universality of the call of grace must be upheld as a postulate of faith against any particularistic understanding, even though we may be unable to show how it reaches all individuals.

Many have asked how the universality of the call can be harmonized with the fact that it accomplishes its goal by a historical development, that is, over time so that also many have departed and continue to depart this world without the call having reached them. However, this question cannot be answered by referring to the call that can be said to form part of God's actual self-revelation to all men in their consciences and in the direction of their fate, nor by assuming that there is a continuation of the call of grace in another world. This call can certainly prepare the heart and give support to the actual call of grace through the law and the gospel, but it in no way replaces a lack of the latter. And the idea of the possibility of a conversion after death cannot be reconciled with the Christian view of the earthly life as the time for grace, salvation, and decision.

We have in the foregoing been considering the regeneration of the person who has matured to the development of full personality. But also for the infant is regeneration both possible and necessary. Its need for such a working of grace is implicit in the concept of sin as inherited sin. And that of which it thus is in need it also is fit to receive. The subjective receptivity for the gracious working of regeneration, which in the adult must first be effected by the call to repentance of prevenient grace, must be said to be immediately present in the child, in whom sin cannot as yet express itself in active opposition to regenerative grace. That longing for salvation that in the adult is suppressed by the power of sin now developed into actuality can still assert itself unhindered in the child. True, its heart also is by nature turned away from God and closed to his Spirit, so that he must therefore here, too, first open the heart before he can enter and take up residence. But, since the child nevertheless does not respond to God's action with any actual opposition, he can also at the same moment as he touches it immediately enter and do his work. From this, the regeneration of the child may be recognized as a gracious action of the Holy Spirit whereby he in a way that is outside an area of experience, and therefore cannot be explained, more closely, opens its heart by nature closed to God and gives it a new direction toward God, corresponding to the adult's faith in God's grace in Christ. He also then thereby enters into the heart, takes the child up into the quickening fellowship of Christ, communicates to it of the fullness of his life, and thus makes it a new creation in him.

The Renewal of the Sinner

The quickening begun in regeneration finds its necessary continuation in the renewal of the regenerated sinner. As a new seed of life, the spiritual life communicated at regeneration is intended for a continually more complete growth. It is therefore essential for the regenerated believer to be involved in a continually proceeding development, a continued "putting on" of the "new man," already in principle put on at regeneration. There must be continued transfiguration or transformation into likeness with God, a steady growth, in other words, that, since the new life also in its continued existence finds its source in faith in Christ, essentially must consist in growth in faith. The essence of the new life as a spiritual life means that the renewal of the regenerated sinner depends upon his own free personal activity. It is no physical development, rather a development of freedom, in which, in the power of the new life that he has received, he himself works on its growth. However, this personal activity is itself in reality impossible without a struggle. At regeneration, a new seed of life has been grafted into the old being of sin, which thus certainly is given over to death, but at the same time, nevertheless, in no way is destroyed. Pushed aside as it is from the dominating position it originally held at the center of the personality, it nevertheless still has its fixed place on its periphery, in the nature that is corrupted by sin. From here it continues without interruption to react against this new life principle, not only by exercising an inhibiting and disturbing influence on all of its outward expressions, but at the same time in working to destroy it. In so doing, the old nature seeks to regain its old domineering position in the heart, by seducing and drawing the new nature out of its fellowship with God. Continued renewal can therefore only be achieved through a struggle of the spirit with the flesh in which the regenerated sinner continually strives to withstand sin's attacks and avoid backsliding, to remain standing in faith, and thus to preserve himself in his regenerated state. In addition to this, he must also continue more and more completely to conquer, lay aside, and eradicate what remains of the old nature, more and more to "lay hold of eternal life" and to penetrate deeper into fellowship with God, seeking to be more and more strengthened and established in faith, and thereby also in his position as a child of God. This struggle can be more or less intense in different individuals, or within the same individual at different times. However, it cannot cease altogether; otherwise the believer will thereby fall away from the state of faith and regeneration. As a struggle of spirit against flesh, a struggle of faith for its own survival and development, it is essentially characterized by a continued, daily repentance from sin to God. It is the believing heart's uninterrupted, continual turning away from sin in heartfelt sorrow over it and abhorrence of it, renunciation of natural desire for it, and a turning to God, seeking and appropriating his grace in Christ. Therefore, the regenerated sinner's life in this struggle of renewal is no undisturbed rest in full possession and unimpaired enjoyment of the essential riches of faith. Rather, it is an uninterrupted continual transformation of the poverty of the longing for faith into the riches of possession of faith.

At the same time as renewal in this way is dependent upon the regenerated sinner's own personal activity, it is nevertheless equally a divine work of grace, a work of God's renovative grace. That which quickening grace has begun in regeneration, it must also continue and bring to completion. The personal activity of the regenerated sinner for his renewal is dependent upon the continued influx of the spiritual power of life communicated to him at regeneration from the source of life, without interruption. He is only able to preserve and establish himself in faith to the extent that he is preserved and established by God. His renewal must therefore also find its continuing foundation and presupposition in the same life fellowship with God that enabled his regeneration. Like regeneration, renewal is a work of "Christ in us," through the Spirit residing in the heart. In the Spirit the regenerated sinner not only has a "seal" of his state of grace and a "guarantee" of the completion of his redemption, which as such strengthens, preserves, and establishes him in faith, but also an objective principle that directs and controls his total will. The difference between the activity of quickening grace in regeneration and renewal is essentially that in the former it appears as creating and thus also working alone, while in the latter it is supporting, and thus also cooperating with the new personality created in regeneration. This description of renewal as a product of cooperation between quickening grace and the regenerated sinner must not be understood to mean that these two elements of this working of grace are placed on an equal footing with each other. Rather the renewing action of grace in the regenerated sinner's heart must always be seen as primary, and his own personal activity for his renewal as secondary.

The spiritual life development that thus is the action of renovative grace consists, in the area of the will, in its continued liberation, being in principle freed by regeneration, and a continued purification of the desiring heart from the pollution of sin that still adheres to it. There is a continually stronger and fuller unfolding of the love that is the fruit of faith and the fullness of the law, and a proceeding development of the holiness communicated at regeneration. This development is known as the sanctification of the regenerated sinner. The struggle by which this process of sanctification is advanced is directed toward the evil desire that still dwells within the "flesh" of the regenerated sinner. In this struggle he must remain in a relationship to lust purely of suffering, where it remains something that is alien to the basic orientation of the desiring heart. Lust must remain something that exercises its inhibiting and polluting influence on his will, against his will. So long as this is the case, his struggle will retain the character of a trial that is assigned to him by renovative grace in order to promote his sanctification. As soon as he begins to allow himself to be drawn away and enticed by evil desires, on the other hand, and gives them room in his heart beside love for God, then the struggle will become characterized by temptation to evil. In this situation, the heart is drawn to both sides at once, and therefore also there is the danger that the process of sanctification might be interrupted by a fall.

A corresponding development is brought about by renovative grace in the area of understanding. The human spirit's natural longing for clear and coherent understanding of everything that he sees as an object for understanding finds new sustenance for the regenerated sinner in that "mystery of God" that with all its "treasures of wisdom and knowledge" has become the possession of the heart by faith. All essential fruit of regeneration is therefore also insight into the truth appropriated in faith that, aided by the thoughts working in the service of faith, cannot but exercise a strengthening and establishing influence on faith itself in return. But this new understanding of truth that the regenerated believer receives is encumbered by the imperfection that characterizes the whole of his existence. The natural limitations of man's intellectual power itself mean that both the clarity and completeness of his understanding is always only relative. In the same way, sin in the flesh and the heart's natural opposition to the truth, whose power in regeneration as yet is broken only in principle, will always exercise an inhibiting and disturbing influence upon the understanding. In this case, renewal will appear as a developing spiritual enlightenment, a continual growth in the understanding of truth as given in the regeneration. However, it will always remain within the precondition of faith, and therefore can only be developed through a struggle. The fleshly mind with all its high and arrogant thoughts must be continually brought into captivity in obedience to faith and thus hindered in exercising its disturbing influence upon the faith life. The growth of the understanding is essentially dependent upon the growth of faith, and thus also upon the progress of sanctification. The power of the regenerated sinner to penetrate the depths of God's being and will by his understanding will always be relative to the power of his faith, by which he can appropriate the truth in his heart and allow himself to be permeated and directed by it, and by which he conquers his self-love and gives himself to God in childlike love.

Also the emotions will gradually be permeated by the power of renovative grace. Here, renewal consists in the renewed heart continually being blessed, and its growth in the peace, joy, and confidence of faith. The normal fruit of faith in God's grace is an assurance of his state of grace that the believer can feel and experience. There is a blessed feeling of inner harmony that in return must exercise a strengthening influence on faith itself and the intellectual and moral life that proceeds from faith. But here, too, it must be pointed out that the regeneration of the sinner is as yet only the beginning of his quickening. The seed of a new, blessed life that thereby has been sown in his heart cannot in its self-development avoid being hindered and disturbed by sin in the flesh. The believer's peace is as yet no perfect peace, nor is his joy as yet unmixed. Just as man's emotions in general are linked to physical stimuli that in no way always are within his power to control, so can there be both in the regenerated believer's physical-psychological nature and in the world around him many different things that could disturb his spiritual peace and joy, and obscure his perceptible assurance about his state of grace, thereby also pulling away from his faith that support and source of strength that it should find in such assurance. When this takes place, that special form of the struggle of faith usually known as the temptation of doubt can appear. By this is understood faith's struggle against the doubts about its truth and reality that appear when the believer misses the feelings that are the normal fruit of faith. It is faith's struggle to protect itself in the face of the despair of unbelief, only conquered in principle in regeneration, which again breaks forth in the heart's feeling of being abandoned by God as it becomes overwhelmed by the pain of conviction of sin. Thus, also, this struggle will appear for the believer's consciousness as a struggle with God who seems to be withdrawing his grace.

The goal for this renovative development can be nothing else than that which originally was set by God as the end of man's moral development: that personal perfection in which the ideal of human life is completely realized. However, man will not be able to reach that goal in this world. That perfection to which he can bring himself here will always remain relative. He can never be free from sin in this life. Therefore, neither will his new life at any time appear here in its true form, no matter how far he may have come in its development. Over against his regenerated and renewed "inward man" there will until the end be an "outward man" who as yet is not penetrated by the Spirit of life. For the same reason, no matter how strongly he may, through his developing renewal, be established in his state and position as a child of God, he will nevertheless never be above the possibility of falling away from it. His new life is not a physical, but an ethical life, always subject to the influence of the will, and therefore always exposed to the danger of being destroyed by sin in the flesh. Thus, his salvation in the sense of his complete quickening, will always, right up to the end, appear to him as something belonging to the future, the objective of his hope. His renewal must embrace his earthly existence in its totality, and continue uninterrupted right up to the end. Where this takes place, where the struggle of faith continues faithfully without interruption until death, there the Lord will also give victory to the one who struggles. Where the struggle is interrupted by a fall, on the other hand, there must of course saving grace also cease to act as renewing. In this case, so long as the sinner as yet has not been completely unreceptive to its influence, its activity will aim to restore the fallen through renewed repentance and regeneration. Here, too, it will therefore essentially appear as grace calling the sinner back to repentance and fellowship with the Lord.

Assuming that the regeneration of the child has been a true regeneration, then also must the life development of the regenerated child, where it is not interrupted by a fall, in its totality come under the concept of renewal. The normal situation is for such a child to grow, as in age, so in wisdom and favor with God and man. Depending on its actual development toward mature personality, the child's spiritual life under the influence of renovative grace will be characterized by daily repentance. As time goes on, he will become aware both of his own sin and of God's grace that is bestowed upon him in Christ. He will come to a clearer realization and a continually greater appropriation of that which it finds objectively given, both in one direction and in the other, and thus also is led deeper and deeper into the spirit's struggle with the flesh. During this development there will therefore be just as little room for any "awakening" in the true sense of the word as for any new regeneration. This is true, even though the less normal course of development in individual cases may mean that the realization and appropriation of sin and grace can seem like a more momentary, more sudden transformation, and thus gain a certain resemblance to the awakening and regeneration of natural man.

NILS LAACHE (1831–1892)

Pastor, revivalist preacher, and local politician Nils Laache was very active in the revival circles in Norway and was responsible for the translation into Norwegian of many of the works of Swedish pietist writer Carl Olof Rosenius. He also edited the Christian magazine For Fattig og Riig *(For the poor and the rich). Laache was decorated Knight of the Royal Norwegian Order of St. Olav in 1885. In 1884 he was made bishop of Trondheim and served in this position until his death. Presented here is a selection of entries from* Book of Family Prayer, *a very popular book of devotions organized according to the church year. Published in Norway in 1883, it was reprinted eight times through 1922 and achieved widespread usage among Norwegian Americans through an English translation.*

Book of Family Prayer

NEW YEAR'S EVE—PSALM 90

"So teach us to number our days, that we may apply our hearts unto wisdom."

It is a sad thought that the days of our life fly so fast. How soon, alas, do the flowers of our youth wither and die! The serious feature, however, the heaviest and weariest part of the consideration, is this, that *sin* is the cause. It would profit us little, at the close of the year, to indulge in melancholy speculations on the flight of time and the rapid revolution of the years; but it shall profit us much to meditate upon our life and to know our sins. Knowledge of sin is the keynote in this touching prayer of Moses. "For we are consumed by thine anger, and by thy wrath are we troubled. Thou hast set our iniquities before thee, our secret sins in the light of thy countenance. The strength of the days of our years is labor and sorrow." Bow, as did Moses, in deepest humility before the Lord, and pray earnestly for mercy. Make up your account at the close of the year, or year will be added to year with unknown and unforgiven sins, and the amount will be appalling at the last; for some time the day of reckoning will come.—During this year you have again received a thousand benefits from the Lord; all that he did was done with the kindest purpose. But you, how have you been minded toward him? How have you received his manifold mercies, and what manner of life have you led during these many days of grace? Make a clean breast of it! You have, mayhap, walked without God and served sin? Though you be old, you may, possibly, not as yet have experienced true conversion and given your heart to God? Or do you, perhaps, spend your days in the enjoyment of worldly pleasures or the pursuit of fleeting honors and wealth? However, let me assume, that you are a converted and believing soul;—how much more faithfully and diligently than you have done it, might you not have employed your time! Consider, how much better you might have thanked the Lord, and how much more you might have benefited your fellowmen; how much sin you have committed, and how much good you have *left undone!* Do, then, weigh this with care, and confess it with sorrow; prostrate yourself before the Lord and cry to him for mercy. And, behold, he spreads his hands above you, and forgives you, and blesses you. He takes away your shortcomings in all things, but crowns your work. You carry, then, no debt of sin over from the old into the new year, but only the grace and good will of God in Christ. Blessed be the Lord, who satisfies us early with his mercy; so that we, who have merited everlasting and voiceless sorrow, can sing and be glad all our days. The beauty of our God is upon us, and he shall establish the work of our hands. We close the year as we began it: *In the name of Jesus.*

> *Accept our poor offering of praise, most high and blessed God. Thanks for everything that we have received or suffered during the year. The Lord gave, and the Lord hath taken away; blessed be the name of the Lord! Amen.*

Thursday after First Sunday after Epiphany —Psalm 119:9–20

> *"With my whole heart have I sought thee: O let me not wander from thy commandments."*

None other has followed the word of God as closely as did our Lord Jesus, and none other has kept his way as clean as he. He loved his Father's ordinances, and delighted himself in them, and kept his word in his heart; and he is lovable in the sight of God, and comely and fair above any other among the children of men. We will earnestly strive to be like him. Dear young people, do you rejoice in the word of God? If you do not, you are on an unclean and slippery path; the trail that you are following does not lead to the home of light and glory. Reverse your steps, and begin to love the word of the Lord. You have a Bible, which you received as a baptismal gift, or at the time of your confirmation; or if not, there surely is a Bible in your home, or you may easily procure one for yourself. Begin to read it daily, first the books of the New Testament in their sequence, then the Pentateuch, the Psalms, and the Prophets; then the New Testament again, and thereafter the whole Bible. Read with careful attention, ask God to enlighten you that you may understand the word, and *obey* it with honest soul. Do not neglect the divine services in the church, and do not let the wicked one come and catch away the word from you while you hear it, or while you are on your way to your home. I beseech you by the love of God and by your precious covenant of baptism, obey my advice, keep the word of the Lord in your heart. Would you not like to keep your way clean? Would you not like to resemble Jesus? You aspire to life and happiness, and imagine that you will find them in the pleasures of the world. David rejoiced in the testimonies, and delighted himself in the decrees of the Lord; and with the deepest yearning of his soul, he prayed that he might behold the wondrous things in the law of the Lord; that he might live and walk according to the word of God. Should not you do likewise? Verily, it is your sworn enemy who shuts your heart to the word of God. You are a child of God from the hour of your baptism; the Father loves you, Jesus loves you, the Holy Ghost loves you, the holy angels, also, love you. Do not pollute your path with ungodliness, but in the way of earnestness, sincerity, and fear of God: "Lord, thy word have I hid in mine heart, that I might not sin against thee."

Teach me, O Lord, the way of thy statutes; and I shall keep it unto the end. Turn away mine eyes from beholding vanity; and quicken thou me in thy way. Amen.

FRIDAY AFTER THIRD SUNDAY AFTER EPIPHANY —ISAIAH 25:6–9

"This is the Lord; we have waited for him, we will be glad and rejoice in his salvation."

Could anything more beautiful be said concerning the glory of our Lord Jesus and the salvation of his people than that which the prophet says in this text? "Many shall come from the east and west, and shall sit down with Abraham, and Isaac, and Jacob, in the kingdom of heaven." The feast shall be prepared for *all* people. All nations shall be there. The Lord of hosts, our Jesus, does not do anything on a small scale. What a feast, what a meal it will be! There the wine is without dregs, and the fat things are all marrow; there is nothing but pure, unmixed joy and bliss, nothing but love, nothing but God himself, who at this feast is all things in all. For the covering that still is cast over all people is taken away, and we know God face to face; we see him in Christ as he is. Then death is wholly and utterly destroyed forever; it is swallowed up in victory, is gone, has disappeared, even as night with its darkness disappears before the sun. And with death there is an end of sorrow, and crying, and sighing, and wailing. Dishonor and ignominy have been buried out of sight forever.—These things has the Lord promised to his church; the mouth of the Lord has spoken it. We still await the fulfillment in its entirety; but in faith and hope we already possess salvation. Thousands upon thousands of the Gentiles sit at the table of God in his church on earth, eat his flesh, drink his blood, live of his life, taste his love, and see him with uncovered face, though still as through a glass, darkly. And who shall number the multitude of those already at home in heaven? But these two, the saints on earth and the saved in heaven, are one people, and stand together in one place, around the same Lord; the only difference being that the saved in heaven see that which we as yet only believe. Who, then, can doubt that the Lord shall do that which he has spoken, and that he shall gather us as one people in the consummation of glory?

Praise be to thee, Lord Jesus! Do thou soon gather into thy church of all peoples as many as can be saved, and as shall furnish thy wedding feast with guests, in order that the glory of the perfect church may come quickly. Amen.

Fifth Sunday after Epiphany —Matthew 13:24–30

"Let both grow together until the harvest: and in the time of harvest I will say to the reapers, Gather ye together first the tares, and bind them in bundles to burn them: but gather the wheat into my barn."

In the visible church here on earth, tares and wheat grow together. We need never think to present a pure community of saints before the end of the world. Christ himself says, Let the children of the kingdom and the children of the devil grow together. Herein there are several important lessons for us. 1) It is not ours to judge; the Lord knows his own; *he* and none other holds the fan in his hand. That the church is to debar from its holy communion them that are manifestly wicked is another matter (1 Cor 5). 2) You shall not take offense, though it come to your notice that there are hypocrites and wicked men in the church. You shall not, on this account, secede; else you assist the enemy in rending asunder the church of God. Conquer such temptations to pride by calling to mind your own littleness; and pay attention to the lesson that the Lord teaches in this test: where there is wheat there always will be tares; it would not be a true wheat field if the enemy did not care to sow tares in it. 3) Do not rely on your being a Christian in name, or on your fellowship with the faithful; examine yourself earnestly before God, and bring forth good fruit unto the Lord. 4) For the sake of his pious children, God spares the world. The great and haughty men of the world in the Christian lands are indebted to the despised saints of God for his long-suffering patience. The believers carry the world and the world's culture on their shoulders. 5) An eternal separation is coming, and the angels shall make no mistake as to who the saints are. Then the present order of the universe shall of necessity cease to be, and every human society on earth shall be dissolved; for all their roots shall then be torn apart. 6) Then the church of Christ shall be purged of all hypocrites, and shall consist of saints only.—Now, are you prepared for the day of judgment? Have you the earnest of the Spirit that you are the elect? Do you keep yourself undefiled of the mind and life of the worldly minded Christians? All who offend and do iniquity shall be cast into the furnace of fire; there shall be wailing and gnashing of teeth. Then shall the righteous shine forth as the sun in the kingdom of their Father. Who hath ears to hear, let him hear!

Lord Jesus, protect us from the evil enemy; preserve us from carnal security, from spiritual pride, from coming with undisciplined and unclean hearts to thy communion table; from sects and schisms, and from judging without charity. Keep us watchful and prepared for the judgment, and let us stand before thee with honor on that day. Amen.

Wednesday after Septuagesima Sunday —1 Corinthians 3:18–23

"For the wisdom of this world is foolishness with God: for it is written, He taketh the wise in their own craftiness."

Persons who are puffed up with conceit have no place in the church of Christ. He that seems to himself to be wise is far away from God; he must become a fool, before he can become wise. He must learn that he knows nothing; in this way, only, can he receive instruction of the Spirit of God. For the Holy Ghost shows us clearly that we are fools, darkened and blinded, without true knowledge of God; but he also teaches us to know God. Furthermore, he leads us into an ever deeper knowledge of self, and keeps our hearts humble, by the very fact of his revealing to our souls more and more of the wisdom of God. As a result we see that we know very little; but, at the same time, we are enabled to surmise and catch a glimpse of a depth of glorious and blessed things, and to understand that we live in the very midst of divine excellencies. What reason have we, then, to be puffed up? Or what have we in which to glory as against one another? We are not one another's masters, but servants; we have not been appointed to rule over one another, but are joint partakers of the wisdom of God, that we may serve one another. And yet all is ours. Each one of us is part owner of the whole. All the gifts that are given to *you* are *mine* also, and mine are yours. For we are one body in Christ. Paul's gifts of grace belong to you, and you belong to the apostolic church. The property of the father is the common property of all the children.—No, the wisdom of God does not lead to conceit and envy. Such things as these come of the wisdom from below. The wisdom which is from above is humble, pure, peaceable, full of mercy and all the fruits of love. O, that no man among us might deceive himself!

Lord God, our heavenly Father, enlighten us by thy Spirit; teach us that we of ourselves understand nothing; and teach us to know thy wisdom from on high, that we therein may serve one another with humility and faithfulness as good stewards of thy manifold grace. Amen.

Second Sunday in Lent —1 Thessalonians 4:1–7

"For God hath not called us unto uncleanness, but unto holiness."

The will of God is your sanctification. It could not be otherwise; for God is holy. Still it profits us to hear and consider that in laboring and striving after holiness we have the will of God with us. Then we may know that victory is assured, even though the path be difficult, and though we seem to be losing ground. Labor jealously for your purification; strive after it with zeal and earnestness. The Apostle beseeches and exhorts us by the Lord Jesus that we would do this. He *beseeches* us; shall we not hear him? He *exhorts* us; shall we despise his exhortation? He beseeches and exhorts by *the Lord Jesus*, in the service and spirit and power of Jesus, by his love, for his blessed name's sake, for the sake of his atoning obedience and death. Shall we not obey him? You made rapid advance in holiness during the earliest period of your Christian life. You displayed great zeal in the work of purging out all sin and of pleasing God. You improved immensely in a short time; your growth was rapid. Shall the blossom not put forth a bud, or shall the bud die without ripening into fruit? You have been taught how we ought to walk. Does not your heart burn within you when the Apostle here speaks of *pleasing God* and of *abounding therein more and more*? "To please God," to walk according to the good pleasures of Jesus;—these are things to touch the innermost chords of the Christian heart. "Not in the lust of concupiscence," God forbid! The holy bride of Christ to defile herself with the uncleanness of the Gentiles! The very suggestion of such a thing gives us a shock.—Out, then, with the unclean desires; purge the heart of them. Immerse your souls in the holiness of Jesus, and in his purity, that you "hate even the garment spotted by the flesh."—It is much to be regretted, if you do not *believe* that he will give you strength to do this; for then the devil has unmanned you. As God is holy, he has in Christ given you grace to become holy; and when you neglect it you grieve the Spirit of God. We also beseech and exhort by the Lord Jesus: be in earnest in the matter of mortifying the lusts of the flesh. You are not called unto uncleanness, as unfortunately seems to the opinion of many nominal Christians; but you are *called unto holiness*. Mark this: *God has called you unto holiness*. Now strive after it with the zeal and perseverance of faith. The commandment of God and his promise to you in Jesus Christ are true and faithful.

Most holy Lord Jesus, give to us thy pure mind. Help us to mortify the unclean lusts of the flesh and to walk in holiness, that by the Holy Spirit we may please thee and the Father. Lord grant us this great mercy, that we increase in holiness from day to day. Amen.

Monday after Third Sunday in Lent —John 18:33–38

"To this end was I born, and for this cause came I into the world, that I should bear witness unto the truth."

Jesus is not the king of the Jews in the sense in which Pilate puts the question to him. Had he made use of his omnipotence in order to wield the scepter of an earthly king, he would not now have been standing before the governor, accused and derided by the chief rulers of his people. The Jews would, in that case, have done homage to him; for then he would have been such a Messiah as they desired.—We, also, have much of this same spirit. It is easy enough to complain of the blending together of the church and the temporal power as being a church-state or a state-church; but it is more difficult to renounce one's own appetite for rule, and to *live* in the truth that the kingdom of Christ is not of this world. We wish to begin reigning with Christ here on earth. To be trodden under foot; to be despised and slandered, and endure it in silence; to walk with him the way that leads through suffering and death; this we find difficult: difficult to understand, and difficult to practice. Our king shall help us.

As he confessed before the council that he is the Son of God, so he confesses before Pilate that he is *king*. He knows very well what will be the result of this declaration; that he will be mocked with dreadful blasphemy, that he will be outraged, and crowned with thorns: but he goes straight onward against all the daggers of death, and steps not aside by the breadth of a hair from his kingly course. He also knows that the heart of Pilate is as a lump of fat; yet with tireless patience he continues to pour the water of his grace upon it, to exercise his royal right to extend mercy, and to preach his truth unto salvation. At the very time when he is being condemned and suffers death for the whole world, he labors with the individual unhappy soul that is before him.—Pilate asks of him what he has done. Yes; what is the kingly office of Jesus? If Pilate had been *in earnest* when he inquired after the truth, he would himself have been made able to give the answer that you and I have learned from blessed experience: Jesus has vanquished the devil and destroyed death; he has founded a kingdom of salvation, in which he gives to the souls righteousness, peace, and joy through his Holy Spirit; he has brought me out of the darkness, regenerated me, given me power to trample sin under foot, given me a heritage in heaven; he comforts and heals me every day, and gives me patience, and sustains me, and never for a moment loses me out of his keeping. Pilate might have answered further:

Christ defends his church, leads his people, guides them through the wilderness; and soon he shall give them for their tribulations everlasting glory. His kingdom endures forever, and his throne does not totter; it is built on the eternal rock of truth. "Every one that is of the truth heareth his voice." It was merely a piece of impertinent pretense on the part of Pilate when he asked, "What is truth?" and therefore he remained a stranger to the kingly office of Christ. Hear it ye, then, who thirst after light and salvation; let it be heard round about in all the earth: Here is truth and victory and eternal life, here and in none other place; nowhere out of the kingdom of Christ is anything but darkness and death. Whom will ye follow and obey, Jesus or Pilate? What shall rule over you, truth or falsehood? Do not wait; make your choice now. For the sake of your soul's salvation, take up the cross, and give your heart to Jesus.

Precious Savior, speak thy word of truth to us, and draw our hearts to thee in true repentance and living faith. Thine will we be; and thee will we serve. Give us this salvation, and accept our poor thanks for thy ineffable grace. Amen.

Monday after Fifth Sunday after Easter —Matthew 6:5–8

"And when thou prayest, thou shalt not be as the hypocrites are."

Prayer is a matter of the *heart*; the *heart* alone is able to pray. The prayer that does not proceed from the heart is no prayer at all. Do you imagine that mere idle words can be a prayer to the Lord? In this Bible lesson Jesus teaches two things: 1) When you pray, present yourself before God, and deal with him only; keep close to him with all your thoughts and feelings. Let nothing else in the world be in your mind; whether it be the beams in the ceiling, or the stars in heaven; your daily business affairs, or your earthly joys and sorrows,—unless, indeed, you happen at the time to be speaking of them to the Lord. Neither shall you be thinking of the people who surround you, nor of the eyes that see you; but you shall be alone with your God, whether you are in your chamber or in the midst of a congregation. The Pharisees prayed in order that they might be regarded as pious men. You are guilty of the same hypocrisy when you want people to know how diligently you pray, and when you rejoice in being praised of men for the fervency and eloquence of your prayer.—How, then? Do the saints never have any irrelevant thoughts in their mind during prayer? Yes, nearly always, alas; but it grieves and humbles them, and they earnestly beseech God to give them grace to pray with proper devotion. 2) Be not concerned about the words in which your prayer is couched; and do not think that you can move God, as you can move men, with eloquent phrases. Speak straight from the heart, whether your words be many or few. It is immaterial whether you often repeat a thought, because your heart is so full of it that you cannot do otherwise, as was the case with David and Hannah; or you but breathe a few words, as did the publican. I have heard long prayers that were so earnest from beginning to end that they seemed not to contain a superfluous word, and I have heard short prayers that laid the whole case before God in a few words. But I have also heard long and idle prayers, from persons with a glib tongue, and from persons who made up for their lack of words by a constant repetition of God's name. The Lord does not prohibit the use of *many* words; but he prohibits "vain repetitions"; and he forbids us to think that God is to be moved by much speaking. "God is a Spirit; and they that worship him must worship him in spirit and in truth." What an abomination is that soulless, idle talk that people sometimes call prayer! But how excellent a thing is true prayer; how strong to force its way into the heart of God, and how sweet and blessed for the hearts out of which it issues! "The best of all the hours we spend while here on earth above the sod are those in which our way we wend in earnest prayer to meet our God." The Lord will and shall teach us this lesson.

Give us, O God, the Spirit of grace and prayer! Forgive us all the sins committed while praying to thee. Let thy Spirit work in us groanings that cannot be uttered. Our own condition strikes us with terror when we appear before thee, thou holy God. Have mercy on us; and let us never more come to thee with idle words, but let us always pray in spirit and in truth. Amen.

Friday after Sixteenth Sunday after Trinity —Romans 5:1–5

"Therefore being justified by faith, we have peace with God through our Lord Jesus Christ."

In vain the devil accuses the faithful on account of the sin and weakness that still cling to them; they stand in grace unceasingly, are clothed with the righteousness of Christ, and thus they all the time have peace with God. The Apostle does not here speak of the *feeling* of peace in their hearts, but of God's relation to them, that he no more condemns them or casts them off, but is to them a God of peace and a merciful Father in Christ. Rejoice, then, in the midst of your afflictions, dear Christian; you dwell continually in "a peaceable habitation, and in sure dwellings" with the Almighty. To have him as your enemy is terrible; but to be his child of grace is bliss; for "if *God* be for us, who can be against us?"—In Christ faith has access to the heart of God. He has taught us to pray to "our Father," and has given us the spirit of children; so that by his blood we have boldness to enter into the holiest, and find help at all times. Glorious estate of grace! Yet our rejoicing is in the hope of the glory *to come*. For this very reason, however, no tribulation can rob us of our joy; on the contrary, we glory in tribulations also. It has been said concerning woman that she "is in pain from the day on which she becomes a mother"; and this can be said with still more truth of a Christian: The world persecutes him, and God disciplines him; and he has labor and vexation and danger and fear every day. Herein we glory, however; for "tribulation worketh patience." It does not only *demand*, but *worketh* patience; and "patience worketh experience." It teaches us to suffer without complaining, and to have brave hearts, and to gain the victory. It consumes our pride and our despondency, and gives our faith the stamp of experience. Saint James says, "My brethren, count it all joy when ye fall into divers temptations; knowing this, that the trying of your faith worketh patience. But let patience have her perfect work." We glory in everything with which our enemies would injure us; for it must serve to injure and destroy our sin only, and to strengthen our hope of glory.—Cause and effect here work beautifully in a circle: *hope* causes *tribulation*; tribulation, *patience*; patience, *experience*; experience again, a stronger hope. Christ has taken away my sin; God has bound me to himself in an eternal covenant of peace; he who cannot lie has from ages eternal promised me everlasting life.

Give us, O God, faith unfeigned; and shed abroad thy love in our hearts by the Holy Ghost. Let our hope wax strong, and sustain us in our tribulations, that we may emerge from them with the genuine stamp of experience; and give us at last the heritage of glory. Amen.

Tuesday after Twenty-Seventh Sunday after Trinity —Revelation 7:13–17

"Therefore are they before the throne of God, and serve him day and night in his temple."

Tribulation first, and then glory! Peter wanted to remain on the mount. "Lord, it is good to be here; let us make here three tabernacles." No, Peter; it is too soon; you must yet a while suffer tribulation; the path to eternal glory leads by way of Cedron and Calvary.

The aged Jacob sighed: "I have waited for thy salvation, O Lord." Naomi lost both husband and sons, David was given tears to drink, and Jeremiah sang lamentations to move a stone. But behold them now before the throne of God, clothed with their white robes, and palms in their hands! There Moses is no longer troubled by the stubbornness of the people; there Job does not lose his riches, his children, his health, and his honor; there the eyes of Peter are not moist with tears; there Paul is rid of his thorn in the flesh; there Nehemiah is no longer a pitiful sight to see by reason of sadness on account of the city of God. Here on earth all believers have their afflictions, and are to be prepared to bear the cross after the Savior every day. But in the world to come they all are forever delivered from all evil; for there sin has disappeared, and with it sorrow and suffering and death; "There is fullness of joy; at the right hand of God are pleasures for evermore." It could not be more beautifully expressed in human language than it is in the words employed by the angel in our text: "The Lamb that is in the midst of the throne shall feed them, and shall lead them unto living fountains of waters; and God shall wipe away all tears from their eyes." The Lamb himself, the Lamb, who now has dominion over all things, and who now owns our heart; he shall care for us, and spread the tent over us. O how safe and how full of bliss shall be our habitation! And he shall lead us unto the living fountains of waters, where we shall drink without hindrance of the living streams of love; and the eternal God shall himself be our abundant comfort for all our tears on earth. Who, then, would not cheerfully suffer, and thank God for it? Fight the good fight for the crown; and the Lord shall give you a most glorious reward. Do not forget, however, that the blest in heaven are they *who have washed their robes, and made them white in the blood of the Lamb*. Ponder this, and follow Jesus!

> *Lord, thou knowest how lukewarm I am, alas; and thou knowest how many obstacles bar my way. Stir me up, and strengthen me; and help me to renounce and cast from me everything which may endanger my salvation. Reveal to me even now so much of the glory to come, that I may rejoice in hope, be patient in tribulation, and continue constant in prayer. Make me faithful, and guide me to the goal. Amen.*

2

DENMARK

NIKOLAI F. S. GRUNDTVIG (1783–1872)

N. F. S. Grundtvig, as he is usually known, was a pastor, author, poet, philosopher, historian, teacher, and politician with a lifelong interest in the Nordic legends and literature, a field in which he published extensively. He and his followers exerted a great influence in the formation of modern Danish national consciousness. It was steeped in the national literature and supported by deep spirituality. Reflecting and distancing himself from academic theology, Grundtvig always called himself a pastor rather than a theologian. He had a deep influence on the religious life of both Denmark and Norway, but that influence is very hard to describe, as is his distinctive understanding of the Christian faith. His basic understanding of the Christian faith sees it as an integral part of the Danish people ("folk"), with a strong interplay of religion and culture. Christianity, as expressed in the baptismal creed, is important in this present life as much as in the life to come.

Basic Christian Teachings

The Christian Signs of Life

Throughout the entire history of Christianity, all serious-minded people who have been attracted to its promise of eternal salvation have been aware that salvation could not have been an eternal concern without an evident influence on our temporal life. Those who deny this and expect from Christianity only a "blessed death" reveal that they are spiritually defunct and that they expose Christianity to the well-deserved scorn of the unbelieving world. If the gospel of Christ were only a so-called word of eternal life that deadened the temporal life even more than previously, no truth-loving person could believe it. Whatever is spiritually dead and powerless or even without spirit in our temporal existence could not possibly be spiritually alive and powerful in eternity. Our Lord Jesus Christ has given testimony that we must be reborn spiritually in the course of time in order to participate in eternal life, and he witnesses that this is a truth about the earthly existence that must be accepted before we can believe the truth about the heavenly experience.

Although the concept of Christianity held by the papists was as dead and powerless as possible without apparent contradiction, even they gave serious emphasis to a so-called Christian life, namely, the monastic life. This was alleged to be the possession of the whole church, and every member could take part in it by believing it and by contributing, each according to his ability, to the maintenance, welfare, and elevation of this so-called godly and Christian monastic life. That this monastic life, even with the halo of saints, was a spiritual and Christian pretense that revealed the spiritual death that it made efforts to hide has been so clearly exposed by church history that it needs no further documentation, at least not among the disciples of Martin Luther.

Turning now to the disciples of Martin Luther, the so-called Lutherans, it cannot be denied that they spoke and wrote themselves out on a limb when they claimed that the basically ungodly and unimprovable temporal life of man must be canceled out in the matters of salvation. They emphasized "a blessed death," quoting the wise preacher who said that the day of death is better than the day of birth [Eccl 7:1]. Like their Calvinistic counterparts, the Lutheran dogmatics were based on the dead letter and on the Scripture principle, and inasmuch as the academic life of the scholars was even less godly than that of the monks, the papists had a good argument when they accused us of having an even more lifeless concept of Christianity than they. But even then the Lutherans have chosen the better part and placed themselves on the side of life, for they left the spiritually dead pseudo-life to the papists and put their trust in the spirit that could make them alive in Christianity despite their apparent death.

Even while the Lutherans condemned the natural life of man, and despite their praise of "the blessed death" and "the blessed corpses," they still make serious demands for a living faith as a requirement for true Christianity. This faith was to demonstrate its spiritual power and its reality in a living confession, proclamation, and song of praise in the mother tongue. We now make bold to declare that we thereby have given name to the Christian signs of life, which must never be entirely absent in true Christianity and that never can be found together except where the spirit of the Lord, which creates life, is the divine spokesman, comforter, and guide to the truth for the congregation.

What caused the everyday catalepsy among even the true Lutherans and stunted the growth of Christian life was the confused and contradictory ideas about evangelical freedom with state church servitude, rebirth in baptism with Scripture living, and finally the Christian renewal of life without the benefit of a previous human life that could be renewed. When we now, by the grace of God, see the light of the Lord, the confession will be more firm and full, the proclamation far more simple and forceful, and the song of praise far more clear and delightful. All of our temporal human life will thereby gain a spiritual and hearty renewal, whose Christianity perhaps cannot be strictly documented but whose nature is sure. For this noble and hearty form of living will only be found where the Christian confession, proclamation, and song of praise are openly present. We have recently seen that this insight is a rarity among us, for when Søren Kierkegaard a few moments ago sought to frighten us out of our wits by his black-chalk drawing of the "mendicant monk" as the only true disciple of Christ, who literally carried his cross and followed him, he was confronted by a deep ignorance about the Christian life. In corners, however, he graciously met the morning light that gives glow to life and that urged him on by the dark cloud to vigorous advances on his heroic career.

In this situation it became clearly evident that all discussion and polemics about the Christian life is futile when we do not presuppose and maintain that the Christian congregation, created by the baptism of the Lord's own institution, has its peculiar source of life in this baptism and in it alone. The congregation's confession of faith at baptism is therefore the one and only Christian confession, and as a living expression of the Christian faith, it is the first and last sign of Christian life. With this basic insight into the Christian life as a faith life, and with this illumination of the confession of faith of the congregation as the true sign of life, it is readily seen that the Christian life can and must be revealed ever more strongly and more clearly in a living proclamation and song of praise corresponding to the confession. The entire history of the Christian church must demonstrate whether the new Christian life is more or less human than the old human life that was lived before Christ, or that human life that is alive today without baptismal faith in Christ and without the rebirth to Christ's human life in the baptism of his own institution.

It could be asserted boldly that this basic teaching (childhood teaching) is contrary to Scripture, for the polemics about the right interpretation of departed writers is endless. Book knowledge and Scripture knowledge differ so vastly that even if all Christians were avid readers, only a few of them could have real grounds for a conviction about the biblical character of Christianity or the Christianity of the Bible. We Christian scribes, however, will correctly and at all times defend the claim that our Sacred Scripture does not contradict our basic Christian teaching about "faith and baptism." On the contrary, there is complete agreement. The confession of faith is even given a wondrous testimony by a Word of the Lord: "Everyone who acknowledges me before men, the Son of man also will acknowledge before the angels of God" [Luke 12:8].

In an outward manner we must therefore necessarily first and last emphasize the confession of faith, even as we inwardly emphasize faith. In the new life the confession corresponds to breathing in the old. Be it far from our purpose, however, to exclude the proclamation or the song of praise as signs of life. As little can they be excluded, where the life born of faith is to thrive, as the life born of faith can gain and grow to maturity without hope and love. These are in relation to the living proclamation and song of praise as faith is to confession. Where confession is the only sign of life, the faith life will be weak and sickly and it will be tempted to death in every trial. This throws light on the fact that the Christian faith was originally given birth by the proclamation of him who came from above and plainly spoke "the Word of God." As the Apostle states it, faith is propagated only by the living proclamation of the Word of faith. He asks, "How are men to call upon him in whom they have not believed?" But he also asks, "How are they to hear without a preacher?" [Rom 10:14].

The Christian confession of faith can be found and has been found alive in a situation where the proclamation of faith largely is dead in the church, but the confession is then moribund and it will take the faith with it into the grave. Or it might be revived to re-create the living proclamation even as unmistakably happened through Martin Luther.

What happened with us in the beginning of our own century had evidently happened all over Christendom in the beginning of the sixteenth century. At that time the living proclamation of the Word of faith seemed to be almost dead or so obviously close to death that it had to be wondrously reborn in order to propagate the faith from generation to generation. It was obviously thus reborn through Martin Luther who proclaimed the "Word of faith" with spirit and life in the mother tongue. Luther thereby enlivened the proclamation not only among the kinfolk in England and the Nordic countries; he influenced even the Romance people, most evidently among the Calvinists but apparently everywhere....

Just as the congregation's confession of faith at baptism is the undeviating rule for all Christian confession and is the core of all Christian proclamation of the gospel, so must all Christian life exclusively be derived from the work of the Lord with his spoken word—in baptism and in communion. Only when the Christian life is thus elevated does the song of praise of the congregation become Christian. It was a sure sign of spiritual death in the papal church that the song of praise of the congregation in the mother tongue had died away, and the congregational song in the mother tongue in the Lutheran church is a clear sign of life and a valid witness to the Christian character of the Lutheran preaching. The song of praise will always correspond to the proclamation, for the song is the congregational answer to the address of the proclamation. The Calvinist preaching in the mother tongue engendered a corresponding song, but this took a Jewish not a Christian shape and thus denied the Christian life of the Calvinistic preaching. The cause for this was the superior attitude toward the fount of life in baptism and the life stream of the Supper. As long as baptism and the Supper were regarded as shadowy images of either circumcision or the paschal lamb or as images of rebirth and nurture, it was not easy dry-shod to cross the Red Sea and enter into the promised land.

To be sure, the Lutheran preaching and song of praise also had their faults and wants, inasmuch as they did not clearly enough relate the "faith" to the "Word of faith" in baptism. Therefore, they could not in a clear and living manner derive the Christian life from its fountain and flow, in the Lord's own Word and action in baptism and communion. Nevertheless, the Lutheran proclamation and song of praise still had a vague understanding and a living expression of a real presence of the Word of God and the life-giving power of the Lord's own institutions. Therefore, the Christian life became more vigorous and more evident than had been the case for many centuries. The shortcomings of the Lutheran proclamation and song of praise have, in a way, straightened themselves out; in other words, they have been corrected by the Spirit in the congregational confession and the life in the Lord's institution. Therefore we claim that the faults had their cause only in the lack of light and power, which can hardly be expected in infancy. It is a matter of course that the newborn preaching and song were tender and frail in the days and in the mouth of Martin Luther.

Hereby it is best seen how objectionable and inappropriate any other norm for teaching than the Holy Scriptures and the undeviating altar book and hymnal have been and must be for the Christian growth of the Lutheran preaching and song. Even in the most tolerable form, all other norms must be likened to a disciplined, monotonous, and restricted diet, which might be appropriate in old age and that can prevent disease and even delay death, but that stunts childhood development and thwarts all further growth. If, therefore, the two blessed offspring of Luther, the reborn Christian preaching and the song of praise of the people, are to grow to maturity by the power of the Spirit so that their glory will ever exist on earth, as we hope and pray the case may be despite all sulking and deviation by deadbeats, then we must give ample room for proclamation and song of praise as the spirit wills it in the realm of confession. This is the right "evangelical freedom," the freedom to eat the fruits of all the trees in the garden except the tree of death, which is that Scripture knowledge and theology that usurp the place of God by judging his words and deeds, namely, his Word to us and his work within us. When we fail to build on and rest within the testimony of the Spirit and the congregation about the Christian faith and confession and about the Lord's institution as actions by his own Word, which is his and his alone, and if we instead doubt this foundation for the faith and the church's fount of life and put ourselves in the judge's seat to determine if we have this Word of God and if this is good and true and can bring us salvation, then we stand like Eve by the forbidden tree, counseling with the serpent about which fruits are good and beneficial for good and evil. Then the Scripture will apply that says, "But I am afraid that as the serpent deceived Eve by his cunning, your thoughts will be led astray from a sincere and pure devotion to Christ" [2 Cor 11:3].

Turning now to the problem of the Christian certainty of the individual in his concern for salvation, which recently has been drawn into the dispute about the validity of baptism administered according to the ritual of the altar book, then we will, as in all matters of Christian information, find no complete answers in any book of dogmatics. Even here, however, the great Lutheran basis for Christian enlightenment, the one of the Word and the faith, is useful and firm. The papists are, of course, right in claiming that the individual must build his certainty of salvation on his participation in the faith, hope, and love of the whole church, but it was Martin Luther's bold stroke to refer the individual to the inner testimony of the Holy Spirit as the only assurance of God's grace and eternal life. This venture was made necessary by the contamination of the concept of the church by the hierarchy and their compulsory baptism. For just as God is the God of the living and not of the dead, so is the Holy Spirit the spirit of the living church and not of a dead one. It is a false and pernicious certainty in matters of salvation to rely on a spiritually dead church where the Christian means of grace, baptism, and communion are distorted or out of function. Such a church is like a priestly insurance company where an annual contribution in an outward way guarantees its members against spiritual fire damage in purgatory and hell. Martin Luther was right when he declared this to be fraud and even murder, as the claim was made to avoid hell or enter heaven. When Luther constantly referred to that external and clear Word of God by which we can learn to know and understand the Holy Spirit, then his mistake was only this, as it was in all of his evangelical service, that he confused his biblical preaching with the confession of faith and the words of institution, as if everything was a clear Word of God whereby we could know and understand the Holy Spirit. We must separate what we, and not the Lord, have joined together. The confession of faith by the congregation at baptism, according to the institution of the Lord, then becomes the clear standard for the congregation and its spirit. It is then evident that as members of this congregation, which is the Christian and spiritual people of God, we can reach the same certainty in matters of salvation as the congregation has in its consideration of the Christian signs of life, the confession, the proclamation, and the song of praise. These signs of life will become clearer and stronger in relation to the freedom these three enjoy. On the other hand, all external compulsion in spiritual matters will weaken the expressions of life and conceal its signs. No one can be certain of the genuine and firm character of Christian confession if the confession is required by law and nonconfession is liable to civil punishment. So then, the Christian proclamation and song of praise will never be the strong expressions and signs that give assurance of strength and growth unless they have external freedom. Opponents of freedom for preachers and hymn writers therefore, consciously or unconsciously, place obstacles in the way of the Spirit who works only in freedom and therefore against the certainty of salvation. When spiritual freedom is a reality, however, we can boldly answer every faithful Christian who questions the validity of baptism, "Why ask me? Ask the Holy Spirit! He who is the spirit of faith and baptism will tell you if you are born of water and spirit to enter the kingdom of heaven. If you are not, he will show you the way."

The Christian, the Spiritual, and the Eternal Life

In our day it is so difficult to be understood when one speaks about the real life, as it is lived daily among us and before our very eyes, that everyone who writes about it can surely expect to be grossly misunderstood by most readers. If we are not believed when we write about earthly things, how can we be believed when we write about the heavenly? It is therefore almost miraculous that some people still speak and write about the Christian, the spiritual, and the eternal life. Apparently no one practices it, and from the time of creation until now, only one person has carried it through, namely, the only begotten, the unequaled, Jesus Christ, who was crucified under Pontius Pilate and is now seated in heaven at the right hand of God, whence he shall come on the final day to judge the living and the dead.

It was therefore no trick for Søren Kierkegaard, as he was applauded by the world, to describe our so-called Christian preaching, Bible reading, worship, infant baptism, and communion as an immense tomfoolery and a merry farce. But this became tragicomical, yea, not only greatly tragic but even mockery, when many people came to believe that we so-called ministers, we "black gowns," were deceiving them. We were telling them that if they would just listen to us with approval, let their infants be baptized, and go to communion on occasion, then they were participating in a secret and incomprehensible manner, yet in a real sense, in the Christian, the spiritual, and the eternal life, as our Lord Jesus Christ had lived it on earth and promised it eternally to his faithful followers.

This was no trick, and Søren Kierkegaard was careful not to write that he, either by his own insight or out of the New Testament, had gained a light and a power to live a real Christian, spiritual, and eternal life that he could transmit to others. On the contrary, he writes that out of his own experience and out of the New Testament he has learned and can clearly demonstrate that all that pretends to be a Christian, spiritual, and eternal life as it is described in the New Testament, the true and infallible account of the life and teachings of Jesus Christ, is a coarse lie and a monstrous delusion, even an enormous blasphemy. By this he has obviously pledged his own honor and the New Testament to the Danish readers to the contention that no Christian, spiritual, and eternal life exists on earth. It is therefore not only up to us but up to that Jesus Christ, whom we confess, and to that Spirit that guides and comforts us, to show the world that such a life does exist, even though it has long been hidden and is hard to recognize.

It is quite evident that the solution to this unequaled task of living can be given only to a small degree by the pen. It is obvious that we cannot by our pens create such a Christian life, when even the Lord's apostles could not to the slightest degree transplant it or communicate it by their pens, even though we assume that their hand was guided by Christ's spirit. It is also clear as daylight that when we claim that the apostolic writings themselves did not possess or lead a Christian, spiritual, and eternal life, we cannot without contradiction ascribe to these writings the ability to transplant or communicate the Christian life that they themselves did not possess or lead.

We cannot without blasphemy or ridiculous pride ascribe to our own writings that divine power of living and transfer of life that we deny to the apostolic writings.

The apostolic writings, however, by being a true description of the life of Jesus Christ and of the Christian life as it was found in those who wrote and those who lived it in the Christian congregation, and by being a prophecy of the growth of Christian life in the congregation until it reaches the goal and pattern set by Jesus' own life, can be useful and illuminating for those who believe in Jesus Christ and participate in the Christian life. In the same manner our writings can be useful and illuminating for living Christians, in part when they give a truthful description of the ways and means whereby the present weak, vague, and obscure Christian life has been transmitted to us, and in part when they are a prophecy of how the Christian life will grow in the history of the church until it reaches the fullness, strength, and clarity of the Lord.

To this end I have devoted a lifetime of writing, seeking as well as I might and with great diligence to give the information that it is by the Word of the Lord's own mouth, as it is spoken at baptism and communion and by nothing else, that his Spirit and his power of living are communicated. His spiritual life disappears where we reject or falsify this Word spoken by the Lord, and the Christian life will be untraceable where we might maintain this Word unaltered, but only half believe it, and expect spirit, life, and growth by other channels as well.

From the perplexity in the days of Søren Kierkegaard as well as the confusion that existed during the recent polemics about "altar-book baptism," it is obvious that the usefulness of my writings has not been as great as I might desire. I had not expected much else, as long as the Christian life, which cannot emerge or grow through book writing, has not been more widespread or more clearly developed through "the Word and the faith" at baptism and communion than all signs show it to be. I hope, however, that my brief description of "the Christian Signs of Life" may have prepared a growing information about the cause of Christian living that we have missed up to now.

It is a Christian insight, which will shed light on the matter even though it does not completely clarify it, that we must and shall sum up the signs of Christian life in "confession, proclamation, and praise" in the language of the people. I have strongly felt the absence of this when I searched for the Christian life in myself and in the congregation, and when I had to defend the Lord Jesus Christ against the dishonoring accusation that he had permitted his life to die in the church or had been unable, with the exception of a brief apostolic period, to bring it out of its swaddling clothes or to nurture it to youthful flowering or adult maturity.

According to the apostolic Scriptures, we assume that "faith, hope, and love" are the spiritual and eternal content of the Christian life, but as long as we cannot differentiate between "these three" according to heathen, Jewish, or Christian speech, nor distinguish between everyday and Sunday understanding, we cannot demonstrate clear expressions of life and clear signs of life that are peculiar to Christianity. All postulates about Christian life therefore seem to be arbitrary. They seem to involve us in a confused polemic about what is spiritual and what is physical in human life, and about the relationship that Christianity, according to the witness of experience, has to that which the human spirit calls spiritual.

We must discover the Christian expressions of the life of faith in the three ways: in the confession of faith at baptism, in the Christian hope as we have it in the Lord's Prayer at baptism as well as at communion, and in the love expressed in Christ's word of submission to his faithful or his declaration of love to his bride, the church, in communion. Only then can we, in our congregational life, show a Christian confession, proclamation, and praise that are the peculiar and unmistakable signs of the Christian faith, the Christian hope, and the Christian love. Then we can speak clearly and judge thoroughly about their relation to faith, hope, and love.

The Christian life in itself will undoubtedly continue to be a profound mystery to us, but the same is true of our total human life, which is separate from that of animals, for no one can make the Christian life known except through comparable spiritual expressions. If someone should object that the Christian signs of life, such as confession, proclamation, and praise, are only words and not action, then we rightly answer that the invisible spirit of man as well as of God can demonstrate its life only through that invisible word that can be heard by the ear and felt in the heart. Every action, by the hand and by all visible things, is vaguely related to the invisible spirit, and we can only glimpse the relationship through a word of enlightenment. Even then we will see darkly in a vague and ambiguous way. The perfect Christian love will seek to express itself in a marvelous generosity and bodily sacrifice, but even the apostolic letter gives testimony that we can give all we own to the poor and we can give our body to be burned and still not have Christian love. It is also evident that many people have done these things without calling themselves Christian or desiring even to be Christians. Even the most dedicated works of love can only be signs of Christian love when they are clearly related to the Christian confession and the Christian song of praise.

This is the outward significance of enlightenment about "the Christian signs of life"; the significance inward and upward is even more important for all of us. We seek in vain to probe the mysteries of the Christian life, whether it be the mystery of the call in preaching the gospel (the cry of the Christmas message), or the mystery of nurture in the Supper. But the Christian way of life does become brighter and easier for us when we discover the company in which we can seek and expect the Christian faith, the Christian hope, and the Christian love, so that faith is strengthened, hope expanded, and love increased. By this we are furthermore comforted about the gap between the shape of the Christian life in the congregation of the present day and the shape in which it is described by the apostles, in part in themselves and the first fruits of the congregation, but especially in Jesus Christ with fullness and purity. We are comforted not as bookworms who depend on the perfection of an alien life whose description they devour but as a bright boy is comforted about the distance between himself and his adult brother or his aging father. When we are turned aright in our living consideration of the Christian life as a spiritual human life, which is just as real and a lot more human than our physical life, then, like the Apostle Paul, we are not anxious about our distance from the goal. Then we see that the Christian life begins with a real conception according to the will of the Spirit, and as the Lord says, with a real birth by water and the Spirit. Then it continues, as did the Lord himself, to grow in age and wisdom and favor with God and man. Then, like Paul, we will strive to forget what is behind us in favor of what is ahead, and by living progress we will reach for the wreath and the crown.

When we regard the Christian life, as also the human life, the mind tells us that there is light behind us but darkness ahead. We can understand no more of life than what we have experienced. On the Christian life way, however, there is an unusual and even superhuman light. The Lord has said that whosoever follows after him shall never be in darkness, for he is the true light of the world. The lantern that guides us through the darkness is, as the Apostle writes, a sure Word of prophecy, which is known by the fact that it corresponds to the rule of faith and mankind's sure foundation.

It is a necessary consequence of the covenant of baptism that the spiritual life to which we are born in baptism can in no way be demonic. In every way that spiritual life has to be divine. Christianity presupposes very clearly that human life in the image of God can only be reborn and renewed by a wondrous separation from devildom. How much of humanity is devildom and how much a person has to contribute during his lifetime to the release from devilry and to the growth of divinity is a puzzle for the mind that can be solved only by experience, and it is no wonder that independent efforts to analyze and determine this matter have led to confusion. The more we listen to the description of the scribes of what is called the "order of salvation," how Scripture calls for us to shed the old man and put on the new, the less we understand the matter. We experience a boundless confusion where it seems as if all of human life must be eradicated as devilry, or contrariwise as if there was no devilry, so that man should either direct the new Christian life or stand beside it as an idle observer.

When a person is a living Christian, even when he has not come of age, he realizes that none of the alternatives is true. If there were no devil, no Satan, no father of lies, no man of darkness, no murdering angel, if he had no power over man, there would be no word of truth in the gospel of Christ, not an iota of truth in the message about the Son of God as the savior of the world from the power of sin, darkness, and death. For this power can exist and be active only in an unclean spirit of the world. If, on the other hand, all of human nature had become demonic at the fall, the Son of God could have become a real human being as little as he could have become a devil. Then the new man could not have been wrought in God's image through a rebirth and a renewal of the old man but only by a brand new creation entirely independent of the old man. How the very complicated matter of sanctification and salvation can take place in fallen and sinful humanity, corporately as well as individually, is hidden from our eyes. The Son of God became man in all respects; he was like us but without sin. His life as man cannot demonstrate for us now the new man, who grows up, is liberated from sin and Satan by being cleansed from the "defilement of body and spirit" [2 Cor 7:1]. If we are to know this, the Spirit of truth as the Spirit of our Lord Jesus Christ must reveal it for us. But, inasmuch as we, during the growth of the new man, cannot dispense with the tentative knowledge of the growth of life, the Spirit of the Lord will also inform us about this when we pray. For it is written about this same Spirit, "He will declare to you the things that are to come" [John 16:13]. When it still does not happen the reason must be that the church's faith in the Holy Spirit is either so shaky or so vague that he cannot be called upon or distinguished from the spirits of delusion. Inasmuch as we have only recently gained a sure and definite belief in the Holy Spirit as a divine part of the Trinity, and inasmuch as we have thereby discovered the nature of that "confession" of the incarnate Jesus Christ upon which the spirit of truth can and shall be distinguished from the spirit of delusion, we have only now received the revelation of the Spirit concerning the usefulness for the whole congregation that we keep the faith, fight, and win the crown. This happened when we placed our trust in the confession of faith at baptism as a word to us from the mouth of the Lord....

It is furthermore a very ordinary bit of human information that the human life that is to be raised is the same life that is under the fall. The same prodigal son who was lost was the one who was found. He who was dead became alive. The same sheep that was lost was carried home on the shoulder of the shepherd. In the same manner the new man is, strictly speaking, not any other man than the old man. He is only another person in the same sense that Saul became another person when he was anointed and the Spirit came upon him. It is quite clear that God's Son acquired the old mankind when he came to earth as the offspring of a woman, of Abraham's seed and David's seed. Even the new human body of the resurrection was basically the same as the body that was nailed to the cross. Yet, all the scribes who stressed the Christian life as that of our Lord Jesus Christ and no one else have more or less cut the so-called new human life in Christ and his church off from the old human life, as if the latter was a physical life of sin that had to be destroyed and eradicated in order that the new and entirely different human life could succeed it. This basic error led not only to all the monastic rules but also to all the orthodox dogmatics books, in which the total and basic depravity and spiritual incompetence for doing good was made the foundation for the work of reconciliation. This was claimed, even though it was clearly evident that the human life that was in the need of salvation, of reconciliation, of rebirth and renewal according to the image of the Creator would be destroyed. The consequences were that the old human life, which was given up, daily went to the devil, while the new life either was nothing at all or had no power or was utterly useless except for the purpose of writing dogmatics and memorizing them. Or else the new spiritual life became inhuman, a demonic life, which battled against humanity and, under all sorts of aliases, raised to the skies that opinionated self-righteousness that always had been characteristic of Satan, the murderer of human life....

It is finally a common human and even evangelical truth that God and his Spirit treat us the same way they want us to treat our neighbor. This means that we must conquer evil by good, and this is, even by human experience, the only way in which evil is profoundly overcome, driven out, and replaced. Even the law of God, which can crush the proudest human being with thunder and lightning, cannot eradicate evil desire and lust. These yield only to the desires of goodness, of which evil desire is a distorted image. Pride is driven out of the heart only by humility; sensuality, which is impure love, only by pure love; and covetousness for the glories of this world is driven out only by a sincere desire for the glories of God's kingdom. But I know of no Christian moralist since the days of the apostles who has described the Holy Spirit in this light and spirit. Such moralists began like the mystics, in the heart, and thus they began in the darkness of the old man that was to be reborn and was to nurture himself with his own love to God and the neighbor. The result was a false and unreal Christianity from beginning to end. Or they began with the law, not as a mirror but as a living force and power that was to demolish the pagan temple and out of its ruins erect the temple of the Holy Spirit. This was done despite the testimony of the Lord that when sanctification begins from without, the result will be a tomb filled with filth and dead bones. This was done despite the fact of human experience that when sanctification begins from within we can put on the whole armor of the law and combat the tiniest evil desire until doomsday without moving it one whit. Christian life in the world is always a life of faith and thereby spiritual and invisible, but inasmuch as our physical conduct is open and visible, the Christian church and all its members must, as the apostle writes, use the compulsion of the law, be it the law of Moses or Danish law, to regulate its conduct. If we wish to live a Christian life, we must guard against a sanctification of our legal conduct. We must also guard against the temptation to change the gospel to a new Christian law, which is to compel the soul to a Christian way of thinking and the heart to a Christian life of love. When we try to do this, we either know nothing about Christian living or we squander it, for we can neither be saved nor sanctified by the law without falling from grace.

The tangled knot of Christian living as a life of faith is seen already in all of the letters of Paul. From the very beginning this knot has, if not strangled the Christian life among non-Jewish Christians, then stunted its growth. It has caused that malady that has been obvious since the days of the apostles. Inasmuch as this knot can be untied only at the resurrection of the body from the dead or by a transformation of the body of the living people who wait for the visible return of the Lord, it is important not to try to cut the knot but to live with it in faith as a thorn in the flesh and to be content with the grace of God whose "power is made perfect in weakness" [2 Cor 12:9].

Even when we hold fast to the faith that the Christian spiritual life, to which we are reborn in baptism and in which we are nurtured at the Supper, is truly an eternal life, we must yet give up the idea that we can become clearly aware of the Christian life's eternal nature in this world. This is so, because it is only in perfect unity with the Lord and his church that this clear awareness can arise, but also because the awareness is impossible except when "the inner becomes outward," when all the senses and the body functions become as spiritual as the Word of faith, hope, and love is spiritual on our lips and in our hearts. Our whole body must become an eternally pleasing habitation, a perfect tool, and a clear, unblemished mirror of the spirit, the divine power that came from the Father in order to begin and complete the good works in all of our Lord's church. This work will be completed only on the day of our Lord Jesus Christ, and it will work toward this end in us only when we really denounce ourselves, give up spiritual independence, and willingly let the Holy Spirit, as a divine person, guide our heart and our tongue. Then we may have the renewed, divine power of living, which alone can create, maintain, and nurture the new humanity in the divine image of Jesus Christ.

Sermons

It is in his sermons that one truly gets the full flavor and force of Grundtvig's presence and religious thought, above all his understanding of the Word of God. For him, this Word was a living, creative instrument that enlivened the whole of the believer's world, as the word the God spoke to create (and re-create) the world. Even more influential than his preaching were his hymns, several of which are still included in modern Scandinavian hymnals and two of which are in the hymnody section of this anthology.

SERMON: ALL SAINTS' DAY (1839)

Holy God and Father! Thy Word is truth! Thy Word is life and spirit, the Word of faith that must be heard. Yes, heavenly Father, thou who until now so wondrously has preserved and, when it seemed dead, through thy Holy Spirit again has quickened thy salvatory Word, O let it never die in our hearts and in the hearts of our children, but live among us from generation to generation and grow through thy Son, our Lord Jesus Christ, to thy glory and praise, and to our salvation! Our Father, who art in heaven!

"The earth was without form and void, and darkness was upon the face of the deep; and the Spirit of God was moving over the face of the waters. And God said, 'Let there be light'; and there was light. And God saw that the light was good" [Gen 1:2–4].

These well-known words from the Book of Genesis may rightly be applied to the days of Martin Luther and to God's great deeds in and with him whom we are gathered to commemorate with joy and gratitude today!

Yes, my friends, the earth was in truth without form and void for the hearts who rejected this world and desired a commonwealth in heaven. For them the earth was more formless and empty than it had ever been since the Baptizer rose up and the Savior came down; since the host of angels proclaimed to God's people tidings of great joy, and the word of eternal life on the lips of the Son of Man reached toward the ends of the earth. For a long time this true Word of God had been infiltrated by so much human learning, so many fables and dreams, that it was difficult to recognize it; but as long as there was life in the dreams about all God's saints who hovered about their enshrined bones and who proclaimed their saintliness with signs and wondrous deeds—life in the fabulous dream about the holy sepulcher where the Lord had lain, and angels descending and ascending with consolation for the penitent who knelt at the holy places, bringing their prayers to the throne of God—as long as there was life in these dreams, people were bewitched as by the evening glow of the day that had brought the glow of dawn from on high. But the hour of delusion had passed; darkness with all its horror had struck. The earth was without form and void, and darkness was upon the face of the deep.

For the earth is indeed without form and void in a spiritual sense when the word about the earth's relationship to heaven—the word about the way to the land of the living—has been silenced or chilled to the point of petrification, rendering it dead and incapacitated. Thus it was at the time when Martin Luther appeared. The Word of the Lord was scarce in those days, and the sun had set on the prophets who had said, "I have dreamed, I have dreamed!" [Jer 23:25]. There were no longer visions or songs, and all prophetic Scriptures were like a book given to someone unable to read, or a sealed book no one could open.

Not only Christianity but also everything else that innately had exalted the spirit of the peoples and warmed their hearts had become dead and impotent. And the affliction was by no means caused by a scarcity of Bibles or other famous books, for through the invention of the printing press they were now easier to find and to possess. But when the living and powerful Word, which the Creator has laid on the lips of man, is silenced, so that heartwarming and eloquent speech deals only with silver and gold and precious stones, eating and drinking, buffoonery and vanity, gambling and dancing and carnal pleasures, or with spears and swords, murder and manslaughter, raging revenge, and sly wiles—then all prophetic scriptures, both God's and man's, dealing with both heights and depths, have become like a closed book no one can open, or an open book no one can read.

Yes, in such spiritless and lifeless times Martin Luther was born and grew up. And there was darkness upon the face of the deep, on the brink of which mortals either sighed or wept, either danced or roared; darkness over the abyss to which death is the door and the tomb a symbol; but darkness first and last within ourselves: the monstrous bottomless emptiness into which human souls sink and are lost, feeling themselves cast away from the face of God, exiled from the land of the living, and bereft of all consolation and joy. There was darkness over the abyss and it was not, as it is sometimes said, merely the darkness of superstition but much more that of unbelief. For there was no lack of people who, to their own way of thinking, were as clever, as captivated by their own reason and intelligence, as anyone can be. Also, there was no lack in many lands of people who had read many books and who knew them by rote, so that if few people knew the Bible it was only, then as now, because they cared not for its content. Nor, finally, was there a lack of artists of all kinds who fashioned beautiful and costly objects, which are still highly praised. And if those who bought letters of indulgence from monks and priests, popes, and bishops, were superstitious, then those who sold these objects for ready cash were yet more unbelieving, and they ridiculed among themselves not only the superstition by which they made a living but also the faith that was thus dishonored.

Thus the earth was without form and void because among thousands one hardly found one, and that one a mute, who cared about things above. And there was darkness on the face of the deep because they who saw it assiduously covered it with conjured darkness. But the Spirit of God still moved over the face of the waters wherever the covenant had been kept by those who baptized in the name of the Father and the Son and the Holy Spirit. Yes, precisely in areas where the papacy bore down on souls as a heavy yoke and made itself felt as darkness over the abyss, precisely there and there alone, the Spirit of God moved over the waters, in baptism. And therefore it was not an angel who descended from heaven and rolled back the stone from the tomb, nor a prophet from other parts of the world using his speech to dispel the darkness from the abyss. No, it was, as we know, a monk who as an infant in swaddling clothes had been brought to the Lord, who took him in his arms, blessing him and saying, "The Lord is with thee, go in peace!" Yes, to him in his monk's cage the Lord said, "'Let there be light'; and there was light."

Yes, my friends, Martin Luther felt the emptiness, found himself on the brink of the abyss over which the darkness brooded, and he detached himself from the world and fled to the monastery, which the serious minded considered the only place one might escape the abyss and with repentance and penance save one's soul. There he sat sorrowing night and day; he read and prayed and tormented his soul, but found neither light nor peace; for it simply is not true that it was by reading he found peace. No, he believed in the Lord Jesus though he did not know him and was unaware of his goodness. And the Lord Jesus, who in baptism had made a covenant with him, fulfilled in him the words of the Gospel for today, "Blessed are the poor in spirit, for theirs is the kingdom of heaven. Blessed are those who mourn, for they shall be comforted" [Matt 5:3–4].

Yes, my friends, never has any mortal spoken in such a way on the strength of his own spirit, for who except a scoffer can declare that those who mourn are blessed, unless he is able to give them comfort and solace? But that the Lord Jesus both could and would do this—no less after fifteen hundred years following his ascension than when he declared to his disciples, "'Peace be with you!' and breathing upon them, 'Receive the Holy Spirit!'"—this Luther learned in the monastery from an old monk, whom the Lord had detained, like the ancient Simeon, in order to see his salvation and a light for revelation to the Gentiles. For when the old monk saw that Luther sorrowed for

God and that it was his sins that overwhelmed and crushed him to the ground, he had compassion on him, searched his own heart for a buried treasure, and opened the sealed lips with the secret of the gospel, "Brother Martin, believe that the Lord Jesus has made full satisfaction for your sins, just as I believe he has done for me, and you will have peace." With these words a light was lit for Luther, a light over the abyss and glory to him who brings souls therefrom. And God saw that the light was good; for it was his own word with life and light, it was the light that shone in the darkness, though the darkness comprehended it not [John 1:5].

Yes, my friends, *finished* was the last word the Savior uttered from the cross before he bowed his head and yielded up his spirit, and this *finished* is the word by which God creates light in the darkness of the soul from generation to generation. That light is good, because it is the true light of the world, Jesus Christ himself, the Lord, our light, our salvation, and our power of life!

Luther still sorrowed, sorrowed all his days, but not without hope and consolation, and less for himself than for the millions who sat in darkness and the shadow of death without seeing the great light that had dawned when the old sun darkened, the great light emanating from the God-given word, "finished," and risen with him who died for us and shed his blood unto forgiveness of our sins! For those Luther now sorrowed, but only as one who finds the sorrow sweet in the consolation and solace that follows according to the Lord's Word—in its fullness only when he rests in the bosom of Abraham, but also here, more often than mortal clay can figure and sweeter than our lips can tell.

Yes, my friends, God saw that the light was good, and Luther saw it; but our forefathers also saw it. Many people saw it and praised God who had given us such a man, had raised a great prophet among us, and had visited his people. And Martin Luther rejoiced as the woman who has sorrow because her hour has come, but who no longer remembers the anguish, for joy that a child is born into the world [John 16:21].

Yes, my friends, the light was so good that it spread abroad because it emanated from the Word of Life as the light for the living. Luther saw that only a living Word in their own mother tongue could enlighten the peoples about God's great deeds, and the light placed such a living Word on his lips for his people. God placed a new song in his mouth that gladdened the hearts and became a living Word also on the lips of our forefathers in our mother tongue. This was not, as is usually alleged, because the Holy Scriptures were translated into Luther's and into our own native language, as well as others. The living Word emanated not from the book, but the Word cast light upon the book so that the book was known by the Lord's light as a work by his Spirit and a masterly picture of him and his house, the house of living stones: his believing church.

Yes, my friends, let us join our forefathers in praise that the light, which dawned for Luther, was good and was communicated through words from his lips to those who heard him; for the light was Jesus Christ who accompanies his Word from mouth to mouth and from heart to heart until the close of the age. Let us perceive and proclaim that through the dawning of that light a new creation began, a new day in Christendom, a creation through which not only the darkness upon the face of the deep was dispersed, but the earth that had been without form and void became bright and alive with the sun, moon, and stars above the firmament, with grass and flowers and all sorts of trees, with birds in the air and fish in the sea, with all kinds of animals, and finally man in God's image and after his likeness!

Let it not diminish our joy, but rather enhance it and our thanksgiving, that once again a period arrived when the earth was without form and void and with darkness upon the face of the deep. For it was evident that this was only a night between the days of creation, evening and morning before our eyes. Or it was as a winter's night superseded by a morn in spring in which we shall rejoice with the birds and look forward to behold the deeds of God toward which he graciously has called us to be coworkers.

Yes, let us thank God for Martin Luther who brought a dawn, this new Abraham, our father in Christ. Let those who now preach the gospel proclaim that word *finished*, which creates light for our souls and peace with God in our hearts, so that they may join the Lord in saying that blessed are those who mourn in his house, for they shall be comforted with heavenly sweetness. May this father of our church, also of our children and grandchildren, become a father until the Lord comes in the glory of his Father, whom Martin Luther encouraged us to call upon freely in the name of him who healed our infirmities and bore our pains, in the blessed name of our Lord and Savior Jesus Christ! Amen.

Sermon: 18th Sunday after Trinity (1845)

Holy God and Father! Thy Word is truth! Thy Word is spirit and life to us, the Word of faith that must be heard. Yes, heavenly Father, let us always sense more deeply and recognize more clearly what a precious and fruitful treasure we have in thy living Word, which not only reveals to us thy secret counsel toward our salvation but, when we faithfully love and hold it fast, links and unites us with thee through thy lovable, only begotten Son as coheirs to the glory that is his at thy right hand. Hear our prayer in the name of our Lord Jesus Christ. Our Father, who art in heaven!

"What do you think of the Christ? Whose son is he?" [Matt 22:42ff.].

Thus, according to the Gospel for the day, Christ himself, with divine calmness, asked his enemies who tempted him with the great commandment of the law—the enemies who would know nothing of a Christ but only of one who was the son of David. And we learn that he bound their lips, reminding them of David's words, "The Lord said to my Lord, Sit at my right hand, till I put thy enemies under thy feet." It is in vain, however, that we attempt to muzzle the mouths of the unbelievers today with David's words, not only because they care as little about David's words as about Christ's, but especially because they take lightly all words about spiritual things and do not sense the strength in the Lord's question, "If David thus calls Christ Lord, how is he his son?"

It is of course awkward when the son lords it over the father, and spiritually speaking it is impossible, because the son must either be without spirit or possess the father's spirit. But the scribes and other learned men of the world today are not perceptive enough to see that, for just as they find it entirely natural in daily living that the son lords it over the father, the young over the old, so they apparently ignore their inconsistency in calling Christ lord in the spirit, while still asserting that his servants lord it over him.

I mention this, however, not just to quarrel with the Lord's enemies either about Christ or about the Word, but in order to remind the Lord's friends that Christ and the Word basically are one and the same; for it is written, "And the Word became flesh and dwelt among us" [John 1:14], and again, "That which was from the beginning, which we have heard, which we have seen with our eyes, which we have looked upon and touched with our hands, concerning the word of life...we proclaim also to you" [1 John 1:1–3]. This basic oneness of the Word with our Lord Jesus Christ, you see, is not merely a profound truth that sheds light on God's only begotten Son, through whom he created and redeemed the world, but it is also a blissful secret that gives the believers the blessed assurance that God's Son, their Lord and Savior, is as near to them as in his Word of faith on their lips and in their hearts, and this Word has the power to conquer the world, defy the gates of hell, accomplish the good deeds of the Father, and, above all, raise the dead to life.

But if it is to be light and life for us that Christ and the Word basically and spiritually are one, we must be on guard lest we become tainted by the world's wanton and slovenly ideas not only about Christ but about the Word. For if the Word loses its constancy and firmness for us, then all our so-called faith in Christ and our fellowship with him are in vain. Then it becomes evident that the only name by which we can be saved, the name of Jesus Christ, is also a word that loses its firmness and constancy, just like the others. And it is therefore the great sorrow for us who seriously proclaim the gospel of God's Son, that in the midst of bombastic twaddle about the Spirit, many of Christ's disciples lose their firm confidence in the Word. Their profound respect for it has been shaken and weakened, if not blown away, so that we hardly know how to build a firm foundation that can support the tower that indeed reaches heavenward.

However, just as it is written that we are to build upon the foundation of the apostles and the prophets, Christ Jesus himself being the chief cornerstone, we also read that the prophet said, "I believed, and so I spoke," and the apostle says the same. The Lord himself says, "If you love me, you will keep my commandments" (words) "and I will...manifest myself to him" [Eph 2:20; 2 Cor 4:13; John 14:15, 21]. We have therefore clearly nothing else to do but to speak tirelessly as we believe, and with all our might exalt the Word of God as the power of God to salvation for everyone who believes, assured that the same spirit of Christ, which compels and strengthens us to do that, can and will also give the Word witness among all those who are of the truth.

Yes, my friends, just as we are convinced that every person's own conscience tells him that in serious matters one must stand by his word lest all assurance disappear concerning intangible things, just so we can and must be confident that the spirit of truth witnesses for all its worshipers. In questions concerning faith and all spiritual matters everything hinges on the Word. If we disassociate ourselves from that and no longer depend on it, the soul is driven hither and yon like a reed in the wind and everything falters under us. For the Word is the spirit's sole revelation and the only barrier between truth and falsehood. When we let go of the Word, we rumble in darkness, losing our bearings and unable to resist any temptation. Just as in daily living, then, our security and confidence are based on the trust that we can rely on the words and promises of the people we associate with, just so is the foundation for all firmness in the faith and certainty in hope that we hold fast the Word that reveals and expresses them; for it becomes profitable to ask about truth and credibility only when we hold fast the Spirit and the thought through the Word.

For what would be the use of asking about the truth of Christianity if we did not have a Word that proclaimed what Christianity is and what we are to believe and confess in order to be a Christian? And of what use is it to have such a Word in the covenant of baptism if we will not, dare not, hold it fast and believe it? Just as it is meaningless to ask people what they think of Christ when they don't know what we think of Christ, so it is useless to ask whose son Christ is according to our Christian faith if we do not hold fast the Word in the confession of faith, which witnesses that he is the only begotten Son of God, the Father, or emphasize the word *only begotten* that sets him apart from other children of God, such as angels or human beings.

Thus we observe in the Gospel for today that the Lord emphasized the words *Son* and *Lord* by saying, "If David calls him Lord, how is he the son?" and so we must also emphasize the words *Son* and *Lord* and all the words in the confession of faith in order to know whether we believe or not and whether or not the Christian faith is the true faith.

My friends, if the Word therefore did not have more to do with Christ than it has with the Spirit and all spiritual things, which are revealed only in words and believed because of the Word, then there could be no Christianity without faith in the Word and reverence for it. But since Christ and the Word are one and the same, we see clearly the shrewdness of the enemy when the world would have us believe that we can retain our Christian faith, our Christian hope, and our Savior's love without the Word, since, says the enemy, it is only the spirit that gives life.

Yes, my friends, such is the enemy's shrewd cunning that he uses truth and freedom as tempting sham. Therefore we must be aware that when we relinquish the Word of the Lord, we dissociate ourselves from him, and then we must either lose all stability and security or we must bind ourselves to our own words about Christ or those of others—words that completely lack the divine vitality found in the Word of God's Son, when he and the Word, through the Spirit, are one. Then the enemy shall not seize or deceive us. Then we bind ourselves to the Word of the Lord, not as his slaves but as the friends of him who says, "If a man loves me, he will keep my word, and my Father will love him, and we will come to him" [John 14:23]. We bind ourselves to his Word because we believe that through it he binds himself to us and gives us a grasp of the unshakable truth, a sure token of his Father's love and a holy temple in which he himself will dwell spiritually among us and reveal his glory. As it is written, "And the Word became flesh and dwelt among us, full of grace and truth; we have beheld his glory, glory as of the only Son from the Father" [John 1:14].

Yes, my friends, just let the learned men of the world and the scribes pity and mock us because we are babes who cling to the Word, too timid through the power of the Spirit to move freely between heaven and earth! From the first moment of our faith we have the consolation from the lips of the Lord that God has revealed to babes what is hidden for the wise and understanding [Matt 11:25], when we lovingly keep the Word of the Lord in our hearts we soon learn that his Word, as he says, is spirit and life. For long before we glimpse the light revealing the deep secret that he himself is in his

Word, we sense it in the security we have in the faith, so that we do not ask, "'Who will ascend into heaven?' (that is, to bring Christ down) or 'Who will descend into the abyss?' (that is, to bring Christ up from the dead)" [Rom 10:6–7], and we find it divinely affirmed by the power of the Word of the Lord within us and through him to whom God the Father said, "Sit at my right hand, till I make your enemies your footstool!" [Ps 110:1].

Yes, my friends, that Word of the Lord to which we refer is the confession of faith with the words of institution both at baptism and at the Lord's Supper, including the Lord's Prayer and benediction. This Word cannot dwell a single day in a believing heart and not reign over its enemies, as it is written about the Lord. And these known enemies—conceit with all its doubts and objections, willfulness with all its ungodly lust, and egotism with all its worldly covetousness—are trampled to death daily under the feet of the Word, just as all enemies of the Lord eventually shall be laid under his footstool while the heavens rejoice: the nations of the world belong to the Lord and his Anointed!

All our trust in the Lord Jesus Christ and all our hope of his glory rest in the faith that he sits at the right hand of God, from whence he shall come again to judge the living and the dead. Just so, our faith is enlivened by our belief that the Word of the Lord reigns divinely within us, and only when we thereby learn that the Lord truly is one with his Word can we also clearly perceive that the Lord Jesus Christ reigns in the midst of his enemies and sits at the right hand of God the Father, while all his enemies are placed under his footstool.

Yes, my friends, when the Word of faith (the confession of faith) as it was in the beginning is on our lips and in our hearts, and when we then consider how hostile the world has been, and is, toward this Word, though it never was refuted or stifled—then we perceive clearly that it has reigned and still reigns in the midst of its enemies. And whenever it victoriously attacked heresy and error, darkness and ignorance, sin and sorrow, and fear of death, it laid enemies under its feet. Thus it is not only within us but throughout the whole earth where the gospel is preached that the Word of faith with spirit and power proves its oneness with the Lord at God's right hand, because he is the Word of the beginning through whom all things are created and in whom both heavenly and earthly things have their deep coherence.

Therefore, let us rest in this faith in the Word, so that through daily experience we learn that Jesus dwells in our hearts and that there exists also on earth, secretly, a heaven where our Lord and Savior sits at God's right hand and does what he pleases. Then we shall never fear the world, be deceived by the enemy's cunning, or doubt that our life, our eternal life, which through Christ is hidden with God, shall be revealed with him in the Father's glory.

Amen! In the name of our Lord Jesus! Amen!

VILHELM BECK (1829–1901)

Beck represents a deep strain of pietism within Denmark, one strongly marked by the eighteenth-century influence of the Moravians. This spirituality was marked by a strong aversion to the things of "the world," a call to repentance and new birth, and the living of a holy life. Beck, like Hauge, was most effective not through his writings but through his personal presence and through the impact of his own life story. They show his deep piety as well as his attempts to breathe new life into the Church of Denmark of his day.

Memoirs

(Old Customs) But to return to conditions at Uby. As an example of how entirely out of touch with spiritual matters the people were, I had decided to begin some Bible studies at the school. But first I had to go about in the parish and ask people to come. They promised to be there, but when Wednesday evening arrived and I went down to the school full of expectation, I found it full of children. There were hardly any adults. Again I had to canvass the parish and approach the people who, in spite of their promises, had not shown up.

"When we heard that it was to be Bible study, we thought that we were to take confirmation instruction from the pastor," they said. "We decided that the children could do this much better than we old folks."

But now they would surely come—and they did. I conducted two Bible studies a week in the school. Later one of them was transferred to the church. During the summer they were held in the church on Sunday afternoons. These Bible studies contributed greatly to the awakening of spiritual life. There was, in addition, the confessional service with catechization of the young on Saturdays and, most important of all, the confirmation class in which young people were frequently awakened to spiritual values.

Youth was a characteristic of the spiritual life at Uby. I was young myself and especially adapted to work with young people.

This good fortune attended me in my more advanced years. So there was a spirit of youthfulness about the newly awakening life. The older people were stubborn, however, and only occasionally was one of them converted. They were firmly bound to one another by old established customs and by parties and drinking. Weddings and funerals were celebrated with eating and drinking lasting three to four days. There was dancing at weddings, and in a neighboring parish there was dancing even at funerals.

I realized that these old, inherited bonds must be broken before individuals could be liberated. At a Bible study soon after a scandalous funeral, where drunken people had accompanied the casket to the cemetery, I spoke out boldly:

"Why do you bury your dead as human beings deserve to be buried while you yourselves live and die like animals? Why don't you place the dead body in the middle of the room and let the young people dance around it while the older folks play cards on top of it? Then throw the carcass over your shoulders like a dead animal and carry it up to the cemetery to be buried like one. But let the pastor and the deacon stay at home. This would be in harmony with your bestial feasts."

This had quite an effect. The people were ashamed; all funeral feasts were abolished, and the Word of God could be heard again at funerals by sober people.

Lent was the worst time of the year. One might truly say that the devil was abroad. On the Monday before Lent a great crowd of young people, headed by a "beggar" who was lavishly bedecked with feathers and ribbons and by a "crone," a young man in female attire, would ride forth, the whole crowd decorated with garishly colored bonnet ribbons. At each farm *they* danced and begged for eggs and money for a feast. In the afternoon riderless horses would be found in the fields, and drunken young men who had fallen off them. This dreadful revelry would continue all week with carousing and dancing.

The first few years, when there were but few believers among the young people, there was nothing that could be done about this. It was an abomination to me to witness this revelry, so I generally tried to go away during this time. One year I rode over to my brother's at Lerkenborg. But on my way back through a town I met a

Shrove clown, a Merry Andrew, who frightened my horse. I became so angry that I drove my horse against him and continued to beat him with my riding whip until with a roar he tumbled off his horse. Tales of this event are still heard after these many years.

Another time I rode to Tersløse in order to avoid the Shrove clowns and to call on my friend Johannes Clausen, who was visiting there with his fiancée. But as fate would have it, at the moment that I was about to enter the parsonage grounds, I met a regiment of Shrove clowns who turned into the gate just behind me. So to the amusement of everyone, I was seen riding at the head of the whole troupe of clowns.

Finally enough spiritual life developed among the young people so I could fight this odious custom. At a Bible study, with the help of one of Brorson's Lenten hymns, I succeeded in putting an end to this kind of revelry.

A great furor arose, especially among the older people, because their customs were overthrown and spiritual life was being awakened. The newly awakened young people were jubilant; not only the church, but roads and streets resounded with their songs.

(A Service at Midnight) One summer Sunday evening my wife and I had visited a believing farm family in the village. As we cut across the cemetery on our way home, we came upon a group of young people who sat outside the church door singing. We stayed and sang with them. Suddenly we heard other music and singing on the road. It was another group of young people from the next town. Among them was a young man who could accompany them on the harmonica. They also entered the cemetery and joined the singing. The cemetery occupied a high spot in the middle of town, and the singing, heard in the houses round about, drew many people, among them some revelers from the taverns, so that the group became quite large. About eleven o'clock I told the young people that it was about time to go home. But they had another hymn they wanted to sing, they said, "If we could only get into the narthex and have some light," since they did not know it by heart. I went home to fetch the key to the church and opened the door. I was not entirely happy, however, because I was afraid that the revelers in the group would defile the church. The idea then flashed into my mind: in front of the altar they will have more respect and keep quiet. I went up and lighted the candles on the altar and said, "Everybody come up here. Here you can sing your hymn."

While they were singing, the words of Luther came to me: "Where children of God assemble, there ought to be preaching." So when the hymn was sung, I preached to them. It was midnight, a beautiful end to that Sunday! In the meantime people on the road had seen the light in the church. Soon the story of the crazy vicar who had now become so stark mad that he held services in the church at midnight was spreading like wildfire.

Neighboring pastors were offended and enraged over what was happening. All in all, I could not boast of their friendship. In reality it was the awakening of spiritual life that aroused their bitterness. These dead pastors were furious because their parishioners flocked to the Uby church and became "crazy" there, while their own churches remained empty. Undoubtedly I was in some way to blame for their anger, for I was young and inconsiderate toward these older men when we met. However, Pastor Lind, at Saeby, was one minister who treated me with great friendship and sympathized with my work. I often called on him. Later when the Inner Mission began, he became more cool toward me.

Pastor Hans Knudsen, at Bregninge, also was very friendly toward me. He was a strange person, somewhat crass in manner, so that most of the pastors did not like him. It was not this that brought us together, however, but our common faith. I soon discovered a warm heart under the stern exterior. Besides, he was a well-informed man who was of great assistance to me. Whenever there was something about which I needed information, I would ride over to see him. I would be given an easy chair and a long East India cigar (he had been a military chaplain and missionary in Tranquebar). Then he would go into his large library and find all the information that I could possibly desire. Only once did he side with the angry pastors against me. That was when I held the first outdoor meeting in the woods about a mile from Kalundborg. This angered the pastors the most, for they considered it ungodly to conduct a service in a forest. This meeting was the origin of thousands of others like it that have been held in the forests of Denmark, where doubtless thousands of people have been saved.

What aroused the greatest bitterness against me in the parish was my occasional refusal to administer private communion, something that the world, then as now, considered the greatest heartlessness. Here is an example of how necessary this refusal was. I was called out in the country to give communion to a man. When I asked him why he wanted to commune, he said, "Oh, I have such pains in my stomach." I told him that the Holy Supper was not a remedy for this condition. It was only for sinners who wanted salvation. I asked him if he was a sinner, to which he answered that he was not. I sat with him a long time, explaining to him the law of God, against which he had to admit he had sinned in many ways.

"But," he added, "you interpret it so minutely, Pastor."

I told him that God interprets it much more minutely, for God said, "Cursed is he who does not keep all these commandments."

"He can do nothing to me," said the man.

"Who can't?" I asked.

"The judge," he answered.

"But the Judge on high can do something to you," I said.

"Well, if you will not give me communion, it does not matter. I shall not die this time, and I can go to the church and take communion."

I told him that since I now knew what he was like, I would pass him by at the communion table if he presented himself there. "But," I added, "you *will* die this time."

I felt the blood rush to my face as I dared to say this. Before evening the man was dead.

This story is only an illustration of the general attitude at this time among the children of the world. The belief was that partaking of the Lord's Supper during an illness would bring about a change, either death or complete recovery.

I found a similar superstition concerning private baptism, which was reputed beneficial to infants who cried excessively.

Against the antagonism of the pastors I had great support from my father who, with his prestige in the parish and among the pastors as dean, always defended the new spiritual life. This was the more notable because it must have been strange for the old pastor to see developing in his parish a kind of life he had never observed during his own pastoral activity. His attitude was no doubt due in part to the fact that I was his son. But there were other factors as well. While otherwise he seemed aloof to the parishioners and would hardly have invited a peasant to sit with him in his rooms, yet it gradually became a joy to him to receive "the saints" as guests. He would sit for hours in conversation with them. To me it was a great joy to see this, for, after all, love of the saints is a mark of a disciple of Christ. But if anyone ventured to disparage the life and efforts at Uby, he had to reckon with my father, who was unsparing when he attacked.

(The First Conversion) One of the first persons to call on me after my arrival was an old childhood playmate named Hans, now a tailor. He was a cripple who had to use crutches. He was somewhat addicted to drink; yet he was also attracted to spiritual things. The devil, who had him in his power, had no doubt realized that he might lose this soul and the night before my arrival had conspired to keep him by inducing him to commit suicide. The poor man did not have the courage for this while sober. So he decided to buy a bottle of whisky, get out of bed at one o'clock at night, and drink the whole amount in order to get enough courage to go and drown himself in the brook. One o'clock came. But in getting up, his night shirt caught the bottle and knocked it to the floor, spilling all the whisky. He became so terrified that the whole room seemed to be full of devils. He jumped back in bed, drew the covers over his head, and did not venture to look out before daylight. Thereupon he immediately came to me.

I soon discovered that he was accustomed to visit the parsonage, where he had been treated as an object of pity. His religion had come to consist in the pleasure of being pitied. This had to be ended.

"Why do you want pity?" I asked. "It is better to go to heaven with one leg than to have two legs and go to hell."

He became angry and left at once, complaining that the new pastor only made fun of him. The next day he returned, but he had not changed.

"What do you have to complain about? You have been given four legs to use. The rest of us must get along with two," I said to him again.

Out the door he went and told people that you could not get help from this pastor. But he kept coming, and he became a converted Christian man, the opposite of what he had been. Hans never touched liquor after that, regardless of how his old companions tempted him. He became a daily guest at the parsonage, a happy and cheerful person, no longer desirous of pity. And through his obvious conversion, he became a powerful witness to many others.

One day our friend Dr. Stricker, from Saeby, came over to ask Hans's help. A drunken man had broken his leg; and now, said the doctor, while I heal his leg, Hans is to heal his soul. Even in the eyes of the world Hans was a marvelous person.

Even so, the devil made one last attempt to win back his lost property. After many years a dullness came over Hans. He began to take a drink with his meals. He did not become a drunkard, but the life of faith was on the downgrade, and his witness among people ceased. Then one day he fell on the street and injured his hip so badly that he had to stay in bed. His old thoughts of suicide returned. But the devil did not get him. Hans's faith was aroused, and he died in peace. This was the first fruit of my work at Ørsløv.

(A Rich Harvest) Finally, after about two years, the fields began to be "white for harvest." Spiritual life was awakening in many souls, not only in these parishes, but in the adjacent parishes also. People from all around started to flock to my two churches. I began to feel at home in Ørsløv, as I had at Uby and at Ørum, happy that the Lord could use me also in this third place. Many of my friends who formerly attended the services at Uby now came to Ørsløv, which was only twelve miles from Uby. It turned out here, as at Uby, that the influx from other parishes was an effective means of promoting spiritual life. Fellowship among the believers developed. They began to meet for conversation in their homes, they began to hold children's services in their homes, and the parsonage became a gathering place for the people of God.

This new life at Ørsløv did not come all at once, as it had at Ørum. Rather it came gradually, step by step. The explanation is perhaps that my stay at Ørum was short, and the Lord's business there was urgent, while my stay in my first and last homes was more extended. One by one people were aroused to new life; it came about slowly, but therefore perhaps more soundly. A beautiful fellowship of converted Christians developed at Ørsløv and Solbjerg, especially at Ørsløv, and my soul is filled with deep gratitude to my Lord and

Master for the service he permitted me to render in this place for twenty-six years.

I have always had the joy of appealing to the hearts of the young. After some time, two societies, one for boys and one for girls, were formed by the young converts, who banded together to keep themselves "unstained from the world." The boys' society, whose membership was continually replenished by my confirmands, later came under the leadership of my vicar. The girls' society was led by my wife. The weekly meetings for fellowship and prayer were conducted by the believers themselves. Very seldom did I participate in these meetings, partly for lack of time, but also from principle. I wanted them to stand on their own feet in case they should ever be without a pastor. There has been a fine fellowship among the people of God. And though this fellowship is now no longer new, it has been spared the difficulties of disagreement and strife that the children of God in so many places have had to endure.

It is common that in a spiritually minded congregation there are—as Paul said of the saints in Corinth—few who are rich, prominent, or famous. So it has been with the congregations in these parishes. They have consisted chiefly of common people. Though it would not seem an extraordinary distinction to be a farmer, yet this position has been prominent enough to keep people of this class from conversion. The few believing farmers here were nearly all converted in their youth.

One exception to this, however, was the conversion of Mr. Andersen, the proprietor of Solbjerggaard. As a young man he had come from the island of Fyn. He pretended to be an agnostic and was an arrogant person who never set foot in the church. One New Year's Day, however, he came, and that was his salvation. In the closing prayer from the pulpit I prayed that, if there were any persons in the church who had wasted their lives in infidelity, at least one of them might be converted during the New Year. My eyes fell upon a young, handsome man who appeared strangely grave. A few weeks later his only son died. This became a time of decision for him. When he came to report the death of his child, I could sense a noticeable change in him. I asked him how it happened that he had become interested in Christ. He answered that when I had prayed in the church on New Year's Day that a person who had wasted his life in infidelity might be saved during the New Year, he had been constrained to pray, "Lord, let it be me."

His prayer was answered, and his was the most wonderful conversion I have witnessed. The arrogant, unbelieving landowner became a humble child of God, a friend and brother to the other children of God, the gentle friend of his servants, and a living witness to his Lord and Master. Solbjerggaard became a pleasant gathering place for the people of God. His wife, our good friend, followed him faithfully in his new life.

After a few years this strong and handsome man contracted a chronic disease that gradually sapped his strength. Once when I had been preaching about the denarius that the workers in the vineyard received at the end of the day, I said that this was the peace that comes to a child of God at the end of his days before the darkness of death overtakes him.

"That was a new interpretation of the parable," he said. "It seems strange to me, although I am quite young, that I already have this denarius; but, of course, I do not know what hour has struck for me."

Not long after this his hour of departure came. A severe case of pneumonia called him away from his young wife and three small children and numerous faithful friends. Though there was great sorrow, his funeral was more like a procession of triumph than a funeral procession. All who belonged to the kingdom of God in these parishes followed this dear brother to his last resting place in Solbjerg Cemetery.

Among the many conversions that have taken place in these two parishes, I thank God for a number of men, ruined by alcohol, who have become living believers. This has been accomplished by the Word of God alone, without any fuss about total abstinence—an impressive refutation of the claim by the total abstinence people that a ruined person is unable to accept the Christian faith. Certainly he who is on high sees also him who has fallen the deepest and is able to reach him, so that when he has turned about he may become a total abstainer, even without joining any association except the communion of saints.

For years we had no mission house. This was often discussed, but I was hesitant. I believed that spiritual life was served best by holding our children's services as well as our midweek meetings in private homes. One Saturday evening, however, after one of their meetings, a group of people came to me and asked if I would be in favor of the erection of a mission house.

"You appear so happy with the idea of building that now must be the right time for it," I answered.

A few days later some of us, mostly poor people and young people, met at a farm. The sum of one thousand crowns was subscribed at once. A poor man donated the building site near the church. The members themselves built it with their own labor, so it was completed at a very low cost. "This must be the way Moses felt when he set up the tabernacle," I heard one of the happy builders say one day.

The dedication was a great festival at Ørsløv. It has been a most fruitful addition to the old church, a workshop for the salvation of men. During the winter it has been in use almost every day or evening. Two years ago a mission house was built at Solbjerg. It, too, was located near the church, where it can serve its purpose as a workshop of the Lord, not as a replacement for or competition to the Lord's house.

God afforded me many joys during the years I served as pastor of the Ørsløv-Solbjerg parishes. His people remembered me with many celebrations. In 1881, when I had served as pastor for twenty-five years, they arranged a great reception for me. The church was so packed that some had to climb in through the windows. My old friend Dean Blume preached. In the parsonage there were speeches by many others, both pastors and laymen. We received rich gifts from the parishes and from many other parts of the country.

Again in 1885, when my wife and I celebrated our silver anniversary, the same love was manifested in a grand festival with many more gifts.

Once again in 1899, when I had served in Ørsløv-Solbjerg for twenty-five years, the same love gave additional evidence that the parishes were not tired of their old pastor.

It would seem that three times were enough; yet in 1899, the year when I reached my seventieth birthday on December 30, the saints from far and near surrounded me with loving words and gifts. My heart was filled with thanks to my Lord and Master that he had permitted me to experience this day as well as the undeserved blessing of retaining a position among his people in my old age.

It was a great joy to me that, when the parish council wanted to nominate a teacher for Solbjerg parish, they asked me to give them names. Of course I chose the names of believers. One of these was nominated and elected. This was a testimony to me of the respect that Christianity had won in these parishes. For several years now we have been fortunate in having three teachers who support the spiritual work here.

Our home life also has been filled with much joy. The greatest has been the companionship of my wife and children. My wife has always been my faithful helper in my work for the kingdom of God. A peculiar blessing has always attended her work with our children, whose rearing has for the most part been entrusted to her. I have been absent from home so often and have been occupied with so much work that I have been able to devote very little time to them. The Lord has used her to lead them to Christ and to help provide the training for their positions in this life. Some of them remained with Christ while they grew up, others returned to him later. Those who have attained independent positions are filling their places diligently and have taken their spouses from among the people of God.

My dear friend Rudolf Frimodt's death in 1879 gave me great sorrow, though mixed with joy. The message struck the children of God in Denmark like a bolt of lightning: "Frimodt is dead!" It brought deep sorrow to many hearts, not the least to me, who loved him dearly. It was difficult for me and for many others to accept in this the inscrutable purpose of God. It seemed to us that there was so much need for him among the dechristianized masses of the capital. At his funeral in St. John Church, where I was permitted to perform the committal service and to speak the last words at his grave, our mutual friend Rudolf Volf asked me, "Who is to be Frimodt's successor?"

I answered, "Jesus," and meant thereby that among the many people whom Frimodt's powerful words had drawn to his pulpit, there were surely not a few whose allegiance extended no further than to Frimodt himself and who therefore had need that Christ should become for them the successor of Frimodt.

(Five Accusations) Some accusations that have been unjustly made against the Inner Mission should be mentioned. The strangest is that by calling ourselves *saints* we isolate ourselves as a special group in contrast to the remainder of the Christian church. It is not strange that the world should utter such nonsense, but that believers do so is incomprehensible.

Saints is the ancient name of the people of God, a name attested in Scripture and embracing all the forgiving grace of our Savior. During all the spiritually alive periods of church history, this name has been used. So it was at the time of the apostles, at the time of the Reformation, and when the work of the Grundtvigians was in full bloom in the middle of the nineteenth century. They also called themselves the *saints*, and those who were faithful to the remnant of spiritual life during the period of rationalism designated themselves by the same name.

The substitution of the word *Christians* for this old confessional name has always coincided with times of decline in the life of the church. *Christian* is also the name that the whole mass of unbelieving baptized people has adopted for itself.

When the Inner Mission reclaimed the biblical name, it never intended to use it as a special name for itself. The Inner Mission is not the saints, but the saints carry on the Inner Mission. We have adopted it and use it as the common designation of all those who belong to the living church. If there are some among these who do not wish to be called *saints*, this is their affair. The Inner Mission can do nothing about that.

Another accusation against the Inner Mission is that it condemns people and makes them censorious. This is one of those accusations about which people cry out without knowing what they are saying. The truth is that the Inner Mission lets the Word of God pronounce judgment: "He who believes and is baptized shall be saved, but he who does not believe shall be condemned."

We who know that anyone who speaks in the congregation must do so "as one who utters oracles of God," drawing a distinct line of division in all our preaching between two kinds of people, believers and unbelievers, saved and lost, in order that each person may decide for himself to which kind he belongs. But we do not point out who is a believer and who is not. We do look upon some persons as believers, and we join them in a holy brotherhood. All believers from the time of the apostles have done this—but we recognize fully that we may be mistaken.

A third accusation is that the Inner Mission "stupefies" people by holding in contempt all other useful enlightenment and everything great and beautiful in human life. To indicate that this is untrue we need only point to the four folk high schools of the Inner Mission where young people are given full instruction in what is profitable and good to know. But in this, as in all its work, the Inner Mission follows the Word of God: "Seek first the kingdom of God, and all the rest shall be yours as well." Therefore, enlightenment about the kingdom of God and work among young people to lead them into the kingdom of God is paramount in these schools, and knowledge of all other things is secondary. It is a sad fact, deplored by the Grundtvigians themselves, that in their high schools the cause of the kingdom of God is not only secondary for many of the young people but is left out altogether.

A fourth accusation, related to the foregoing one, is that the Inner Mission teaches that the image of God in natural man is completely obliterated. This would be equivalent to saying that in our natural state we are no longer human beings but have become demons or animals, for the image of God in us consists in the human element that separates us from all other creatures on earth. Had we become demons or animals, there would never have been any possibility of our salvation, and it would be the height of unreasonableness to carry on mission activities for the purpose of saving demons or animals.

The Inner Mission does teach, however, that "nothing good dwells within me," that all the remnants of the image of God that are still found in sinful man are corrupted by sin—our understanding as well as our emotions and our will power. Everything must be born anew—sanctified, cleansed, and purified by the Spirit of God—that man may once more become the true image of God. So it is also with everything great and beautiful here on earth. They become really great and beautiful only when they are brought under the influence of Christianity so as to be ruled and cleansed by it.

Finally, the Inner Mission has been accused of localizing sin in certain external activities, such as dancing and card playing, and of making abstention from these activities the criterion of faith. Only ignorance of the Inner Mission and of the mind and life of its friends could be the explanation of such an accusation. The Inner Mission knows no other difference between believers and unbelievers than faith and unbelief. Every believer knows, however, that with this difference goes a different life. A person of faith will necessarily gain new friends among God's children, and friendship with the world becomes impossible. A person of faith necessarily acquires new joys, and old pleasures lose their allure. In most instances such pleasures come to be taken as sad and miserably empty.

The unfortunate Grundtvigian assembly halls with their tawdry pleasures are an impressive warning that these things may be a great temptation and stumbling block for believers. Yet the Grundtvigians continue, undismayed, to advocate dancing and all other worldly pleasures. The Inner Mission, on the other hand, maintains that we have something better with which to amuse ourselves.

(The Future and the Perils of the Inner Mission) It has often been said with a certain self-satisfaction, as though it were especially profound, that the goal of the Inner Mission must be to make itself superfluous. Like many other false profundities, this is a mere phrase. The Inner Mission can never become superfluous, once Christianity has become the people's religion through baptism. There will always be a mixture of believers and unbelievers, and if this is true of the people, the same will be true of their pastors—they will be a mixture of these two categories. For this reason Inner Mission activity has always appeared as a complement to the work of the pastors. The mendicant friars of the Middle Ages, pietism, Methodism, Moravianism—all were forms of Inner Mission activity to promote the spiritual life of the church.

For this task the Lord will make use of laymen as well as clergy. We saw this at the time of the apostles when laymen cooperated harmoniously with the apostles as deacons and evangelists. The Lord himself sent out seventy laymen as witnesses in addition to the twelve apostles. Not only in times of stagnation will there be a need for the Inner Mission; the more life is awakened, with all its temptations to commit excesses, and the more extensive the need "for the equipment of the saints," the more will faithful pastors sense how insuperable is their task and feel the need of aid from the Inner Mission.

No one can predict the future of the Inner Mission. The finest future would be one in which the happy fellowship and cooperation of believing pastors and laymen continues. This fellowship has been the strength of the Inner Mission in Denmark.

The first peril facing the Inner Mission of the future is that of becoming a sect. This was a danger that pietism, Methodism, and Moravianism did not avoid. Originally these movements were inner mission activities for the purpose of awakening new life in the church. Later they isolated themselves as special communities or brotherhoods with special teachings in addition to the doctrines of the general fellowship of the saints in the church.

Up to now there has been no danger for the Inner Mission of Denmark in this respect. It has no special teachings that are different from the doctrines of the Lutheran church, and it has never had a partisan leader, such as the Grundtvigians have had. The name that a pastor gave to the Inner Mission, *Bekkasinerne* ("disciples of Beck"), is too ridiculous to merit consideration. I am clearly conscious of never having been, or wanting to be, the instigator or leader of a party. But the existence of a danger to the Inner Mission at just this point has not eluded its enemies. They have seen this clearly and have continually charged the Inner Mission with standing apart, after the manner of a sect. Of this the people in the Inner Mission should beware.

The same variety exists among the representatives of the Inner Mission in their views of Christianity as one finds among pastors. There are men with a cheerful outlook on Christian life and men with a more somber outlook; there are men with an emancipated attitude and men with a narrower attitude toward the life of a Christian. The Inner Mission accommodates all these differences because it is not a sect. It is only an activity for the purpose of awakening spiritual life and assembling the awakened people into a communion of saints.

3

SWEDEN

HENRIC SCHARTAU (1757–1825)

Henric Schartau, a Lutheran pastor in southern Sweden, represents the older, "churchly" piety of eighteenth-century Sweden. Not very well-known during his life, his influence spread after his death, mainly through a collection of his sermons, two of which are excerpted here. Schartau urges an "enlightened" piety that combines a faithful reliance on God's plan of salvation with a living life of obedience by the believer.

Sermons

SERMON: FIRST SUNDAY AFTER EPIPHANY

These things have I written unto you, that ye may know that ye have eternal life, even unto you that believe on the name of the Son of God. Thus the Apostle John speaks of faith to them that believe (1 John 5:13).

First Part: The Measure of Faith Granted by God as a Criterion of One's Spiritual Condition

The first and least measure of faith embraces the whole Christ and appropriates all his merits, bringing with it complete justification, which cannot be increased, and an entire renewal of the heart. Just as a spark is as real fire as a large flame, so the first spark of hope in Christ, arising in a contrite heart, is as real faith as the most confident reliance on the victorious Lord and Savior. Though ever so weak, a true faith embraces Jesus, "who was made unto us *wisdom from God*," and it expects to learn of him to know his word and ways of life. It accepts him "*unto righteousness*," expecting forgiveness, not by virtue of any contrition or repentance of its own, but by virtue of the suffering and obedience of Jesus. It accepts him "unto sanctification," expecting to receive from him a changed heart and strength to follow him in newness of life. It also accepts him "unto redemption," hoping by him to be delivered from the misfortunes of life and to be saved from the torments of hell.

Whereas even the first feeble faith fully embraces Christ, it brings with it complete justification, so that such a believer is considered quite as justified before God as the greatest heroes of faith, and, indeed, quite as pure from sin as "the spirits of just men made perfect," for he is considered quite as righteous as his Savior. The merits of Jesus, by which the believer has been justified, cannot be increased, nor enlarged by any growth of our faith; so neither can the justification of a true believer be increased. It is quite as complete with the first beginning of faith as it can ever become.

The first measure of faith is that point when a person begins to inquire about faith, though he cannot then perceive that it is faith at all. The beginning takes place when a person who has been frightened by the law begins to ask for salvation in Jesus Christ. Though the unclothed and wounded Redeemer is altogether too insignificant for a proud reason, he nevertheless is the first fountain of comfort to a grieved soul. Hungering and thirsting after righteousness, such a person begins to search in the Scriptures for the things concerning the Savior. He then finds that it is by faith alone that one enters into fellowship with the Savior, for he finds that God's promises everywhere have no other qualifications than this, "Unto every one that believeth." This inquiry about faith implies a vital concernment and an earnest seeking, which find expression in prayer that the Lord might grant a true faith. Every desire of such a soul is, "Alas, if I could only believe!" When he hears the Word, he listens carefully to hear if the preacher has anything to say about faith, and when he reads the Word of God, it is as though his heart addressed the authors of the Scriptures in this wise: "Ye dear apostles of the Lord, ye beloved prophets, teach me to know my Savior. Alas! Bring me to him. Show me how I shall acquire a true faith in him." That this already is true faith is evident from the word of promise in Jeremiah: "Run ye to and fro through the streets of Jerusalem, and see now, and know, and seek in the broad places thereof, if there be any that doeth justly, that seeketh truth; and I will pardon it." God promises pardoning grace to everyone that "seeketh truth." An honest seeking after faith must be faith, for "without faith it is impossible to be well-pleasing unto God." It is quite as impossible that one who is well-pleasing unto God should be without faith as it is impossible to be well-pleasing to God without faith. The mystery of faith is hidden from the reason of the natural man. No one concerned about his salvation inquires about faith until there is faith in his heart, for the concern of an awakened sinner is fixed on the hardship and wretchedness of sin, to the extent that there is no room for such inquiry unless God himself directs him to seek this only means of attaining righteousness and eternal salvation. And why is an awakened soul so deeply concerned about obtaining faith? He longs for a part in the merits of his Savior. He is concerned about entering into fellowship with Jesus. He yearns for true righteousness. But what is such concern, such longing, if not faith? Jesus himself pronounces such a person blessed: "Blessed are they that hunger and thirst after righteousness." It is then certain that he is on the way, coming to Jesus. It is also evident that he has come to Jesus, for Jesus himself is the way. Yes, a person who is on the way coming to Jesus, has already come to him, for Jesus has assured such a soul that he shall in no wise be cast out. But there can be no question of any casting out, except from a room where one already is and has his dwelling.

We find another measure of faith where a person has grown in enlightenment to perceive *that* he has faith, to which belongs a deep sense of joy, though this is not the real measure of his faith. When a person diligently beholds Christ in the Scriptures, he begins to reflect "the glory of God in the face of Jesus Christ," and he is thus enlightened to know himself as well as Jesus. When one enters aright into the Word, one finds shooting forth from all of God's promises beams of light, which, as it were, find their focal point in one's heart, so that one is enabled to see clearly how the Word in its entirety acquits one of guilt. Thus enlightened, one finds that his faith is such as the Word of God describes and that he has become converted in the manner prescribed by the Word of God.

Upon such enlightenment follows deep joy, for how should a person become aware that he is covered with the robe of righteousness, and yet not rejoice in his Savior? How should he be able to find that he has been clothed with the garments of salvation, without being joyful in God? Spiritual gladness follows the assurance of grace, as the shadow follows the body, but we must not imagine that the shadow is the body itself. When the sun shines or a candle has been lit, the shadow appears, but in darkness and gloom it does not appear. It would be foolish to doubt the existence of the body, merely because one cannot see its shadow, for when the sun begins to shine, the shadow immediately appears. As long as the Sun of Righteousness appears to them that fear the name of the Lord, he brings the perception of "healing in his wings," but when he appears to set and shine no more, even they that fear the Lord may walk in darkness, without joy or any clearly discernible peace. We must not then conclude that faith has been lost, merely because we do not experience the joy of faith. After the storm has passed, God again lets the sun of grace shine, and then

> Light is sown for the righteous
> And gladness for the upright in heart.

A greater measure of faith is this, that a person is able to believe in spite of everything his heart feels or his reason sees. The beginning of such faith takes place when the Holy Spirit trains and teaches a person to believe without any heartfelt emotions. On the one hand, God removes the emotions before a person has time to rely on them, and, on the other hand, he leads the soul to the gospel and to a hearty reliance on the promises of grace. In this way a person becomes trained in faith and enabled to believe the Scriptures, even though he finds no corresponding feelings in his heart. By such means he eventually obtains so great a stability of faith that he is able to believe the Word, although he finds the opposite in his heart; that he is sure of the promises in the Word, although his heart speaks to the contrary; and that he has perfect assurance of forgiveness, grace, and salvation through Jesus Christ, although in his heart he finds condemnation, wrath, and unblessedness. If our heart condemns us, we still know that we are of the truth, and are able to assure our heart before him with the confidence that "God is greater than our heart, and knoweth all things." By this training in faith a man attains such an increase of faith that he can believe quite the contrary of that which his reason sees; that he is able to believe that God will provide for his temporal wants, though there be no visible means for his support; that he may feel sure of help, though he sees before him only want and distress, and expect great goodwill of men, being enabled to live with them in peace, while it appears as though he were hated by all.

Second Part: How a Person Must Judge of His Spiritual Condition by the Measure of Faith Granted by God

The Apostle says in our Epistle text, "Let no one think of himself more highly than he ought to think, but rather soberly, according as God hath dealt to each man a measure of faith."

If you have not now, nor ever had, the first measure of faith, you cannot have attained to any of the other measures. You then have full reason to consider yourself unconverted, not having any faith at all. An unconverted man is very strangely minded. Occasionally he speaks of his faith as though it were very weak, and then, again, as though he had arrived at the highest measure of certainty and courage. In spite of all this, let it be remembered that you have not as yet prayerfully and diligently searched the Scriptures and inquired for faith. Nor is this strange, for you have never been seeking for Jesus, nor realized that you are without him. If you really felt, as you say, that your faith is weak, you would be grieved, and again if, as you sometimes pretend, you had a strong faith in the Lord, you would have experienced the lack of both faith and grace. But when you say that you have always had a good faith, it immediately becomes apparent that your faith cannot be of the right kind, for you have not grown to such stability of faith in the manner that other children of God do. Furthermore, when your faith is compared with your manner of life, it becomes evident that your faith is a monstrosity. When one organ of a newborn babe is as large as it should be in an adult, while other members of the body are like those of a normal child, this child is deformed. So, too, when faith, which is the chief part of a newborn convert, at once is as large as that of the fathers in grace, while other characteristics and gifts of grace are as small as those of the weakest beginner in Christian life, then this "new man" is without due proportion, a monstrosity. When your knowledge is so slight that you need to learn "the rudiments of the first principles of the oracles of God"; when the light that is in you is so faint that there scarcely is twilight or dawn of enlightenment; when love is so lukewarm as to give place to carnal jealousy and strife; when conditions are such, and you nevertheless boast of a good and strong faith in the Lord, then your whole religion is a monstrosity, and your faith is deformed. It is not a work of the Holy Spirit. Satan has given it to you, or you have taken it yourself. It is not the work of God, nor a true faith—the faith that embraces Christ. It is not the faith that appropriates the forgiveness of sins. It is not the faith by which Jesus dwells in the heart. It is not the faith that brings with it the Holy Spirit. It is not the faith the possession of which in time is followed by unspeakable blessedness in eternity. No, it is a false, imaginary faith. With this faith you have no part in Jesus; you are far from him. If you get no other faith than this, you will never get rid of your sins. If you keep this faith to the end, this very faith will become the cord, the chain, by which the evil spirit will bring you into eternal destruction.

If, on the other hand, you notice in you some of the things pertaining to the first measure of faith, then you may consider yourself on the way to Jesus, and if you have received the comforting insight into the Word that you have come to him, you must not cast it away. When you realize that you have received the first measure of faith, God thereby grants you the greater measure, namely the assurance and certainty of a true faith. When a person has been truly converted by the Holy Spirit, he will also be brought forward on the way of life. Though you have unconsciously come to faith in Jesus, God will enlighten you to know that you have the true faith. The Spirit of God will thereby strengthen your soul against approaching temptations and confirm your resolution to belong to Jesus forever. If you have not resisted the beginnings of God's work of grace, you must not resist the perfecting thereof. If, by the Word of God, you find that you have the first measure of faith, a sincere longing for faith, an inquiry about faith, and a seeking after faith, then this very insight is an enlightenment of the Holy Spirit, quite as much so as that of your awakening when you saw that you had no faith. This light cannot deceive you nor lead you astray. Hence, if in this way you become kindly persuaded and comfortingly convinced that you have the true faith, God grants you the second, greater measure of faith by assuring you that you have the first measure. "Cast not away your boldness," for you shall in this way receive an increased measure of faith, just as surely as faith has been begun in you.

If you have the assurance of a true faith, you must not become proud, imagining that you have come to the greatest measure of faith, nor demand that you shall always have this assurance and become impatient when you lack it, for you ought to know that it is God's purpose to thus bring you to a greater measure of faith, enabling you to believe without feelings and in spite of feelings. If you have found that your faith is real and true, then you may thank and praise the Lord for this gracious refreshing. Let your heart be strengthened thereby, but be not puffed up. You have indeed received an increased faith, but not the greatest measure. Jesus blesses those who "have not seen, and yet have believed." It is to guard you from pride and to train you in faith that the Lord soon deprives you of that assurance. Remember that God's ways are such with his faithful ones, and be content therewith. Do not rush willfully along, endeavoring to regain the certainty of mind, for you cannot find it in the recesses of your heart. Go rather to the Word of God and look for insight into its promises, and ask the Holy Spirit to teach you to rely on these. Behold, you have a greater faith, when you are able to believe without consulting the feelings of your heart; for God is greater than your heart. Your faith thus gains stability and certainty, for the words of promise are irrevocable and unfailing, while your feelings are changeable and unreliable. You thus eventually obtain a durable peace, and you are being prepared for the future beholding of God's face in heaven, while God frequently hides his face from you during your earthly pilgrimage.

Finally, you must also take warning and remember that it is quite as possible to recede as to advance in the measure of faith. By neglecting the means of grace and growing sluggish in prayer and careless in his manner of life, it may happen that one who had attained the stability of the fathers can be set back to the weakness of spiritual children, so that, while before he could believe in spite of the condemnations of his heart, he now finds it increasingly difficult to feel at ease without the conscious enjoyment of the sweetness of grace. It may likewise happen that one who had attained certainty, can, by the neglect of grace, fall into protracted wavering and lose the assurance of his state in grace, to the extent that there remains only a seeking after grace, like that at the first awakening. A person in this state considers himself without any part in Jesus, just as he did at his first awakening, but he is still remaining in the state of grace, though near falling away from it.

In conclusion, let me instruct the upright in heart that the great measure of faith cannot always be perceived, but only now and then, between the spiritual battles. When the devil cannot prevent your growth in faith, he tries to deprive you of the joy that you should have when you become aware of your spiritual growth. The Lord permits this. The evil one is allowed to cover you with darkness and to obscure from your vision the measure of faith attained; for it is one of the great wonders along the way that a lack of assurance increases faith, and that faith becomes greater by seeming less. If you find yourself unexpectedly set back in your faith, without any previous neglect on your part of the Word and of prayer, this is no evidence of a diminishing faith, but rather of a new spiritual battle, which thus almost imperceptibly begins. You have the less reason to fear that you have erred from the faith if you notice that your conception of the Redeemer is retained, working on your mind, sustaining your hope, and urging you to obedience. This is an evidence that you are grasped by your Redeemer. Be content with this very slight measure of faith. The Lord who has helped you to the lesser faith will also help you to the greater. Only continue to press on, that you may apprehend that which you have not yet apprehended, and you shall not forever miss the goal, though you have not yet attained it, but you shall reach the goal which God has set before you and to which you are aspiring, since you are able to say with Paul, "I press on, if so be that I may apprehend that for which also I was apprehended by Christ Jesus." Amen.

Sermon: Seventh Sunday after Trinity

Lifting up their eyes, they saw no one, save Jesus only. In this way Matthew concludes his story of the peculiar occurrence described in the seventeenth chapter.

First Part: Jesus Only. In the Awakening, as Its Object

It is Jesus only who has provided that the Holy Spirit works upon a secure heart unto its awakening. Paul says that the awakening takes place with reference to Jesus, in connection with, and as a result of, his redemption, which was perfected when God awakened Jesus from the dead. The blood of Jesus was shed even for those who have "counted it an unholy thing," and it bespeaks mercy even for them. God is jealous for the honor of his Son; he desires to show that the atonement is valid and powerful, and he therefore permits his Holy Spirit to quicken the slumbering consciences. Jesus gave his life for the wandering sheep, and he "goes after that which is lost." It is the suffering of Jesus that pleads for pardon. It is his prayer that quickens the movements of grace in dead hearts, and it is by virtue of his merits that gifts are provided even for those who have fallen away.

Jesus only is the basis of a sinner's awakening, but he is also the object thereof, for it is the object of the law to urge sinners to accept the grace offered by the gospel. Paul teaches that Christ and justification through faith in Christ are the objects of the law: "Christ is the end of the law unto righteousness to everyone that believeth." Then again he describes the end of awakening as follows: "The law has been our tutor unto Christ, that we might be justified by faith." Hear then, O man, that the law causes grief in order that you may eagerly accept the comfort proclaimed in the gospel: that Jesus has paid for all your sins. The law frightens you, threatening you with eternal torment, in order that you may take the refuge that is being offered you with Jesus. When God, in his law, demands perfection in everything, his true object is that you may become a partaker of the righteousness of your Savior, who has fulfilled the law for you.

Second Part: Jesus Only. In Justification and the New Birth, as Its Foundation

A person becomes justified through faith alone, but Jesus only is the foundation of faith. He has provided that an awakened sinner can come to faith. Therefore an apostle says that "Jesus is the author and perfecter of our faith." Jesus has not only atoned for sins and purchased righteousness, but he has also provided that a sinner shall become a partaker of this grace. And since this is done by faith, Jesus has also provided that the Holy Spirit shall work to that end and grant a true faith, in order that the works of grace may be perfected and that man may appropriate and enjoy the fruits of redemption.

Jesus is the foundation of faith, for it is he of whom the gospel says that he has purchased all the good that the gospel offers to those who are rightly awakened. It is only through the gospel that a man can come to faith, for the gospel speaks of Jesus and, indeed, concerning Jesus only. Any doctrine that does not speak of Jesus, whatever experience and glory it may proclaim, is not the gospel. So then Jesus is in the Word. His suffering, his blood, his obedience and death are proclaimed in the Word, and this is the only means of coming to the right faith.

It is Jesus only whom faith embraces and on whom it relies. When a person, after seeing the awful depth of his own misery, has once caught a right vision of Jesus, he cannot turn his thoughts from him. Jesus becomes everything to such a one, and everything else is "counted as loss and dung." He seeks for Jesus, comes to him, longs for his righteousness, prays in his name, and hopes in him alone. He presses on that he may grasp Christ more securely, and that he may trust him with more certainty and with greater boldness.

Jesus only is the basis and main cause of justification. Jesus only is considered by God when he makes a person righteous. God merely sees that the sinner has accepted Christ and that he is in Christ, in fellowship with him. God does not wrathfully count such a person's sins, for they are covered with the blood of Jesus. The Savior is sinless, and a justified man is considered quite as free from guilt as Jesus was when he had paid the whole debt of sin, and as pure, free from the corruption of sin, as Jesus has always been. Nor does God graciously look upon a person's good deeds; no, he looks only on his beloved Son. If he were to look upon our good deeds, he would also see the sins wherewith these good deeds are contaminated, and he would by virtue of his righteousness be compelled to exact punishment. God looks upon his beloved Son only, in order that he may find something perfect to rest his holy eyes upon. The atonement and righteousness of Jesus only are then by God attributed to the justified sinner. Nothing else will avail and satisfy an awakened soul. Nothing else suffices for our salvation from eternal fire; no other righteousness is valid and pleasing before God than that of his beloved Son in whom he is well pleased. It is by reason of this alone that God forgives sins and receives us into sonship with him. Sins are forgiven, because Jesus "blotted out the bond against us" with his pierced, bleeding hand, and for the sake of his childlike obedience, every one that believes on him becomes a child of God. For Jesus' sake every child of God is considered like Jesus himself, and a like verdict is rendered in heaven at the time of every act of justification as was proclaimed with reference to Jesus at the transfiguration: "This is my beloved son [this is my beloved daughter], in whom I am well pleased."

Jesus only is the basis of the new birth, for it is faith in him alone that brings regeneration of the heart. Paul expresses this in Ephesians 2:6, saying, "God made us to sit with Christ in the heavenly places." When a man fixes his attention upon Jesus alone and upon the holiness that he purchased and perfected when he had "his delight in the law of the Lord," he receives the Spirit that grants full enlightenment in the Word of God. The believer then becomes like the Lord Jesus, being "transformed into the same image." The light of the glory of Jesus enlightens the soul to see aright and to perceive clearly the heavenly light in the Word of God, when the Sun of Righteousness arises and God takes his dwelling in the soul. God then also grants the believer a new mind, "the mind that was also in Christ Jesus." His will becomes our will, and we thereupon always desire to be humble like Jesus, meek like Jesus, obedient like Jesus, pure in heart like Jesus, and occasionally we are also able to be thus, for in the new birth we received "a clean heart and a right spirit" and a mind like that "which was also in Christ Jesus."

Third Part: Jesus Only. In Sanctification, as Its Power

It is in sanctification that the power of our Lord Jesus Christ is best shown, for it is Jesus who provides the power to put off the old man and put on the new. If you are to get rid of your wicked thoughts, if you are to quench your evil desires, if you are to succeed in overcoming your old sinful habits, verily, there is no other help for this in heaven or on earth than that provided by Jesus only. He has conquered sin, and "in all these things we are more than conquerors through him that loved us," for he is "the Lord that sanctifies." "The sanctification of the spirit" is a sure result of his redemption. If you were unable to resist sin, if you were compelled to fall therein again, then the forgiveness would be useless and the atonement in vain. But his merit is complete and perfect, and he has arranged that the merit imputed to you at once and immediately in justification shall also gradually be wrought in you in sanctification. Jesus has not only stood in your stead as a just man who has had his delight in God's commandments and whose righteousness is imputed to you as though you had always been just, but he has also brought about that you actually become just and obtain more and more delight in God's law according to the inner man.

The more a person grows in faith in the Lord Jesus, the more he will also increase in good works. You do not, as you may suppose, receive more faith and grace from God by virtue of your watchfulness, meekness, patience, and devotion, but quite the reverse. In the proportion that Jesus becomes great and glorious to you, in the proportion that he becomes indispensable, you will increase in all the virtues that derive their strength from him. The more faith, which is the origin of love, increases, the more will also love, which is the result of faith, increase.

Love for Jesus is the chief motive unto sanctification in a converted soul. It is love for Jesus that makes the believers submissive to him in trials and sorrow, enabling them to bear his cross when the Lord finds it needful for their sanctification. Paul designates the knowledge of the love of Christ as the most immediate cause leading to one's being "filled unto all the fullness of God." In like manner it is love for Jesus that makes the most pleasing sins abominable and the most grievous duties light. It is love for Jesus that enables us to love all men, because he has deigned to make them all objects of his love. It is love for Jesus that opens our heart so that we may have confidence in those who are known to be partakers of that same love of Christ. It is love for Jesus that quenches our anger when we are offended, that kills hatred and enables the believer to love his enemies, since Jesus has loved them too, precisely as he loved us even while we were yet his enemies.

Jesus is the most splendid and only perfect pattern to follow in sanctification. Do not ask to become like this one or that one, but pray that you may become like Jesus. Do not attempt to imitate the talents of others, nor their measure of grace, but walk in the footsteps of your Savior. Along that way you shall more and more attain to that whereunto by your election you were ordained, namely, to be "conformed to the image of his Son."

Application

Do you, O confident sinner, know whom you are warring against, whom you are scoffing at? It is not the servant who proclaims the message that you contradict, not human beings whom you mock for their spiritual interests, but Jesus only, Jesus, whose words are being spoken to you and whose members they are whom you vituperate. Rest assured that Jesus alone is able to overrule your wickedness and to judge and punish you. How dreadful it will be for you when you lie upon your death bed at the end of the way to realize that the Son's wrath is upon you! How awful the mere appearance of Jesus when, in the resurrection, you raise your head from the grave!

Take heed to what you have heard, O mournful souls, remember that Jesus only is the object of your awakening. Do not therefore seek for more regret nor for an immediate improvement in your course of life, but seek for Jesus only. Where, indeed, can you look for salvation except to your Savior? Where can you find salvation except in him? It is nowhere else to be found. When you have found him and in him righteousness and strength, when his righteousness is your support in temptations, when his might is your succor, lo, then you have enough in him, for you have all in him. If then it should ever happen that you, like the first disciples, should in spirit see somewhat of his glory and "taste the powers of the age to come," and if this glory should thereupon disappear, then do not look for Moses or Elias, but be contented with the grace granted to those early disciples of whom we read, "When they lifted up their eyes, they saw no one, save Jesus only."

When the peace of Christ has brought you reinvigoration and his promises have given you assurance of grace, then it shall also be your lot, at the approach of death, when your eyes can no longer see the things of this world, then the vision of your soul shall be opened and endowed with heavenly light to see the great glory, world without end, face to face,—Jesus only. Amen.

CARL OLOF ROSENIUS (1816–1868)

Besides his public preaching, Carl Olof Rosenius's main work was literary, and his main vehicle to bring spiritual care to Sweden was through the publication Pietisten *(The pietist), which he founded in 1842. His writings were soon translated and compiled into various collections that found wide circulation throughout Scandinavia as well as among Scandinavian-Americans.* The Believer Free from the Law, *of which excerpts are presented here, is a selection of spiritual writings from* Pietisten.

The Believer Free from the Law

May all Christians, therefore, lay to heart the final admonition given by the Apostle to the Galatians, when he explained to them the freedom from the law. With this admonition we, too, now wish to close. It reads as follows:

> *"For freedom did Christ set us free: stand fast therefore, and be not entangled again in a yoke of bondage"* (Gal 5:1).

Even many upright Christians are still so ignorant of the real nature of the spiritual life that they do not attach much weight to this admonition, do not understand that it is essential to life and salvation, but imagine that the good Apostle by this only reveals the particularly devoted interest that he takes in the peace and well-being of the Galatians. For even in our own day a preacher of the gospel is often estimated in that same manner. They do not understand that their spiritual life is in any danger if the conscience is dragged down and made captive under the yoke of bondage. May God awaken all such souls out of their error! The Apostle has another understanding of the case. He makes this admonition so exceedingly important that he says that if you only lose your freedom of conscience and become captive under the law, and begin to seek your righteousness in your own works, or expect life and sanctification from the law (Gal 3:2, 5), you have made "void the grace of God" (Gal 2:21) and crucify Christ afresh (Heb 6:6; cf. Gal 3:1). Then you "are perfected in the flesh" (v. 3), you are "under a curse" (v. 10), you are a "son of the handmaid," and after all your service you shall be "cast out" (4:30). You "are severed from Christ," you "are fallen away from grace" (5:4). And he says that this point is so delicate and sensitive that if you intentionally and purposely include ever so little of your own deeds as necessary for salvation, and do not let Christ alone be sufficient for that, faith is spoiled, "the lump leavened"; for this is what he means when he says, "A little leaven leaveneth the whole lump" (v. 9).

When our whole nature now leans so strongly toward self-righteousness, se1f-significance in spiritual things, through the self-idolatry with which the serpent in the fall filled man, so that nothing is so foolish to the reason and mortifying to the heart as this that we are wholly incapable of the good, but as utterly lost must receive everything by grace, and as a gift, through Christ; then each one ought to understand that the danger of being made captive under the law is not so slight as the ignorant think. Add to this, secondly, that our enemy, the devil, knows well that whatever else he may do to us, he has gained nothing essential so long as we still remain in the faith, in Christ our city of refuge; that then only will there be death, when the devil has succeeded in leading us from the love of Christ to our own labor in legal servitude and unbelief, so that life in the Son of God ceases. Yes, then there will be death, even if we retained the most beautiful life. Therefore we can in truth say that all the devil purposes with all his attacks and temptations, with all his hellish zeal, his deceit and power, finally aims at this, that he may lead us away from the good child relation to God, from "the freedom for which Christ set us free," and bring us into bondage and unbelief. Not without reason does the Apostle use the word *entangle*—it is a hunter who would "entangle" us—and if we only become entangled in the yoke of the law's bondage, we are also immediately bondservants to the inner life of sin, yes, to the devil and death. The devil can bring less experienced Christians to this bondage in a very simple way, by merely pointing out that they still are sinners, and that God hates and judges sin. Here he now has two truths, by which, however, he permits us to lead us from the sound truth. Although we are truly born again, and have a holy and willing spirit by which we have become new men, the flesh, the old heart, is nevertheless filled with all the corruption of sin that the fall of Adam brought on, and that operates in countless directions, in thoughts, feelings, desires, words and deeds, in sluggishness toward the good, in cool indifference of the heart toward God and our neighbor, disinclination toward the Word and prayer, sinful emotions, and the like. Then the Word of God arises and condemns all this, and still I am unable to free myself from it; how shall I then be able to believe that I am in a constant grace and friendship with God?

The temptation to despair and unbelief becomes especially severe when the devil puts before me *God's own words* that seem to condemn me. First of all the Bible contains a great number of terrible threatenings against the secure, ungodly hypocrites. Since the world is full of these, the Word of God must, of course, contain a good deal for them. But a soul that is poor in spirit, who is chastised by the Spirit, feels, indeed, all kinds of evil in himself and he says, "Yes, precisely, *I* am secure, *I* am ungodly, hypocritical, and so forth—for all this surely lies here in the old heart." This the devil then uses to murder and destroy my poor faith. Further, since every Christian must hold in reverence the commandments of the law as unchangeable rules of guidance, even though he is continually condemned by those very commandments, how can he then still believe that he stands in a constant grace and friendship with God? We were not only to know but also to fulfill the will of God, were we not? But in spite of everything that grace has worked in me, I can still not find that *I fulfill* the commandments of God; and so the judgment of the law immediately comes upon my conscience. Oh, what grace and wisdom are here required, nay, what a miracle of God, what a mighty help of God, if we are to be able to remain firm of faith in God's grace!

It will here be quite necessary to consider deeply and thoroughly what God's *covenant of grace* implies, namely that all these judgments and threats fall only on *them* who are *without Christ—or* fall merely on *the sin itself* and *the outward man*, but do not at all touch *the state of grace* itself, as long as I am under Christ; and further, that God, to be sure, wishes by his law to punish and correct that which is wrong in my life, yes, even by external punishments and plagues pursue and slay my sins; but that I at the same time am in an eternal grace; that he is angry only at my enemy, sin, which I, too, after the spirit hate, but that he is not angry with *me*, who in Christ am perfectly free from all wrath, all the judgments and threats of the law, have a constant forgiveness and am already inscribed in heaven as his child and heir. Christ very plainly indicated this when he rebuked his disciples for their strife as to who among them was the greatest—a most disgusting sin—but at the same time, as if nothing had happened, spoke of their seats of honor in heaven (Luke 22:24–30). So also John says, "These things write I unto you, my little children, that *ye may not sin.* And *if any man sin, we have an Advocate with the Father*" (1 John 2:1, 2). It was this alone he wished—that they might not *sin*; but if, alas, they did sin, they were to know, however, that they had an Advocate in heaven; of this comfort they should let no one rob them. How necessary is it not to *consider this distinction deeply and thoroughly*, this, to let the commandments and threats of the law fall only on the *sin*, but not on our *child-confidence* God, and to retain our certainty of everlasting grace through Christ. This is the true freedom from the law.

The pious Spener has spoken of this with much thoughtfulness and caution. He says,

> The believers are free from the Law in this sense, that they have a perfect and *constant forgiveness* of their sins. And it is to be noted that this forgiveness consists of two points. First, that *those* sins which man committed before his conversion when he was not in a state of grace, and those sins by which, peradventure, he once lost his state of grace, are, if he again becomes converted and comes to Christ, so perfectly forgiven, however great they may have been, that of them shall no more be made a remembrance. Secondly, the forgiveness consists in this, that as long as man stands in the faith, and consequently does not willfully serve sin, all his indwelling corruption and his sins of frailty, which still cling to him and through which he errs, whether it be through omission, or imperfect doing of the good, or through sinful desires, thoughts, words, and deeds (which if he were not in Christ, would be condemnable), all these sins God by His divine grace does not

reckon against him, but for Christ's sake passes over them, just as if they had never been committed. This is the fundamental thought in the words of Paul: "There is therefore now no condemnation to them that are in Christ Jesus—who walk not after the flesh, but after the Spirit" (Rom. 8:1, 4). Consequently they still have the flesh remaining, which in and by itself is subject to the curse of the Law; the flesh still incites them to walk after its instincts, awakens in them therefore evil lusts and desires, and at times even gains some advantage over them, so that actual sins arise, which in themselves would merit a curse. But because they still are in Christ Jesus, from whom nothing but unbridled sinning and unbelief can separate them, such sins are to them, for Christ's sake, not unto condemnation. For they themselves are not under the Law. There exists here a matchless bliss, without which our other comfort would be altogether too weak. For even if we otherwise knew that our sins, even such great sins which now are long since past, were forgiven us, when in true repentance we acknowledged them and sought forgiveness, we could, however, not even one single moment do anything else but pray for forgiveness, because no moment passes during which we do not notice, or otherwise must fear, that we have sinned in one way or another, or at least have neglected some good, and hence our present sins would always be at hand. This would then keep us in continual anguish and discouragement and never allow us to turn our faces with joy to God; and this would diminish our power for good. But this is our glorious comfort that as long as we stand in the faith (and consequently do not give sin the freedom it seeks), we are *completely free from the Law*; that the Law is not permitted to condemn us for our sins that still beset us, but God simply forgets them for Christ's sake, as if they did not exist. As was said before, sins are in themselves always condemnable, but they are not reckoned against those who are in Christ. This does not do away with their humility and piety, on the contrary it increases them, and gives to the believers a glorious

> boldness of faith, which is the ground of all spiritual power.[1]

Only it behooves us here not merely to understand and know this, but also earnestly to begin using this wisdom of ours when the actual warfare is on. And here we must make mention of a very destructive fault, which especially clings to certain younger and unsteady Christians—that they do not earnestly utilize their knowledge of God's covenant of grace, when the enemy assails them through the law and the conscience, but walk mildly subject to every suggestion, and consequently are dependent on temporary impressions. This is not what is meant by keeping the Word of the Lord and establishing the heart in grace. We cannot sufficiently praise the wisdom speaking in a sermon of Luther,[2] where he teaches us how we may answer the law and the devil when we are unrighteously attacked in the conscience (Luther, Third Sunday after Trinity). With many and powerful words he here shows how necessary it is to distinguish between two things, conscience and life, faith and walk. When it is a matter of faith and conscience, we are not to give room to any law, provided we wish to stand fast in the freedom, but let that be perfectly settled that in us there is sin constantly, and that before the law our righteousness is at an end, but that we have an entirely different righteousness, in which we can stand before God; namely, that the Son of God has been under the law for us, and has also become a curse for us. On the other hand, when it is a matter of our life and walk, we are to accept with all submission the reproofs and corrections of the law, and can then never give sufficient heed to God's commandments. In the faith and in the conscience we are to live as free "as if no law had been given on earth, neither one nor ten commandments," but when it is a matter of life, we are to be as slaves, not because of the threats of the law or because of the promises, but of fervent desire and love, of joyous, hearty thankfulness for our precious freedom from the judgments of the Law.

1. [Ed. note] I have not been able to locate this quote with any accuracy.
2. The sermon to which he refers is from a sermon of Luther for the Third Sunday after Trinity. An English version is found in "Sermon for the Third Sunday after Trinity: Luke 15:1–10," in *The Precious and Sacred Writings of Martin Luther*, ed. John Nicholas Lenker, vol. 13 (Minneapolis: Lutherans in All Lands Co., 1904), 66–96.

"In this way," says Luther

> a Christian must learn so to rule his conscience before God, as not to permit himself to be ensnared by any Law, but whenever anyone seeks to assail his faith by the Law let him defend himself against it, and do as Christ does here and in other places where He shows himself in His course so firm, singular, and strange, that neither Moses nor any zealot of the Law can move Him, although He otherwise is the most humble, the most gentle and friendly of men. Let us do likewise. But it is a difficult and great art, which no one but our Master knows perfectly. For the devil sports with our flesh and blood, when he grips man in his conscience and takes him to task for what he has done and for what he has not done.

Especially is this so if he has first succeeded to lead him into some grievous sin. He now tries to bring him to think that he is thereby completely fallen from grace and that he must experience something peculiar in his heart as the sign of a new pardon. And then this peculiar experience does not come, but rather, as is common when the conscience becomes bound in unbelief, the law only works a peculiar dryness and deadness in the feelings. Or if a Christian, one beyond doubt in grace, is beset by a disposition very troublesome in certain respects that he never quite escapes, but, with all his weeping, praying, and use of the means of grace, is still surprised by the sin that always "besets him," and the devil suggests to him that this is the same as the *rule* of sin, or to "*do* sin"—oh! In both these events the hellish enemy can frightfully torture a man and fill his whole soul day and night with a roaring din of threatenings by the wrath and curse of God, so that he believes that he is the most monstrous sinner on earth.

How shall I in such severe circumstances escape being made captive under the law? Aye, now it is a question of being furnished with the proper arms and of being able to "withstand the devil, steadfast in the faith," and to answer, "If my sin even were still more terrible, my Lord Christ shall not be made a sinner. I will, none the less, render honor to his blood and his truth. I still remember the words of the everlasting Father: 'Though your sins be as scarlet, they shall be white as snow, though they be red like crimson, they shall be as wool' (Isa 1:18). Even if I for a long time may not feel anything special in my heart, I will, none the less, let his words be divine truth. Get thee hence from me, Satan! Sin shall not condemn me, as long as Christ lives. And if the sin were, as thou sayest to me, my own doing, I would no longer weep over it (Rom 7:20). And how dost thou, false spirit, wish in such a perverted way to make a saint of me, since thou speakest of my having sinned? Why, I have never pretended that I was sinless. My own righteousness before the law is a thing of the past so that, as regards my pardon, what I am, or do, or have done counts for nothing. The only thing that counts here is what my Lord Christ has done for me, what he still is, and what he does as my Advocate with the Father. We are now in the bridal chamber, where only the Bridegroom may be with the bride."

But the law continues to knock at the door and says, but you ought nevertheless yourself to be pious and holy and keep the commandments of God, if you wish to be saved. Answer: It is true that I ought to be holy and keep the commandments of God; but merely because you add the words, *If you wish to be saved,* I will not now listen to you at all. Because my conscience is attacked by a condition for salvation taken from the law, I wish to be rid of you entirely. For in the question as to my salvation my life does not count at all, simply because it is already settled that I am lost before the law, but also that I have a perfect righteousness, in the abundant merit of my precious Bridegroom. He has for me fulfilled all that the law could ever demand. I neither can, nor do I wish to appear before God with any other righteousness. Come at the right moment, when it is a question of my life, with your reminders. Remind me, for example, to be merciful, patient, humble, chaste, forgiving, and so on, when my neighbor needs anything of the like from me. But here, when it is a question of my relation to God, I will not listen to you, for then I have quite another righteousness, a perfect, yes, divine righteousness. Praised be the name of my Lord Jesus.

In this way a Christian may defend himself and prevail against the suggestions of the devil and the threatenings of the law, whether for past or present sins; in this way, namely, that when the law tries to attack the *conscience,* and to deny my *state of grace,* I then daringly beat him off, and say, I shall gladly do good works when I am among my fellow men, who need them; but here when my conscience is to stand before God. I will know nothing of that. For here my life and walk do not avail, but only my Lord Christ.—"But if it is here that I am lacking, that I do not do these good works among men as I ought, what then?" This is certainly to be deplored and here it were well if some improvement took place—by a more watchful walk your conscience would also experience less severe attacks. But if you are to be *saved*, it is, nevertheless, needful, that you with all your power pierce through the thick cloud of contradictions and, despite all, let Christ count for more than all your poor being. Otherwise you will forever perish. Through faith everything can be remedied; through unbelief there is naught but death and condemnation.

Much more ought to have been said on this precious subject, yet we must leave it. We wish only to add that this lofty grace, freedom from the law, is not at all proclaimed to the hard, presumptuous, and unbroken souls who know the art of believing and of being secure all too well, or to those who with a pretty evangelical confession also wish to retain full freedom for the flesh and to live as it pleases them. No, thus says the Apostle: "As free, and not using your freedom for a cloak of wickedness, but as bondservants of God" (1 Pet 2:16). As to the flesh, true Christians are, alas! Indeed, weak, so that they, too, can err and fall miserably, but there is in them however a God-fearing spirit that cheerfully accepts admonition and seeks improvement. But they, on the other hand, who wish by their advocacy of evangelical freedom to defend a carnal life conformed to the world, have not the Spirit of the Lord.

But the Apostle Paul admonishes even the believers not to allow the false heart to lead them astray into the misuse of this precious freedom. He says, "For ye, brethren, were called for freedom; only use not your freedom for an occasion to the flesh, but through love be servants one to another" (Gal 5:13).

Oh, that all the children of God might in time take to heart also this admonition! It is a common sickness, or perversion, of our minds, that we are bound where we should be free—in *the conscience*; and altogether too free where we should be bound—in *the flesh*. Let us watch! Since we have an everlasting freedom from the judgments of the law, let us fervently love the commandments of the law so that with cheerful mind we serve our neighbor in love with words, deeds, and patience. Let us beware lest we grieve the Holy

Spirit by sins against his holy commandments. Watch and pray and flee when you see the temptation approaching. Flee cheerfully and willingly, since God is eternally gracious toward you and opens his bosom to you. But if you have been so hapless as to fall, know that you have an "Advocate with the Father," and you shall not perish if you flee to him and seek restoration, grace, and comfort, and a new purpose to watch more earnestly hereafter.

Such, then, our whole way will be. The Lord be with us on that way, and protect us both on our right hand and on our left hand!

A Faithful Guide to Peace with God

Though he sought to study for the ministry, circumstances prevented Rosenius from acquiring the necessary education. Instead he became a lay evangelist, preaching, teaching, and writing all around Sweden. A Faithful Guide to Peace with God, *a compilation of excerpts from Rosenius's writings made with the assistance of Norwegian bishop Nils J. Laache, shows his deep personal concern for the spiritual struggles of those wrestling with faith and doubt. He attempts here to show the path for the sinner to the renewal of faith and life that he saw as the center of the Christian life.*

The Revelation of the Mystery: The Third Day

Should anyone ask the question, "Does not salvation really take place before I come to faith and before my sins are blotted out?"—the answer is, salvation in reality took place nineteen hundred years ago on Golgotha, the place of execution, outside the walls of Jerusalem. Concerning this historical event, we read, "When Jesus therefore had received the vinegar, he said, 'It is finished': and he bowed his head, and gave up the ghost" (John 9:30). Mark you: "It is finished." Behold in these words the salvation of the world! When these words were uttered by the dying Savior, God's eternal justice was satisfied. Humanity was redeemed and ransomed by the blood of the Son of God on the cross. Then occurred the "blotting out of the handwriting of ordinances that was against us, which was contrary to us, and he took it out of the way, nailing it to the cross, and having spoiled principalities and powers, he made a show of them openly, triumphing over them" (Col 2:14–15). Behold on the cross the price of the redemption of mankind! No man can lay another foundation.

The death of the Son of God is an atonement for sin so perfect that the triune God according to the law is absolutely satisfied. No sinner who comes to God in the name of Jesus will be turned away. Atonement has been made for the sin of the world. The punishment for all the sins of every sinner has been suffered by Christ. He bore them all in his body on the tree. Now God calls out everywhere, Return, all ye backsliders, and ye shall receive double at the hand of the Lord for all your transgressions. Your sin is taken away. Your iniquity is atoned. Eternal righteousness has been purchased for you by the blood of the Son of God himself. "Come unto me, all ye that labor and are heavy laden, and I will give you rest" (Matt 11:28).

All that remains now is to believe. "He that believeth and is baptized shall be saved, but he that believeth not shall be damned" (Mark 16:16). He who would know himself to be saved must turn in faith back to that which transpired nineteen hundred years ago on Golgotha.

> *"My soul is saved from sin and shame, For I believe in his dear name."*

He who would be saved must turn his faith to the suffering Christ on the shameful cross. He must look to what took place there—not to that which may take place in himself.

"But," you remonstrate, "I read in my Bible, 'Repent ye therefore, and be converted, that your sins may be blotted out, when the time of refreshing shall come from the presence of the Lord' (Acts 3:19). Granted, that repentance is not the same as regeneration, sanctification and the cleansing of the heart, for which we find no strength under the law, yet God requires repentance, that is, contrition and sorrow for sin. I am afraid that I am not as repentant as I should be. I am callous and hard. How, then, am I to believe?" Answer: Repentance is indeed necessary. It begins with a sensitiveness of conscience, a feeling of sinfulness. Under the various attempts at betterment, this feeling of sinfulness develops into the living knowledge of sin, soul poverty with no substantial and abiding comfort in anything. In order that you may know whether your repentance is as it should be, you must consider its purpose; for that which attains its purpose is sufficient.

What is the end and purpose of repentance? God's purpose in your repentance is by no means that you are to make yourself fit and worthy of his pardoning grace, but rather that you be driven to Christ. Paul, the Apostle, says, "Wherefore the Law was our schoolmaster to bring us unto Christ, that we might be justified by faith" (Gal 3:24). If, then, you are capable of remaining away from Christ, away in your carnal security, with no desire to beseech God for mercy and pardon in the name of Jesus, your knowledge of sin and guilt before the all-seeing eye of God is certainly shallow and superficial. If you still seek salvation in your own betterment, the improvement of your character, your remorse, and your prayers, your knowledge of sin and guilt before the living God is sadly defective. But as soon as you find no peace; as soon as you cannot conform to the ways of the world, uncertain about the mercy of God, with no comfort in your heart, in your contrition, in your self-improvement, throwing yourself upon the mercy of God in Christ alone, just as you are, then is your repentance as it should be; for it attains its purpose, which was to drive you to Christ. In him you find peace and rest and safety. You are secure in the city of refuge. "He who hath the Son, hath life."

You understand, friend, that in order that your knowledge of sin may be right, it must not be of your own making. You might find comfort in your own remorse. All such artificial comfort must be taken from you. True repentance involves dissatisfaction with your repentance. It comprises a sense of spiritual callousness, imperviousness to the approaches of the Spirit of God, carnal security, and the inner corruption. You are constrained by the facts in the case to judge yourself as worldly minded, secure, ungodly, condemned by the righteous law of God. Not until you have reached this stage of self-damnation are you ready to give Christ the honor of saving your soul.

If anyone should ask, "How much remorse and sorrow for sin must I have before I am fit to come to Christ?" the answer is, You need only so much sorrow for sin as to feel your need of Christ, that you cannot live without him, that you can find no peace before you come to him. No greater sorrow for sin is required—and no less will suffice. It is an error, though, to believe that remorse must first have its time; then there comes the time for faith; then the time for peace, joy, and holiness. Begin, friend, by believing in Christ. Then follow him in a daily renewal of your life and conduct. One result will be that you will know the sin in your flesh more keenly than you ever did formerly.

However, one of the shrewdest tricks of the devil is the following: A man believes in a general way that the Bible is the inspired Word of God. The book is God's Word from cover to cover. In it he seeks comfort and encouragement for his heart, light and strength for his daily life and walk. But there is one particular sin weighing upon his conscience. Then comes the devil and suggests to him the following line of reasoning: "The gospel is the very truth of God. The grace of God in Christ is universal and comprises all sinners. All sin has been atoned for and taken away by Christ, so that ordinary sinners may be pardoned and receive mercy at the hands of God. But you are an exception to the rule: you know yourself what you have done. If it had not been for that particular sin or many sins against the fifth, sixth, or seventh commandment, you too might be forgiven. But your sin is too black. You are an exceptional sinner. You do not come within the scope of God's merciful compassion." The phrase, *You are an exception*, is the most venomous thrust of the ancient serpent. Truly, as Jesus says, "He was a murderer from the beginning, and abode not in the truth, because there is no truth in him. When he speaketh a lie, he speaketh of his own; for he is a liar, and the father of it" (John 8:44).

The truth is that there is no exception among sinners. The mercy of God is over them all. There is no sin that has not abundantly been atoned for by the blood of the Son of God. All that is necessary is that the sinner, whoever he or she may be, or whatever he or she may have done, repents of the sin or the sins, turns to Christ and of him receives grace for grace. The pardoning grace of God in Christ is the very heart and core of the gospel. Both the Old

Testament and the New Testament testify to the universal grace of God, and that by word and example without number. "Come, now, and let us reason together, saith the Lord: Though your sins be as scarlet, they shall be as white as snow; though they be red like crimson, they shall be as wool" (Isa 1:18). King David, guilty of adultery and murder; Manasse, the robber on the cross; the woman who was "a sinner in the city;" Peter the denier, all these are striking examples to prove that with God there are no exceptions among sinners. He invites them all to share in his grace, however sinful and guilty they may be.

Indeed, it was precisely for the blackest sins and the vilest sinners, for whom there is no salvation anywhere, that the Son of God became incarnate, bled, and died, in order that "whosoever believeth in him should not perish, but have everlasting life." To summarize: You have never sinned so horribly, never sunk so low, but that the blood of the Son of God can cleanse you, providing only that you repent and accept the forgiveness of God in the Savior. But that your heart and conscience may find rest and peace, it is a blessed privilege, in the case of gross sin especially, to make confession to your pastor or to some other Christian. The pressing burden will as a rule fall from the conscience.

The Revelation of the Mystery: The Fourth Day

A sincere Christian may find himself in perplexity upon realizing that, even though he trusts implicitly in the grace of God as revealed in Christ Jesus, he has no vivid feeling of this grace in his heart, but is instead troubled by the consciousness of his sins and shortcomings. Here we would let Doctor Luther answer by an excerpt from his sermon on Easter:

> Now comes the question: Since Christ has died and taken away our sins, how does it come that we still feel that sin and death are within us? For sin gnaws at the conscience, and an evil conscience causes us to fear the judgment. Answer: I have already said that it is one thing to feel, and quite another thing to believe. Faith clings to the Word in spite of feelings and reason. Feeling operates against faith,

and faith against feeling. For this reason you must set reason aside and listen only to the Word, permit the Spirit to inscribe the Word upon your heart and believe it. Hold to the Word, even though you have no feeling that your sins are forgiven, and even despite the fact that you feel the power of sin within you. You must not go by your feelings. You must hold fast the truth that sin, death and the devil are conquered, even though you feel that you are held back by sin, death and the devil. For though there still is in you a feeling of the strength of sin, that should drive you all the more to faith and make you strong in faith. Disregard your feeling of sin and guilt before God and take Him at His word. Then let your heart and conscience rest in Christ. Thus faith leads us, in spite of our feeling and the strictures of reason, through sin, death and hell. As a consequence, you shall see God's redemption. You shall realize thoroughly what you formerly believed, namely, that sin, death and all evil have been taken away from you.

Let me draw a comparison from the fish in a net. When they are enclosed in the net, they are drawn so gently on shipboard, that they do not realize that they are caught. They imagine that they are in the water. Very quickly, however, they begin to squirm and tumble about, realizing that they are in captivity. So also with the souls that are caught in the net of the Gospel. Jesus compares the Gospel to a net: "The Kingdom of heaven is like unto a net that was cast into the sea, and gathered of every kind" (Matthew 13:48). When the Gospel takes possession of the heart, it binds the heart to Christ, and leads it so quietly and unnoticeably out of hell and the love of sin, that the soul scarcely realizes that it has been delivered from the power of sin and death.

Presently a conflict arises between feeling and faith. The more faith increases, the more the remonstrances of feeling decrease, and vice versa. Sin still clings to us, in spite of our faith and trust in the promises of the Word of God. Pride, avarice, anger, and other sins, still torment us,

> but only to drive us to faith, in order that faith may increase and grow stronger day by day.

Thus far Luther.

Jesus taught his disciple Thomas the same lesson when he said, "Thomas, because thou hast seen me, thou hast believed: Blessed are they that have not seen, and yet have believed" (John 20:29).

There are spiritual perplexities of a more puerile character. The following is an example: "I certainly believe that my sins are all forgiven. But I do not conduct myself in my daily life and conversation as I ought to do, according to the Word and will of God. The result is that I am a little uncertain as to whether I stand in the grace and friendship of God." Answer: It is, in the first place, a great error to think that only in your great conversion did you receive the forgiveness of your sins, particularly of the sins that you committed in unbelief and spiritual darkness, and that you after that event would be enabled by the grace of God to live so sinless and pure, that by your holy life you would retain the friendship of God. You must know that the greatest saints have always stood in need of the daily forgiveness of their sins. For this reason Jesus taught them to include in their daily Lord's Prayer the petition, "Forgive us our trespasses as we forgive those who trespass against us." The holiest saints have daily committed sin, real sin, not imaginary sin. "If we say that we have no sin, we deceive ourselves, and the truth is not in us" (1 John 1:8).

But it is equally certain that in Christ we have a perfect righteousness before God. This righteousness covers not only all our former sins, but also our present daily sins, that is to say, all the defects, faults, and shortcomings of our daily life. The Apostle Paul writes, "For what the Law could not do, in that it was weak through the flesh, God sending His own Son in the likeness of sinful flesh, and for sin, condemned sin in the flesh, that the righteousness of the Law might be fulfilled in us, who walk not after the flesh but after the Spirit" (Rom 8:3, 4). Observe: We have already now in Christ the righteousness before God that the law demands. The defects of your daily life are precisely the sins for which you have daily forgiveness.

"According to what you have just said," someone interposes, "we do not need to live the Christian life. We do not need to leave off sin and sinful habits, since we have begun to believe in Christ. Since through faith we possess the righteousness of Christ that we could not produce by our good works under the law, we may live as we please, may we not?" Answer: You may not live in sin if you would live in Christ. That would be the same as repudiating the merits of Christ. Paul says, "I do not frustrate the grace of God: for if righteousness comes by the Law, then Christ is dead in vain" (Gal 2:21).

We are bound to live the Christian life for an entirely different reason, namely, gratitude to God for his pardoning grace. Christ says, "He that loveth me, he will keep my Words, and the Word which ye hear is not mine, but the Father's which sent me" (John 14:23, 24). In other words: There are two things in the life of a Christian that must be kept apart. The one is his life and conduct, his thoughts, desires, words, and deeds. As regards his life, the Christian can never be too severe and critical. Self-criticism in the light of God's Word and law will be his daily and continuous practice. The other factor is his state of grace with God. The adoption into the holy fellowship of God and all believers is attested by the Spirit of God. In this state of adoption as a child of God, he deprecates his own works and merits, but magnifies Christ. He looks away from his own merits and excellencies, and sees nothing but the crucified Christ.

As regards our life and daily conduct, we need to be circumspect and exacting. As a rule, however, we are only too gentle and merciful in judging ourselves. As regards our state of grace we should be happy and secure in the merits of Christ. But here, again, we are inclined to be legalistic and fearful. This condition is intimated by the Apostle: "My little children, these things write I unto you, that ye sin not. And if any man sin, we have an Advocate with the Father, Jesus Christ the Righteous" (1 John 2:1).

Romans: A Devotional Commentary

Paul's letter to the Romans has always been a central text for Lutheran piety. It was the object of great importance to Rosenius, who worked for seven years on this devotional commentary, which he finished toward the end of his life. This selection is from Romans, chapter 5, in which Rosenius expounds on the nature and centrality of justification to the life of the believer.

Verses 1–2: Therefore, since we are justified by faith, we have peace with God through our Lord Jesus Christ. Through him we have obtained access to this grace in which we stand, and we rejoice in our hope of sharing the glory of God.

The requisite that God requires is that one be totally justified, made wholly righteous before his perfect law. Divine justice will be satisfied with nothing less. But the justified person does not claim such perfection that he is no longer rebuked in conscience by the law. He does not claim that he has perfected his own righteousness.

Yet the justified person does claim to be "justified by faith." He confesses that he is justified through the perfection of another. He has discovered that his only righteousness is in Christ, who died and arose again in his stead.

The first great treasure of heavenly gold claimed by the justified sinner is "peace with God." This peace is given reference oftentimes as peace within the heart that comes as a fruit of the forgiveness of sins. However, it holds another meaning relative to one's relationship with God. The war has come to an end. The judgment of God that rests on the unbeliever has been nullified, and now the holy favor of God is bestowed upon the believer. It signifies a condition of peace wherein God's wrath has been repealed; then it is a blessed consequence that inner peace of the soul follows.

The subsequent teaching of this text is that every soul who is *not* justified by faith is under the wrath and judgment of God unto death. There is no neutral zone between the friendship of God and his wrath. We possess peace with God only if we are justified by faith. Conversely, one who has not come to be justified by faith is warring against his Creator.

Nothing else will avail as long as a person will not subordinate himself to the righteousness of God offered in Jesus Christ. Trying to bring about one's own righteousness without honoring the Son is futile and of no avail. All who have not sought reconciliation with God through Christ are under sin and its judgment.

It is not so with those whose reconciliation with God is resolved through faith in Jesus Christ. God has justified them. Their sins are pardoned, and they are clothed in the righteousness of Christ. The new status brings peace with God, cessation of wrath, imputation of Christ's holiness, the "best robe," the "fatted calf and the feast of joy."

Think of it...God beholds us only as we are in Christ! God sees us garbed in the divine perfection of Jesus. Therefore it is not correct to say that because of our sins God barely tolerates us. The opposite is true. God no longer imputes our sins to us. Rather, "Blessed is the man to whom the Lord imputes no iniquity" (Ps 32:2).

Here and there are individuals who sincerely seek after faith and righteousness by grace alone, but who remain in a confused state. They scarcely know why. Sometimes a physical ailment may underlie the mental frustration and anxiety. This is not an evil sign in a life committed to God. On the other hand it would be strange if faith and peace were never shaken. The lives of the saints confirm this.

"Through him we have obtained access to this grace in which we stand." There is a blessed comfort in these words for those who will claim it. Because we have "access to this grace" we may realize the meaning of the words written by the writer to the Hebrews: "We have confidence to enter the sanctuary by the blood of Jesus, by the new and living way which he opened for us" (Heb 10:19–20). This is truly a consolation that applies to any condition in life. Whatever I may discover as it pertains to my spiritual life, the assurance of open and free access to the throne of grace is a healing comfort to me.

As long as there is a "today," all ills can be resolved. This is because we have access to grace today. Therefore the words of encouragement are timely: "Let us then with confidence draw near to the throne of grace, that we may receive mercy and find grace to help in time of need" (Heb 4:16). This access is through Jesus Christ and through him alone. "He is able for all time to save those who draw near to God through him, since he always lives to make intercession for them" (Heb 7:25).

The assurance of being able to "stand" or remain in grace is based on the firmness of grace itself. This firmness rests upon the truth that grace is available "through our Lord Jesus Christ." If grace and righteousness before God were based on merit in ourselves, we could not be in a state of grace. We are never without sin and never perfect under the scrutiny of the law. Were we to possess the favor of God only when we felt guiltless, but be dispossessed of it when we felt guilty, then righteousness would come by way of the law. Christ alone is our righteousness before the Father. He has accomplished for us all that the law requires. Hence, God's righteous wrath and judgment are terminated for those who believe. Then we remain in the friendship and favor of God because we are clothed in the righteousness of Christ. We remain in Christ only through faith.

This is further emphasized by our church fathers as recorded in the Formula of Concord:

> The believer must be assured concerning the meaning of faith in his Christian life. Paul writes in Romans, chapter five, that it is by faith we remain in grace. It is by faith that we can rejoice in the glory of God. Paul ascribes to faith the beginning, the continuation, and the perfecting of our faith-life. It is by faith that we stand in faith and rejoice in the glory that is to be. (Solid Declaration, art. 4)

Deficiency or weakness, or iniquitous moments, cannot mar the grace relationship. Anything sinful that may injure our pilgrimage is healed and balanced by the divine institution of grace based upon the Lord Jesus Christ. John wrote, "If any one does sin, we have an advocate with the Father, Jesus Christ the righteous; and he is the expiation for our sins" (1 John 2:2).

This covenant of grace and our defender who provides it are mightier than anything that may befall us. If we doubt that all the iniquity that dwells in us can be covered by grace, then we base our hope partially on ourselves, or we believe that the Son of God is not a perfect Savior and advocate before the Father. Therefore it is fundamentally important that we cling to the words, "through our Lord Jesus Christ." This must be deeply inscribed upon our hearts.

Verse 2: We rejoice in our hope of sharing the glory of God.

A Christian not only embraces hope for glory, but also rejoices in it. The reference to "rejoicing in our hope" signifies that there is a triumphant assurance in the believer's heart. This rejoicing is based on God's Word and his works, not on human achievement.

One who has come to recognize failure in his own works and merit before God, and now believes in him who justifies the ungodly, knows something of joy in being a child of God. There is joy in knowing that he is an heir to eternal glory. Jesus said, "Rejoice that your names are written in heaven" (Luke 10:20).

It is worthy of note that before the Apostle Paul had spoken a single word about sanctification, he said that believers rejoice in the hope of glory. This assures that the hope of glory is not based on sanctification. As soon as a person is justified he is possessor of both peace with God and the hope of glory. Newborn children of grace, that is, those born anew in Christ, take possession of their heavenly inheritance immediately. The very second that a sinner receives grace through faith, he is clothed in the wedding garment, the righteousness of Jesus. He is made ready to enter the eternal glory. The robber on the cross, and John, worn out in the service of his Lord, received their gift of eternal life from the same grace. Paul wrote the Colossians of "giving thanks to the Father who has qualified us to share in the inheritance of the saints in light" (Col 1:12).

If we are truly waging battle for the Lord, we will become weary often, and we will be sorely wounded. Many fiery darts of the evil one will pierce us. What comfort it is then to be refreshed in our spirits by "the hope of glory." If that goal becomes obscured the crown of glory may seem lost; but hasten then to the fountain of living waters, the blessed hope. God who is faithful and all-powerful will not let us be put to shame.

Behold what God has done and ask yourself, "Did not God create man for a higher purpose than a period of suffering on earth to be terminated in annihilation? Would God give his Son only for a bit of temporal good? Has God ordained the Sabbath and given us his Word and Sacraments only for this life? Finally, God having given us the promises of eternal life...would he at last deceive and betray us?" We need to pray, "Lord, increase our faith." Then may the cheer of hope and rejoicing in the Lord be kept firm to the end.

Verses 3–5: More than that, we rejoice in our sufferings, knowing that suffering produces endurance, and endurance

> *produces character, and character produces hope, and hope does not disappoint us, because God's love has been poured into our hearts through the Holy Spirit which has been given to us.*

How blessed it is to be a friend of God! What a glorious light is shed into our hearts when the love of God is poured into our hearts through his Holy Spirit! This sacred relationship with God makes possible a truly blessed comfort for all who believe.

However, those who know nothing of this relationship with God and the comfort received will deride Christians because they are persecuted. Minucius Felix in his *Octavius* said, "You are an impoverished and helpless people. Your God gives sanction to this. Either he will not or cannot help you. Threatenings, rocks, and crosses surround you. Where is your God who is able to give life to the dead? You are deceived, and you disdain the life that you might have."

The Apostle hastens to reply that this suffering is only an evidence of our salvation, and we are being nurtured for heaven. Not only do we endure these trials, but we "rejoice in our sufferings."

The hope of the very glory of God is certainly sufficient to overshadow the temporal sufferings of this present time. We ought to be willing that martyrdom be endured if necessary, since we know that all eternity with its unending bliss will follow. This assurance, resting on the truthfulness and faithfulness of God, ought to dispel anxiety and fill the heart with peace in the midst of tribulation.

No one can "rejoice in suffering" unless he knows the secrets of Christian suffering. There is something unseen and unfelt in suffering of which the glorying sufferer must know. Suffering in itself cannot offer consolation. Believers can feel and know sadness. Paul expressed this clearly to the Corinthians: "I was with you in weakness and in much fear and trembling" (1 Cor 2:3). Sensitivity to human suffering is often expressed in the psalms of David.

Sometimes Christians become dejected in time of trial, and comfort seems to have taken flight. But they should rely on other resources than their feelings and senses. They should remember that which comes to them exclusively through the Word of our heavenly Father. He has revealed his heart of compassion through his Son who has told us that nothing can happen to us without the Father's knowledge. Not even a hair will fall from our heads unless it is in the will of the Father. All suffering regardless of magnitude is visited upon us by our gracious and wise Father. What is more comforting than this?

The Apostle tells that trial has a purpose in us. But we must see God's motives in chastising us. The Word says, "The Lord disciplines whom he loves....It is for discipline that you have to endure" (Heb 12:6–7). The fruits of suffering are like links in a chain. They complement and follow each other in strengthening "our hope of sharing the glory of God."

Another link in this progression, as stated by Paul, is this: "Endurance produces character." This implies development of capacity to stand the test. This also reflects God's faithfulness and power to help in time of need. It refers to his work through his Spirit in us. Only steadfastness in the grace of God tested by the storms of life shall prove that the work within the heart is of God and not of flesh and blood.

A believer endures many trials. He learns how helpless he is in his own strength, and finds how fainthearted he is in times when reverses beset him. But he holds to the promise that he is protected and upheld by the power of God. He clings to the promise that God will never forsake him, and that "his power is made perfect in weakness" (2 Cor 12:9).

God's sacred work within the soul is tested often in the furnace of trial and suffering. We may be unable to discern or understand this work of the Spirit, but we shall understand it in the future when there will spring forth renewed strength in our hope of eternal life (see 1 Pet 1:3–21).

God has sacred and wonderful plans for our lives. Our present experiences are prelude to the better life. We may be assured that when God works in us his discipline and nurture in every circumstance, he will not leave us, and when we are called from this life, he will not forsake us.

When faith has stood the test of suffering as the work of God's Spirit has been in progress, the hope of glory is strengthened. See the words stand out in bold print: "Character produces hope." All this relates to the opening statement of this chapter that the hope of glory is the fruit of believing in the finished work of Christ. Character-producing hope does not preclude earlier hope. When Jesus turned water to wine (John 2) it was said that his disciples believed in him. This does not mean that the disciples had not believed earlier; but it means that their faith was increased. Character-producing hope implies the increase and growth and deepening of hope. Luther wrote that the Christian who relies on God's help in his trials will be strengthened, and God will continue to help all the way through life.

The outcome is assured in these words of Paul: "Hope does not disappoint us." Some who have imagined that they possessed sufficient righteousness in themselves will be put to shame on the day that they appear before the righteous Judge. But believers who have felt so unworthy that they scarcely dared hope, but have longed for the grace of Christ, will meet with a surprise beyond all expectation. They will be filled with awe and wonder that they have entered into the state of heavenly glory.

God's love poured into our hearts is the basis and source of our hope. It is his work inspiring hope within us, and this hope will not fail us. True hope is born of the love of God. This hope born of the Spirit yields comfort and assurance in time of trial, tribulation, and death. The vitality of this hope spawns from the love of God poured into our hearts by the Holy Spirit. A description of the sun will not cause it to cast its rays of light and heat upon us. The sun itself must give its light and heat. So—what we hear about God's love will be meaningless unless we receive it, an active force working in us by the Spirit. We cannot lay hold of it, but God gives it by his Spirit. Every evidence of repentance and seeking for God, or hoping for his grace through Jesus Christ, is always a result of the working of the Holy Spirit.

Let us remember that the Holy Spirit works mightily through a knowledge of God's Word. This is the means through which God's love comes to us, and through which it can be retained in our hearts. Such work of the Spirit comes as a gift for us to receive. This pouring of God's love into our hearts is most convincing proof that our hope will not meet with disappointment. What folly it would be for God to pour his love into our hearts, and encourage us to hope, unless he intends to give us the realization of this hope.

The Holy Spirit is specified as "the guarantee of our inheritance until we acquire possession of it" (Eph 1:14). Would God in his eternal faithfulness give us the guarantee of an inheritance and refuse it? Would God fail the faith and hope he has worked in us? No, the love of God has been poured into our hearts working divine assurance. How firm a foundation we are given for the hope of salvation.

> *Verses 6–8: While we were yet helpless, at the right time Christ died for the ungodly. Why, one will hardly die for a righteous man—though perhaps for a good man one will dare even to die. But God shows his love for us in that while we were yet sinners Christ died for us.*

Since our unworthiness plagues us, and our consciences accuse us, we may be terrified at the suggestion of God's wrath. Consequently it is difficult for us to think affirmatively of God's love. This is a universal weakness. As long as we live in this world we shall never be able to feel and sense God's love as we ought because our hearts are darkened. Nevertheless we could experience more of the sacred joy of God's love if we would seek it more earnestly. This is God's will, and he has the might to pour his love into our hearts through his Holy Spirit.

The most convincing proof of God's love for us is that he gave his Son to die for us. This is magnified in the light of these words: "While we were yet sinners Christ died for us." There is a universal condition indicated in these words, a weakness of all humanity, helpless under sin and unworthiness. Human nature is perverse to God, as Paul wrote in Romans 8:7–8: "The mind that is set on the flesh is hostile to God…and those who are in the flesh cannot please God." But the love of God reaches into this helpless state to save and redeem because he "who is rich in mercy, out of the great love with which he loved us…made us alive together with Christ" (Eph 2:4–5).

> *Verses 9–10: Since, therefore, we are now justified by his blood, much more shall we be saved by him from the wrath of God. For while we were enemies we were reconciled to God by the death of his Son, much more, now that we are reconciled, shall we be saved by his life.*

Here are mighty words that, like a fulcrum and lever, are able to lift the heaviest burden from believers' hearts. Since God gave his Son to die for us while we were without justification, we are given the greater assurance that we shall be saved because the blood atonement has been completed.

Awakened sinners are often afflicted with thoughts of God's displeasure toward them because of their sins. But the Apostle reminds us that our heavenly Father, after justifying us through the blood of Christ, will not ignore this grace when dealing with us.

It is in the counsel of God that we are saved through Christ; therefore we are not judged according to the law. God will not deal toward us in a manner contradictory to his love and to his decree of salvation wrought through the Savior. Thoughts to the contrary are found only in our hearts, injected there by the old liar, Satan. There dwells in the heart of God an eternal grace that is guardian of them who believe in Jesus.

Justified through the blood of Christ, the believer is immune to punishment before the law. This is not through piety of our own. Neither is there an act of clemency on the part of God. But shedding of blood was required (Heb 9:22). This requirement has been met through the atoning blood of Christ.

Faith lays hold of the atonement, not as a merit, per se, but as the hand reaching out to receive the gift procured by the finished work of Christ. Faith receives the gift of Christ's victory and his righteousness.

Let no one, however, suppose that God would reckon a person righteous who is not righteous. God will not cancel one iota of his holy law to justify a soul. Every requisite of the law must be totally and perfectly fulfilled. God's holy judgments are as unshakable as his love. They have been satisfied fully for us by our great Mediator and High Priest. This is perfect justification, not an imagined thing but one that bears all the standards of the law. It is this: "The blood of Jesus his Son cleanses us from all sin" (1 John 1:7).

When we are justified through the blood of Christ, should not God's great love be upon us in its holy fullness? Now that we are cleansed from sin, should not God love us even more deeply when the impediment of sin is no longer hindering? Further, then why should he not love those whom he has justified? This is the weight of the words, "Much more, now that we are reconciled shall we be saved by his life."

Even though my heart may be troubled with fears, and my peace may be disturbed by thoughts of God's judgments, I know that these anxieties arise from my unbelieving nature and from the fiery darts of the evil one. I shall have to endure these disturbances while here on earth; but I am assured that there are no such threatenings in the heart of God. Rather, in his heart there is his eternal unwavering grace.

PAUL PETER WALDENSTRÖM (1838–1917)

Paul Peter Waldenström, a Lutheran pastor, was the most prominent leader of the free church movement in nineteenth-century Sweden. He was called to become the editor of Pietisten *in 1868 after the death of Carl Rosenius. Influenced by newer evangelical thought, Waldenström moved away from traditional Lutheran theology and piety at several points, especially regarding atonement and justification. Though he and many of his followers remained nominal members of the Church of Sweden, their "Mission Covenant" movement tended toward independence.*

The Lord Is Right: Meditations on the Twenty-Fifth Psalm

FIRST MEDITATION: "O MY GOD, I TRUST IN THEE."

1. This psalm is one of the most beautiful in the Psalter, and has, therefore, always been dear to the children of God. It speaks so good, so heartily good, about the Lord and his uprightness, or righteousness; and to rest the uneasy heart in his righteousness,—that feels so inexpressibly safe. Our righteousness is only piecework, wretched and miserable. It can give no rest to the heart. "All our righteousnesses *are* as filthy rags," and to rest in them is to rest in death. To have peace in thinking oneself good and righteous, to be satisfied with one's own repentance, sorrow for sin, prayer, and sanctification, this is a piety with which innumerable souls are deceiving themselves. They may appear earnest, but they are building their house on the sand, and then it is of no use to decorate the walls of their house with mirrors and golden ornaments. When the floods rush upon it, then all depends on *the foundation*, and if this gives away, then also all wall decorations are lost. Yes, the fall of that house will be great.

2. On the contrary, happy are they who have come short as to their own piety, so that they must cast themselves on the Savior of

the lost. It is indeed not pleasant, or happy, to feel oneself to be a wretched sinner, and to come to naught in all that one undertakes in godliness. To know how we ought to sorrow for sin, and nevertheless feel our heart hard; to know how we ought to love God, and yet feel how full the heart is of love for the world, of covetousness, pride, and other abominations; to know how we ought to walk in godliness, humility, meekness, love, and so on, and also how we ought to put off all defilement of the flesh and spirit, but yet, in the meantime, daily see how also we transgress in innumerable ways, yea, how may fall into gross sins, and this in spite of the admonitions of the faithful Spirit,—this does not feel pleasant. But it is in this way that it is good to hear of the goodness and uprightness of the Lord. Not as though God's children would by the hearing of this seek rest in sin. No, this is the way of hypocrites: with the story of grace they would *silence* their consciences, in order that they may continue in sin. On the contrary, God's children seek, in the story of God's goodness and uprightness, help against their sins. For them grace is important because it is the only means that can cleanse their consciences, and help them out of their misery. This we see from all history of the saints. Of this also this psalm bears witness.

3. David begins by saying, "*Unto thee, O Lord, do I lift up my soul.*" These are words by which he expresses the attitude of his heart to the Lord. Such a longing the ungodly man does not know. He indeed wants to go, or get, to heaven; but he does not long for *the Lord*. To be happy, this he wants; but to be with *the Lord*, this is not the happiness he seeks. No, just listen when he talks of happiness: freedom from suffering and trouble, the meeting with dear departed relatives, and so on,—this is what he thinks of as happiness, or salvation. But to see God and the Lamb, to be like Jesus, to be forever with Jesus, free from all sin, to be permitted eternally to praise God and the Lamb,—that is not what draws his heart toward heaven. If there be in him any fear of God, or if he do any works of piety, or of devotion, it all comes from his fear of hell. Were there no hell, he would not at all care about the Lord. Any need of the Lord, any love for or delight in the Lord or his will he knows naught of.

The children of God, on the contrary, have such a disposition, that they long for the Lord. As also David in another place says, "O God, thou *art my* God; early will I seek thee: my soul thirsteth for thee, my flesh longeth for thee in a dry and thirsty land, where no water is" (Ps 63:1). And again: "My soul longeth, yea, even fainteth for the courts of the LORD: my heart and my flesh crieth out for the living God" (Ps 84:2). And again: "Cause me to know the way wherein I should walk; for I lift up my soul unto thee" [that is, "I long for thee"] (Ps 143:8). And in Psalm 91:14 the Lord says, "Because he hath set his love upon me, therefore will I deliver him." The same desire, or longing, for the Lord we see also in the words of Asaph: "Whom have I in heaven *but thee? and there is* none upon earth *that* I desire besides thee. My flesh and my heart faileth: *but* God is the strength of my heart, and my portion forever" (Ps 73:25–26). The same mind also Peter expressed when the Lord asked the disciples if they would go away from him, and he answered, "Lord, to whom shall we go? Thou hast the words of eternal life" (John 6:68).

Such a desire, or longing, for the Lord comes only from a soul's having learned to know its sins. It can never be counterfeited, or produced by artificial means. In all outward ways a hypocrite can make himself like a Christian, but still he will always remain a stranger to this *desire* for the Lord. It is only *the need of a Savior* that awakens in the heart a desire for the Lord. Therefore we always see that, as long as sin is not felt, a man may indeed hear the gospel, but it does not affect him. With hearing ears he hears nothing. He may regard it as beautiful, he may admire it, but all the while *his heart remains averse to the Lord.* On the other hand, as soon as one gets into distress over his sins, quickly his heart begins to cry after the Lord; and if one has found peace in Jesus, then also he has such a desire for the Lord that he can no longer live without him. He may indeed often feel his heart to be dead and cold, but to say farewell to God—that, however, is impossible for him. Therefore, also, his life is never so dreary and heavy as when he does not clearly know how he stands with the Lord. The apostles of Christ, and the other disciples, were, surely, never so burdened as in the days when they thought that their Lord had been taken from them. But what was it that then so burdened them, if it was not this—that their hearts so clung to him, that they thought they could not live unless they might have him?...

6. It is indeed very sad that our hearts can be drawn to the Lord only through need. If anyone in days of prosperity had not at all cared about another, but had despised him, and had been hostile to

him, but afterward, when need came, turned to him, then he, the latter, would very likely answer, "Nay, since you have despised me in your days of prosperity, so now help yourself in your days of adversity." But such is not the case with the Lord. For him it is delightful that there, after all, is *something* that can drive the lost children home again to him. Yes, for this very reason, also, he himself sends want. When the prodigal son came home, his father indeed knew that if the son's money had held out he would have remained away still longer, but nevertheless he was glad that the son came home. Had he come before, it would indeed have been the more gladsome to the father's heart; but since he did not come before, it was delightful that he came at least *now*. In the history of Israel, also, we see how distress alone, time after time, could turn the hearts of the people to the Lord; but still he was always alike glad to attend to their want and wretchedness. Never did he say, "Since *you* in the day of your prosperity departed from me, so will I in the day of your adversity turn away from you." Nay, he was nevertheless their Father. Therefore it was even he who made the evil day, and put it as a closed gate in the way of his erring people, in order that they might turn about to him.

7. But where such a desire, or longing, for the Lord has been called forth by distress, there also it manifests itself in the soul's crying after God, just as David does here and in all his psalms. He who no longer needs to call upon God, he has no desire for him, but is dead, and is not a Christian. The children of God have daily needs. Now it is something bodily, now it is something spiritual, that presses. Therefore, also, there is in their hearts a daily crying unto God, for he is their Father, their Redeemer, and their refuge. Whither should they go with their needs if not to him? Of this it is said in a psalm (46:1), "God is our refuge and strength, a very present help in trouble." Thus David says, "Be merciful unto me, O Lord, for I cry unto thee daily" (Ps 86:3). And again, "In the shadow of thy wings will I make my refuge, until *these* calamities be overpast" (Ps 57:1). And Isaiah says, "The LORD hath founded Zion, and the poor of his people shall trust in it" (Isa 14:32). And again, "Thou hast been a strength to the poor, a strength to the needy *in his* distress, a refuge from the storm, a shadow from the heat" (Isa 25:4): So Joel says (3:16), "The LORD *will be* the hope of his people, and the strength of the children of Israel." In short: in joy and sorrow the Lord is their

strength, their rock, their fortress, their deliverer, their God, their consolation, their shield, the horn of their salvation, and their high tower, even as David says in Psalm 18.

8. Thus the life of the believers remains here upon earth a life of daily looking unto the Lord, and a daily crying unto the Lord. Not indeed as though their mouths were always crying, but in their heart there is an unutterable sighing. As Paul says, that when "we know not what we should pray for as we ought," then "the Spirit maketh intercession for us with groanings which cannot be uttered" (Rom 8:26). And this cry God most surely hears. For "the Spirit maketh intercession for the saints *according to the will of God*," says Paul (Rom 7:27). Yes, where no man hears a sound, there God hears a strong cry. As he said to Moses at the Red Sea, "Wherefore criest thou unto me?" while Moses indeed did not say a word, but only went about oppressed in heart and full of need. When a sick child, on account of its weakness, can no longer speak, but only lift up its eyes to its mother, then is this to the mother just as much as a strong and powerful cry. And in this, as in a mirror, you can see what the sighing of the distressed and lowly is before the Lord. And yet a mother's heart is as nothing, compared with the heart of God.

9. Therefore David in all his psalms gives us an example how also we ought to turn to the Lord in all our need. For the Lord is "the same yesterday, and today, and forever" (Heb 13:8). And far from his being tired of us, it is, on the contrary, his very highest and most sincere desire, that we every day and hour bear to him all our need and misery. Hence he is called, and he is, "a helper in need," and to such a one we ought to go when we are in need. Therefore, never any evening lie down in your sins or troubles, but before you go to rest do bring them, your troubles and sins, to the Lord, and when you have brought them there, then let them lie there. Think, if any one every night when he went to rest were to lay a great stone upon his breast, or every morning when he went to his work were to place a great stone on his back,—surely it would not be strange if his work went hard and his rest was poor. Why, one would say to him, "Put away from you that stone!" So also here: "Cast your cares, your sins, and all your need upon the Lord—he is your Savior." Needlessly to go and torment oneself is beyond measure foolish. To have a God who is willing to bear everything, yea, asks to be allowed to bear

everything,—think of having such a God, and nevertheless you go about and bear misery and troubles and cares, and thereby destroy all your rest and quiet in the Lord, and all power to walk in his fear and footsteps! Why, that is altogether too bad.

10. If I have a temporal matter that I cannot understand nor manage, but that only oppresses me, and unfits me for everything else that I ought to do, then I am glad if any one who understands the matter and can manage it comes to me and says, "Look here, that matter is really destroying you. I will help you; leave it to me, and trust me." Yes, if I find such a helper, then I become lighthearted, and at once feel a new desire and power to live and attend to my work or business. And if any one comes and talks with me about the matter, I say with cheerfulness, "That matter is now off from me, and is put into the hands of one who understands it. It at last became too heavy for me to be burdened with it. But he took it off my hands, and now I am doing nothing about it, but trusting him." Yes, thus I would think and speak if in a temporal matter I had found a reliable helper. But who can be more reliable than the Lord? And now he has promised me that I may cast upon him all my cares, both bodily, or temporal, and spiritual, and that I may go to him with everything, from the smallest trifles that concern my daily bread, even to the most terrible sins in which the devil perchance has ensnared me or brought me to fall. Yes, he also says that he will rejoice over me to do me good (see Jer 32:41). Then how can I act more wisely than simply to put my trust in him, and allow his words to mean just what they say? Of this David here further says,

11. *"O my God, I trust in thee"* (verse 2); that is, I am trusting in thee because thou art my God. This is true faith. Just as children in all things trust their parents and rest themselves in their word without thinking that they will be deceived, so faith here is nothing else than such a childlike and simple trust in the Lord. Children do not carry about with them many cares: they eat, drink, sleep, work, play, are at times obedient, at other times disobedient,—but with any cares they do not concern themselves. Where money is to be gotten for food, clothing, and so on,—with such a thing they do not burden their hearts, but leave it all to their parents. If the parents have said that they will take care of them, then the children believe it even so far as to the point that they themselves forbear being anxious, and do

not trouble themselves with any cares. If the parents have forgiven them their disobedience, then they no longer go and burden themselves with this sin; but as the parents desire it to be forgotten, so the children do forget it, and in a few moments they are glad again and jump and play as if nothing had happened. *For they trust the word of their parents.* And if they be asked how they can have such trust in them and their word, they know of no other reason than this, that they are their parents. But if they be asked how much they have to pay for such a right to trust their parents in all things, they do not at all understand such a question. They have never heard of such payment, neither have they themselves ever thought of it. No, they believe and have believed for naught, freely; and the parents never had any objections to their doing so. Both for parents and for children it has been and is the most natural thing in the world that all should be free and for naught.

12. Thus also the Lord desires that you in all your need look into his word, and see how he has spoken in the matter, and when you see it, just trust in it right away. For the word cannot disappoint. And the more simply you take it the better it is for you. "Yes," you say, "if I only had faith!" No, no, say not so; but instead, say "*Amen.*" Think, if a poor man received a trustworthy communication that a great inheritance had fallen to him, and he, instead of believing it and rejoicing, let his hands fall and began to sigh, "Oh! If I only had faith!" Why, one would be greatly amazed at such folly, and would say, "What ails you? Do you not see how it is written?" But equally foolish it is when we have a word of God that can never disappoint, then, instead of believing it, to sit down and sigh, "Oh! If I only had faith!" God would rather that you looked to his word and let it hold good and said to him a simple, "I thank thee." For that would be the faith that would please him.

13. Also, such a right to trust the Lord costs nothing. For it you need not have wrought good works nor have any worthiness nor come with great promises. For your worthiness lies only in this, that the Lord is your God. And when you are most unworthy, then you can still always appeal to this, that the Lord is your God. He at all events is the one who has created you, he who has also undertaken to redeem you, and is not ashamed to call himself your father, but esteems it an honor for himself that you cling to him as your own

God. This fact and relation, that he is your God, is not changed by your being sinful and wretched, just as indeed the fact that children are disobedient cannot change the relation that their parents are still their parents. "What are we to do?" they would say; "They are still our children; they have sinned and offended, so that, perhaps, none will have compassion on them and help them; but we, we must do it, for we are nevertheless their parents." If the Lord God would not be the God of those who are unworthy, sinful, and wretched, then he would be altogether without children. But with what earnestness he considers himself the father of the lost and fallen children, that you can see by the sacrifice he has made for their salvation when he laid all our sins, "the iniquity of us all," upon his only begotten Son (see Isa 53:6).

14. Therefore, when you get into distress in any way, whether the distress be self-caused or not, and you see that you cannot help yourself or get out of it, then *trust the Lord*, turn to him, and say, "Dear Lord God, this and that has now happened, thus and thus have I sinned, by reason of which I am greatly distressed, and I cannot help or clear myself, therefore I come to thee, for thou art my God and dear Father; have mercy upon me, and forgive me all my sins." But if the devil comes and terrifies you, holding up before you your unworthiness and the wrath of God, which you have well deserved, then do you hold up against this the fact that God delivered up his only begotten Son for your salvation. If he had thought of destroying you because of your sins, he would not have sacrificed that which was dearest to him to help you out of your sins. Yes, if it had been his intention to destroy you and deal with you according to your sins, then would you long ago have been in hell. Hence, that he is still giving you a day of grace, this is a new sermon in which he is saying that he rejoices to do you good, and that it is his delight to have mercy upon you (see Jer 32:41).

15. It seems indeed altogether unreasonable that I should thus, year out and year in, keep on trusting in that way, when yet I see and know how I daily, in many ways, sin and deserve naught but punishment. It appears to the heart as altogether too light and frivolous thus wholly to trust to grace. But what am I to do? When David had sinned with Bathsheba,—what other course had he then than to bewail his misery before the Lord, and according to the word of the

prophet believe in grace for everything? When Peter had denied the Lord,—what other course had he then? It would have been better that he had not sinned; yes, afterward he likely would have been willing to have given his life, if he could have had that sin undone. But now it was all done, and then—what could he do but bewail before the Lord his need, and believe in the forgiveness of sins? "Yes," you say, "but such things are not often related of the saints mentioned in the word of God, but I—I fall time after time, now in one way, now in another." Well, that is indeed dreadful, and without doubt it would be better if you paid more heed to your life, as Paul says: "Walk in the Spirit, and ye shall not fulfil the lust of the flesh" (Gal 5:16). But now it has happened again, if you had watched better, if you had not been so remiss in prayer and in the use of the word of God, then it would not have happened; no: it is altogether your own fault, but now, however, it has happened, now you stand there again guilty, as an offender; yes, perchance through your sin you have brought reproach upon the Lord Jesus. What then will you do? Do you know of any other way than again to take your sin and need to the Lord, and again to believe in his free grace for it all? "No," say you; "but in this way one might begin to sin while trusting to grace, and then it would be nothing but hypocrisy with all of one's piety. Thus indeed do all hypocrites." Yes, altogether true; but what will you do? If hypocrites destroy themselves by abusing grace—why, it is not on that account right that you should destroy yourself by thrusting away from you the grace of God. Nay, here the great matter is to persevere—perseveringly and stubbornly to believe, in spite of the devil and all his angels believe in grace and say, "Nevertheless I will remain with thee, O Lord. I *cannot* leave thee, I have no one else to go to, for thou alone art my God, and thou hast promised 'to have pity on the poor and needy, and to save the souls of the needy'" (Ps 72:13).

Squire Adamsson: Or "Where Do You Live?"

One of Waldenström's most popular works, Squire Adamsson, *was an allegorical novel written in 1862 and first serialized in a Swedish magazine. The novel itself satirizes conventional Swedish religion of its day, especially the unconverted clergy, and compares them unfavorably with the uneducated but deeply religious character of "Mother Simple." In this excerpt, Squire Adamsson is imprisoned under God's law, but finds salvation in God's free mercy and grace.*

THIRD CHAPTER: IMPRISONMENT

In a city called Holiness, there ruled at that time a mighty king by the name of Justus All-Powerful. There were many peculiar rumors circulating about him among the citizens of The World. Many considered him to be an inhumanely strict man, which is why they feared him tremendously. Others were of the persuasion that he was a good-natured master, of whom there was nothing to fear. Some even wondered if he really existed, or if he wasn't just some kind of saga hero. In short, everyone had their own ideas about him, but no one truly knew him. Because of this, it often happened in The World that one could hear people mock his name, as well as mock anyone "who was foolish enough to believe all those fables about him, spread by that former councilman Conscience and his kind." At the same time, there were others who were at a loss for how they were supposed to be able to praise and exalt him for his "goodness" and "mercy" and "leniency toward their faults and weaknesses." There were also plenty of people to be found who, out of fear of him, lived an arduous life, expending all their energies in an attempt to escape his wrath. While there were still others who gladly and with a cheerful spirit worked to make themselves right with him, in the expectation that they would earn some reward by this service.

Even Mr. Adamsson's household had dealings with Lord Justus in certain matters. To be specific, Adamsson owed an enormous amount of debt to this man. All these debts had been carefully recorded by the bookkeeper Conscience in the squire's account books. After some time had passed, Justus All-Powerful sent his faithful servant Moses to demand payment on the entire amount. Mr. Adamsson was just then sitting at home with his wife, peaceful, glad at heart, and with his mind completely at ease. Kind-Hearted had just returned from his rounds, and Complacent had started in with reporting on all the day's activities to his parents, especially all the remarkable things that his brother had accomplished. With steamy eyes, his father blessed this "precious treasure" of his (a nickname he had for Kind-Hearted), and declared himself happy beyond measure to call such a child his own. All the while, he humbly admitted that he was not worthy of such an altogether enormous grace.

It was into this scene that Moses had intruded and delivered his master's certificate of debt. Astonished by this, Adamsson curtly replied, saying that he did not believe himself to be indebted to Lord Justus at all, "beyond a few small trifles, which he well knew Lord Justus did not keep such close accounting over, but instead would gladly remit." He therefore did not understand how Moses could come in his name with a demand of ten thousand talents; neither could he acknowledge that such a debt existed, nor believe that this demand had come from the good and righteous Lord Justus. Instead he kept insinuating that "this must be some fraud or mistake."

With this response, Moses made his journey back home. Enraged, Lord Justus sent him out again with the same certificate of debt, threatening this time that if he was not immediately compensated, then Adamsson should expect to have all his assets promptly seized and himself thrown in prison.

This all occurred on a dark and chilly fall evening. Adamsson felt nervous and even a little bit sick to his stomach. Earlier that day, he had been out on his customary rounds among people of the estate. While he had been on his stroll, he had run across Mother Simple, with whom he had struck up a conversation.

"How do you do?" he asked.

"I am getting along the same as ever," had been her reply. "Wretched and miserable as I am in every way, I cannot seem to accomplish a single thing. But despite this, I am still content and glad, since the gracious Lord Justus has just offered me a refuge and dwelling place in his holy city, Evangelium. There I will have everything that I need, at no charge. And though I am so old, poor and feeble, nevertheless, I am not above living on grace. But how is the Squire?"

"Well, thank you. Very well!"

Mother Simple turned away and dried her eyes with her apron.

"Why are you sad?" asked Adamsson, bewildered.

"Oh, dear Squire—but why is the Squire out and about in this nasty weather?"

"Well, you know one has to work while the daylight lasts. But tell me this, at least—why are you crying and depressed?"

"Oh, because I am deeply concerned for the Squire. He has always been so good to me, that I guess it just brings me to grief when I consider his situation."

"Brings you to grief? My dear old girl! Why should that be?"

"Because I worry that the Squire will not take advantage of the great grace that is available to him, before it is too late—I mean, to leave his property and move to Evangelium. I have heard from his bookkeeper, Conscience, that the Squire's affairs are not standing on as firm a foundation as one might hope."

"Oh, don't you go on worrying about my affairs! Each of us will have to answer to his own master; so, you can stick to worrying about yourself. My affairs, I trust, are secure enough. And I have my debts, just as well as I have debtors."

After this they parted company. Adamsson continued on his rounds. At first he was somewhat bewildered by the little old woman's unusual behavior. Although he well knew that she sincerely cared for him and wished him the best, while he walked along he began to feel himself become all the more troubled by her words.

"My affairs," he said to himself, "my affairs...how...could they be that bad? I say, Conscience!" he called out, when at that same moment he caught sight of his bookkeeper in the distance, "my affairs surely are resting on a firm foundation, right?"

After his fashion, Conscience said nothing; for he usually never answered half questions of this sort, which more expressed a wish to be set at ease rather than to receive a true answer. Thus when his squire did not ask him straight out how things actually stood, but instead if they were not really right, he acted like there was nothing wrong and went his way.

This struck Adamsson as peculiar and increased his state of alarm. In order to find some assurance and to calm his nerves, he sought out Pastor Shepherd-for-Hire. And he began to confide with this man, explaining his troubles and the conversation with Mother Simple. In turn the man, puzzled, asked how something like that could bother him.

"The Squire," he asked, "isn't thinking of leaving Industriousness? Why? In order to move to Evangelium? In order to be lazy? Whatever for? No, no. Christianity calls for more seriousness, for more life and activity, than exists there. One cannot help but be filled with zeal when observing how often—sad though it is—people can be tricked and led astray by sanctimonious preachers of falsehood like this. Such preachers are talented in the art of hiding their sloth, incompetence, and idleness under a mantle of beautiful talk about grace. No, dear Squire, remember that beautiful verse:

If we've lived by God's command, we shall there in heaven stand.

Furthermore, the Squire can always speak with the bishop. He lives on Pious Street in the city The World. He certainly knows more about these things than a cotter widow."

A few moments later, they parted. Adamsson felt himself somewhat comforted by Pastor Shepherd-for-Hire's words, but not entirely set at ease.

"The bishop," he thought, "yes, the bishop! Did not Luther once say, 'If the devil takes the pope, who then will take you?'"

He felt a chill come over him, and so he hurried his steps in order to warm himself up. On the way he met Mrs. Praise.

"Can it be that the Squire once again is out delivering blessings, even in weather like this!?" she exclaimed.

At this the squire was once again overcome by anxiety, for he was well aware that on this trip he had hardly accomplished one good thing. But just then, he also met his son Complacent, who reminded his father that when one is producing Good Deeds, one should not so much look at the outward results, but instead concentrate on the good will and noble intentions behind them. Once again he felt partially calmed down, yet not fully at ease. Mother Simple's words weighed heavily on his heart. As he walked and pondered them, he happened to have the misfortune of tripping and tumbling into a mud puddle, so that he ended up soaking wet and managed to catch a cold.

He had no sooner returned home from this worry-ridden outing and taken out his best clothes in order to change when Moses came calling for the second time, bearing with him his master's stern and threatening certificate of debt. One can easily imagine Mr. Adamsson's horror when he read this letter, especially since his bookkeeper had also arrived with the account books, and verified that the debt really was as great as it said.

"Why have you never shown me this before?" the deathly pale squire asked his bookkeeper.

"This is the Squire's own fault. For he has paid so much attention to other people's accounts that it has never crossed his mind to review his own. Every time I have wanted to show these to the Squire, he has been preoccupied with matters pertaining to the mission, or visiting the poor and sick, or prayer, or the study of God's Word and the like. Lately, I have, for this reason, considered it pointless to try to bring any of this to the Squire's attention."

Horrified and shaken by this answer, Adamsson immediately set to writing a humble petition to this harsh moneylender, explaining that if the payment of the principal could be deferred, he would be willing to make annual payments on the interest. His letter sounded like this:

"Most austere and mighty Lord Justus!

With all my heart, I humbly confess that I have dealt dishonestly with you and have incurred all of the debt that you have demanded. But, Lord Justus, as much as I wish that I had not done all these things, and as much as I sincerely wish that I could pay my debt, it is nevertheless impossible. Therefore I beg you that you would look with grace on my distress, my prayers and my tears, and allow these old debts to be deferred. In the future I shall strive to improve myself, and will offer to pay the yearly interest. Have compassion on your miserable, but honest, servant, Adamsson."

In response to this petition, Adamsson only received a renewed threat to seize his assets and send him to prison if he failed to pay the entire sum immediately. What was he going to do now? Well, he tried once again, with the greatest humility, to write another request that Lord Justus might reduce the principal in some way, just as much as would allow him to pay.

"Is it your will to altogether ruin me and cast away your servant?" he wrote. "Oh, master, I stand before you and promise that I will, with faithfulness and diligence through your grace, work and strive to make right the wrongs I have done. And I beg you, that you, in your mercy, would reduce or remit that which I cannot pay."

But to his horror he received an even harsher answer than before. Now there simply was no way out of this, other than to pay. He tried in vain, partially through work, partially through loans to come up with the requested sum. His property was sold, and he and his wife and children were thrown in the prison Sinai. Oh, to hear their cries of distress! It was here that they would sit like this, until everything was paid. And how could any payment ever be made when they sat there with chains bound fast on their wrists, and without any means of earning a single crumb? But that was hardly the extent of their sorrows, for it was in that prison that Kind-Hearted would die.

That poor father who sat there, bound hand and foot, was in utter despair. His suffering was only worsened by the fact that in this prison his wife bore two twins, Hateful and Bitter, seemingly to take the place of their lost child. At the same time, a strict order was issued from Lord Justus that he would pay his debt or else risk being thrown into an eternal prison, Gehenna. Oh, that poor man! He begged that someone would remove his chains, but no one did. And now he realized that he had no other way out, but would face an eternity of imprisonment.

"Oh," this poor prisoner thought, "if only I could bring Mother Simple here as an advocate! She is on good terms with Lord Justus, and I am sure that she would be able to give me advice."

"Wouldn't it be far better," answered his wife, "to call for Pastor Shepherd-for-Hire, instead? He is certainly a good helper, and surely he knows Lord Justus better than Mother Simple does."

"Do not speak like that," retorted Adamsson, through his tears. "Shepherd-for-Hire has misled me long enough. He has preached peace where no peace was to be found, and by this he has lulled me and others into the false belief that everything was fine. Oh, that I had just listened to Mother Simple earlier! Then I would not now be sitting in this prison. But perhaps even now she has some advice, if only I could bring her here."

"Well," sighed his wife, "that would certainly be good. But we have offended that little old woman to such an extent that she can't possibly ever want to see us again." And so they sank back into their despair.

Poor Adamsson! He had never experienced distress like this. He had certainly read and heard much talk about Sinai, but never had he been able to imagine that it could be as bad as what he now experienced. All of the great spiritual knowledge that he had absorbed from his reading was of no use. In this prison, he met many companions for his misery, and every one of them was just as in need of advice. The cells echoed with their lamentations. Every day, new prisoners arrived.

"Oh, how is all of this going to end?" he asked his wife, time and again. "Sometimes I feel that I am altogether brokenhearted; sometimes I feel as hardened as these stone walls. How will it end?"

"Yes. That I don't know," answered his wife. "This is certainly going to be the end of us."

And so their gaze of despair fell to rest upon the cold, hard floor.

FOURTH CHAPTER: Liberation

In the meantime, Mother Simple had received word as to how grave the matter had become concerning Adamsson and his family. Setting out at once, she found them in their desperate situation in prison.

"Oh, how are you all getting along here?" she asked.

"Well, as you can see, it really could not be worse," was the answer.

"Well, then—how long are you intending to remain here?"

"Remain here?"

"Well, precisely. For you must be aware that you could leave; I know that much about Lord Justus."

"No, no. My dear old girl—how could that ever be?" sighed Mr. Adamsson, while tears of despair streamed profusely down his cheeks.

"Well," replied the little old woman, "all that the Gracious Squire would need to do would be to simply submit a plea to Lord Justus, that he—out of his own free grace and mercy—might cancel the entire sum of the debt."

"Oh, you must not address me as *Gracious Squire* any longer! I am a poor, lost prisoner. I have offended both Lord Justus, as well as you, yourself. My debt, he cannot possibly cancel. Early on, I asked him to defer payment on the principal and allow me to pay the interest. But even that he refused to do, and he continued issuing his dreadful threats. Then I asked him simply to decrease the debt only a little, but that prompted him to have me sent here, saying that I needed to pay everything immediately. And now, you suggest that I should go and request to be liberated from the entire debt—oh! What could he possibly say to that? No, be serious, now. Tell me what I should do."

"Hmm, hmm! I see that the Squire is now in such a state of mind that it is going to be very difficult to accomplish anything at all."

"Yes, but otherwise I will be forced to remain in prison forever!"

"Oh, no. Follow my advice, and the Squire will be set free for eternity."

Oh, you have no idea the degree to which Lord Justus despises me for my misconduct toward him."

"No. He loves the Squire."

"How is that possible? How could he love me?"

"Well—because he does. Lord Justus is love itself, and love cannot help but love. It is for this reason that his son, Immanuel, has been sent to save the Squire."

"Love me?—me? What? I have never, never had any affection for him."

"But how would this prevent him from loving the Squire?!"

"Yes, if only he would, despite it all! Then I will do as you say. Oh, if only his grace now was as limitless as I have often heard you claim—though it used to annoy me so. If that were to be the case, then even I would have some hope for salvation."

"Do try," said Mother Simple, with a knowing smile. "Of this I am certain, ever since the moment Immanuel revealed to me the nature of his father's heart."

"My goodness, how happy and content you seem," sighed Adamsson. "But you have no idea how things are for me. If you did know, you would be in tears."

After this, Mother Simple excused herself, promising to return another day.

Now Adamsson, with much trepidation, made ready to write to Lord Justus by way of a man named Doubt, who had offered his services. But when Mother Simple returned, she found the squire in the same miserable condition.

"Now all hope is lost!" he exclaimed. "I have done just as you told me to do, but have been denied again."

"How did the Squire go about it?"

"Well, I sent my greeting to Lord Justus, carried by Doubt—you must know him, right? He is a very humble gentleman. Anyone can see that about him. He always hesitates in his speech and trembles in his boots. He never crosses the threshold, never presumes to just walk up and present himself. It was with him that I sent my message, that if Lord Justus would cancel my debt and liberate me, then I would forever be his humblest and most obedient servant."

"Well, well. Then it is no wonder that the Squire was denied."

"But, I did as you told me I should do!"

"No, the Squire did no such thing; I never told the Squire to propose some kind of an exchange, for Lord Justus is not in the practice of selling his grace—not for old services done in the past, nor for promises of Good Deeds to be produced in the future. And I certainly did not tell the Squire to send Mr. Doubt. He is a lousy messenger. And particularly since Lord Justus has such a low opinion of him. Doubt once stated that Justus cannot really be taken at his word; and there are few things that displease him as much as shameful slander like this. Instead the Squire should send Bankrupt Faith, the husband of Mother Prodigal, and he can make a request for pure grace and mercy. Bankrupt Faith always receives what he requests. Whenever he knocks, the door is opened for him at once."

"Oh," sighed Adamsson, "Bankrupt Faith—well, if anyone was deserving of the nickname *bankrupt* then it is surely poor old Faith. I have never known him, but I have heard people speak of him. Do you really believe I should send him? People have said that he is a bit presumptuous. He has been known to shake the hand of Lord Justus and even look him straight in the eyes. And that is going too far, you know? But—perhaps people are lying about him. I will do as you say."

Despite all this misery, Mother Simple could not keep from smiling when she heard these words. Instead of giving an answer, she read to Adamsson from the tale of the prodigal son. When she came to the line where the father "had compassion, and ran and fell on his neck and kissed him," she pressed her index finger under every word and read the verse five times through. Upon the fifth reading, Bankrupt Faith peered in through the door of the cell, and Adamsson's heart was jolted by a beam of hope. When the errand had been explained to Faith, he began at once to prepare himself to set off on the assignment. Countless times before he had visited Lord Justus, and for this reason he knew the road quite well.

The little old woman dismissed herself and Bankrupt Faith set off. It was very dark. While on the way, he stumbled upon Doubt, who in his rage attacked Faith. For a time it looked as though Faith would yield, but at last he gained the upper hand. Nevertheless, for a long time afterward he walked along, shaking in his boots. Then he remembered a song from which he had often found strength, and he began to sing!

Rock of Ages, cleft for me, let me hide myself in Thee...

His courage restored, he continued and hastened on his way through the deep darkness.

After a while the sun began to rise, signaling that the dire situation had passed.

With dread, Adamsson awaited his response. Even so, he did not have to wait long. It was Immanuel himself who came and liberated him from his shackles, assuring him that his debt had been forgotten and it would never again be demanded from him. Upon this, he began transporting Adamsson along a newly paved road called New Birth, through the so-called Narrow Gate, and up on into the city Evangelium....

It was to this fair city that Adamsson was brought by Immanuel, and it was here that he received a dwelling place assigned to him in one part of the city, a district that had an inscription over its gate that read, *Room for the Lost.* This district contained three subdivisions, namely an infirmary, dwelling rooms, and a banquet hall for the inhabitants of the city, who all lived there at Immanuel's expense and patronage. At the entrance, Adamsson had asked Immanuel what this district was called, and received the answer that it was called The Forgiveness of Sins.

"Here is where you may live," added Immanuel, "as long as you need; and here you will be lacking for nothing that you need for your well-being."

"But," Adamsson chimed in, "you must remain here, too, of course, for otherwise, how can I really thrive here?"

"I do live in this city, although I often spend my time in a hidden room, which keeps me out of sight," answered Immanuel. "The residents here must diligently train themselves in the art of believing without seeing. Keep that in mind."

"Why, everything will be fine—that is, as long as you do not venture off."

"No, no. Rest assured that I will remain here with you all."

"Well, can we count on you for that, then?"

"You of little faith, I am with you every day, I have called you by name: you are mine, and hereafter you will no longer be called Adamsson, but instead Abrahamsson."

With these words, they both crossed the threshold. And just think of the joy upon meeting Mother Simple and Mother Wounded-Hip with her sisters! They were sitting there just then, feasting on God's Love at a richly set table, which they called The Bible. Now our former Squire and his wife were mighty glad to sit down and join their company and share this meal. And neither did these dear little old women restrain themselves as they wished our gentlefolk welcome. At the side of Mother Simple limped Mother Wounded-Hip, followed by the other two, to greet their friends and newcomers and embrace them; and their mutual joy found voice in moving songs of praise in honor of Immanuel. It was a moment that one might be able to experience, but which is impossible to describe. Abrahamsson felt as though he were a brother to these women. For now, he was their equal in poverty.

"Who would ever have believed," said Mother Wounded-Hip afterward, "that even the Squire himself would come here!"

"Well, I for one have believed that for many years," Mother Simple chimed in. "And now it has come to be so. May he always remain here in peace."

When Abrahamsson went to bed that first evening, he felt such an indescribable bliss that he could not fall asleep until well into the night.

"What a wretched fool," he said to himself, "what a wretched fool I was, not to have understood this earlier. Oh, if only all of my friends would also decide to come here! First thing in the morning, I am going to write to them. There is no way that they would not come, once they hear how things really are here."

And so he reveled in this hope.

* * *

But in the city The World and on the estate of Industriousness a tremendous commotion had arisen when the Squire had been taken into custody.

Mr. Admirer was completely beside himself. His wife had arranged a coffee hour where everyone could have the opportunity to express their sympathy for this family that they had previously esteemed so highly. Everyone was able to tell some splendid story, some extraordinary aspect of the former lives of their dear Squire and his wife. One person pointed out his generosity and self-sacrifice, another pointed out his uncommon zeal for everyone's spiritual and physical well-being, and yet another praised the institutions she had established, and this went on and on.

"And now all of this has regrettably come to an end!" burst out Mrs. Admirer, amid her heavy sobbing, while the faces of all the others bore the mark of a deep sorrow and distress.

Never had there been such a display of sorrow there on the grounds of Self-Activity. Pastor Shepherd-for-Hire led a moment for devotions, which made a deep impression. Dismayed, they parted ways, and Mrs. Sensible felt that the one lesson that everyone could take away from this sorrowful event was to learn how essential it is to be cautious about taking things to extremes and to remain moderate in everything.

"If Adamsson," she added, "had remained in the city of The World, then he would have certainly still been doing just fine. But he wanted to be better than others. That is why he moved out of the city. For a while he was even able to shine like a star out on his estate, admired by all, but like a star that is on the verge of burning out. Now everyone can see the consequence of such striving; for a while this light can be dazzling, but in the end it will expire."

And all the ladies from The World agreed that Mrs. Sensible was correct in her assessment, though Mrs. Admirer thought that it was somewhat one-sided.

It was in this way that Abrahamsson lost his former friends. Others defamed him and his reputation. His name was no longer printed in a large font in the reports of the mission society. He would not be re-elected to the board, and the following year he was excluded from the society, like someone who had fallen away.

During the initial part of his stay in Evangelium, Abrahamsson managed to not be affected by all these darts that had been thrown his way. In his heart there was no room for worrying, for Immanuel remained within his sight all day long in one way or another. Abrahamsson took delight in his time there, unlike at any point in his previous life. And when Immanuel one day had spoken particularly loving and graceful words to him and his wife, they were both brought to their knees and exclaimed that they were unworthy of all this grace, unworthy to serve him. But yet they begged that, if it were possible, they should like to be allowed to go and perform some service for him on account of his mercy. This request was granted to them gladly, and so they were directed to the other side of the city, which was called Sanctification, and over the gate to which is inscribed the words *Workshop for the Redeemed*. This district was made up exclusively of work stations and workshops. Unlike in The Forgiveness of Sins, in this district there were no sleeping quarters or dwelling places, and neither were there any meals served there. It was also in this part of town that Mother Wounded-Hip held the meetings for her work society. Mrs. Abrahamsson was now more than pleased to be able to be a part of this society, and her husband became a member in another mission society, comprised of several poor brothers.

4

FINLAND

PAAVO RUOTSALAINEN (1777–1852)

Paavo Ruotsalainen was born the oldest son of farmers, and he retained the outlook of a peasant all his life. He learned to read but not to write, so what we have from him are letters dictated by him, sent to individuals and publications. As a lay evangelist, he led and represented the spontaneous awakenings of rural Finland, an often fractious movement. For Ruotsalainen, the Christian life was a hard road, a continual struggle to obtain and retain an inward awareness of fellowship with Christ.

Letters

A Few Words to the Awakened among the Peasants: December 16, 1846

The following is a brief message to the honored peasant class on the question of why all whom the Lord awakens are not saved. The reasons have already been written and published, but you, my brethren, are a stiff-necked people; you haven't loved the truth as it is written in the Bible. In this little booklet I've made known to you in great weakness the indifference and deceitfulness of the peasants. No one can understand the bad faith of the peasants except I, who am the most wicked of them. Therefore, I've written a few lines in the Lord, lest you go astray.

In the meantime let the Lord be the judge and the witness. If these few lines are false, say so and forgive me my slander; but if they are true, repent at once before God, in his righteous judgment, hardens you.

Good-bye, dear congregation, in the care of the Lord who on the cross cried out, "It is finished!" What's finished? The work of reconciliation, so that the greatest sinner who comes to the Savior, the crucified one, will not have his sins remembered. With this message, our dear low estate, good-bye.

Dear friends:

I come to you, peasant class, with a little question. Why aren't all that are awakened saved? The chief reason, I think, is that even though awakened, they haven't entered through the narrow gate that stands at the very beginning of the way of life. Now comes the question, Why haven't they entered through the narrow gate, even though they've been awakened? The reason is that this people is a stiff-necked people. It happens to them as happened to the people in Moses' time who against God's will began to push toward the land of Canaan without the Lord's guidance. The peasant class of our day is of a similar mind. Now comes the question, How does it happen among them? It happens this way, that after they've been awakened from darkness to light, that is, into an awareness of sin, they're humble and repentant, as Bunyan writes of them, "When the flames of hell beat around their ears they are repentant." Question: Why does this happen when they've been awakened by God? The chief reason is that when the judgment of the law in their conscience grows weaker, they take heed as one should of the righteousness of life that now ought to follow their imagined faith. But when the righteousness of life doesn't follow according to their enlightened conscience, some of the people lapse into slavish fear that begets unbelief. Others who are wiser express sorrow when they are called and admonished but in everyday life are quite reckless and indifferent. Question: Why are they like that? Because they haven't entered through the narrow gate that, as was said, stands at the beginning of the way of life, about which Bunyan talks and of which Christ himself says, "Many strive to enter by the narrow door and will not be able" (Luke 13:24). The reason is the one mentioned earlier, that they leave too soon the sorrow of repentance for pious practices, some by their singing, others by their prayers, and in this way they quench the godly fear even though they're breakers of the baptismal covenant. And in this way they lose the true awareness of sin that God had begun to create in them.

Well, doesn't Finland have awakened ministers today? Can't these guide them? They can't guide them at all for they deceive the ministers, coming to them as those who have already done what is required. They demand from the ministers pleasant nourishment for the soul. The awakened minister has a compassionate heart and begins to feed them in their slavish fear with the bread of the gospel, but it doesn't last long. Why not? Because they haven't entered on the way of life through the narrow gate.

Now comes yet another question: What is that narrow gate of which the Bible speaks so much? Isn't this the narrow gate, that when the sinner is aware of God's wrath resting upon him and knows himself to be a breaker of the baptismal covenant, he is willing to stand before the Lord with all the reproaches that fill his conscience, to stand still before the Lord until he is inwardly aware of grace being his? Well, why don't the awakened ministers tell them this? The reason is that they're prevented by their philosophy (theology). They themselves know best how difficult it is to humble oneself to walk the way of the cross as life in Christ's kingdom requires. But my purpose isn't to talk to philosophers or to the highly educated. They themselves know their way best, whether it's the right way or the wrong.

But now comes yet another question: Can it be that there's still grace for those who have fallen into the above errors? We answer that according to the Lord's own promise, there is much grace; if they return to the Lord wholeheartedly, the Lord himself testifies, "In the day when the greatest sinner returns to the Lord, his transgressions will not be remembered." The Savior himself has revealed his love through the thief on the cross and the prodigal son as encouragement to all who are afraid.

You peasants would like to know the simple order of salvation. I tell you briefly that during this time of great light you must acquire true knowledge from God's Word as to the order in which God wants to justify even the greatest sinner. You must learn to understand the reasons for the redemption in Christ. Although ministers talk a great deal about this redemption, they never point out to the simple peasant the true beginning. If we are to get the right understanding, we must return to the Bible where the words read, "In the day that you eat of the forbidden fruit you shall die" (Gen 2:17). Well, what happened? Man disobeyed and didn't fear God's righteous wrath. Well, you want to know why God couldn't have forgiven Adam his crime, for it's written of him that he is merciful. He couldn't do that without violating his holiness. Well, God did show mercy to Adam for Christ was promised, who then paid for Adam's crime before the righteous God. Now comes the question, What kind of Christ is he? This, good friend, you've learned already in childhood, especially in confirmation school. The Almighty himself gave his own Son who had to suffer and die. But why couldn't an ordinary saintly man do this? The debt was so great that an ordinary man couldn't pay it, as you know from the catechism. Here then is the reason and the fault why our righteousness doesn't mean anything before the Lord. Since no mere man was able to pay Adam's debt, our holiness has no meaning without new birth. But this knowledge you treat lightly, even though the ministers preach about it very often.

Well, I suppose you want to know what this new birth might be. The first step toward new birth is this, that as soon as you are more or less keenly aware in your conscience that you can't be saved in your present state, then you can be sure that this is God's call, so honor that call. But how can you honor it, you who are spiritually dead? Here's a bit of advice. Set the omniscience of God before the eyes of your understanding; you don't know him but he knows you. And if you don't know how to pray as the Word requires, then yearn for the Lord to look upon you in his grace. Don't run here and there if you receive no answer, but continue to yearn before the Lord until you know inwardly that now you can have Christ as your own helper, no matter how great a sinner you are. This is what the Bible calls the right of sonship. And if the Lord sees fit to let you linger a bit longer in the house of sorrow then that's what you need, so that already in the beginning you get to know your corruption, for the Savior says of this sorrow, "Blessed are those who mourn; blessed are the poor in spirit" (Matt 5:3, 4).

But why are you so impatient? When you aren't comforted and refreshed according to your own mind, you lapse into slavish fear that begets unbelief in you, and in this state you run to men for help and not to the Savior for the simple thing, even though you have known about the simple way from the beginning. Well, how can it happen that you seek help from men? It happens in this way, that you enumerate to the learned all the accusations and deceptions of your conscience with the idea that from them you should receive rest and peace for your soul; but these things are to be enumerated to the all-seeing Savior alone and not to men. You've made your deceitful heart into an idol, contrary to the warning of God. How does this happen? In this way, that when there arise good thoughts in your heart then you have courage to go to the Savior, but when evil thoughts arise, for the heart is a nest of evil, then you hide from the Lord as Adam did in paradise. In this state you'd rather seek help from men than from God, as we just said. Well, don't the learned show the way to Christ? Why doesn't that guidance help you? It doesn't help because you label the grief that is pleasing to God as unbelief, so that you wouldn't be refreshed in the least even if a hundred Saviors were promised to you. Read the letters of the apostles where you find a statement like this: "For see what earnestness this godly grief has produced in you" (2 Cor 7:11). As long as you are impatient under godly grief, you are obedient to your deceitful heart that constantly begets slavish fear of God and total unbelief.

Now, dear friends, I turn to you in great weakness. I too am troubled by all these same temptations about which I warn you, but I haven't become their slave. I've considered the example of the old saints, whom the Lord had to chasten to subdue the flesh, who exercised faith toward God and wrote such precious testimonies as this: "Though he slay me, yet will I trust him" (Job 13:15). This is their testimony. My hope for you, my friends, is that if you can't take the way of the cross, you'd turn openly to the world. Dear friends, I've wanted to write these few lines to you not to offend you but to point out to you your natural dullness and your little love for spiritual books that describe the simple way of salvation for us. For example, the books of the sainted Fresenius[1] contain all that a Christian needs to know. And now in conclusion I say, "Humble yourselves therefore under the mighty hand of God, that in due time he may exalt you" (1 Pet 5:6), as he has promised. I leave you, dear brethren, in the care of the Lord who has awakened you.

P. R.

Addressee Unknown: 1825

Many thanks for all the love you have shown me in the past. I long very much to know how it goes with you in regard to the inner man. It seems to me that, especially because of the improper behavior of many weak awakened souls, you have the kinds of problems that often show up in connection with the initial awakening, as in the case of speakers in tongues, which cause great confusion among people that are easily moved. Dear friend, if your position allows, look after such people with great care and admonish and keep them in check with all considerateness within the limits of reason. Let it be far from us, however, to set ourselves against God's wise purposes in matters that stem from the right spirit, even

1. John Philip Fresenius (1705–61) was German Lutheran pastor and spiritual writer.

though many weaklings abuse this gift to build their own proud selves. It is these people, therefore, that must be reproved and not the Spirit that has moved them. For God has not sent his Spirit that men might boast; it is man's own fault. Adam in paradise wasn't satisfied with the Creator's will, so it's no wonder that corrupt man now abuses even the most powerful calling of God.

I suppose you have all kinds of trouble with the separatistic spirits. But don't give up, dear friend, even though it is very burdensome for you in your office to show the proper kind of zeal against them. Dear friend, we must not give in even an inch to impatience, no matter how numerous these separatistic spirits might become. You yourself know that the Apostle once said, "By this it may be seen who are the children of God, and who are the children of the devil" (1 John 3:10).

I have had much to do with such speakers in tongues and other visionaries, but I have been victorious without too much trouble, so that in our area we are in no danger from them. If because of these things you should experience sorrow inwardly or outwardly, don't become impatient and don't let their faith go out, so that they begin to doubt the gracious help of God. You yourself know that in these matters the best thing is a living and inward knowledge of God; and no matter how feebly it may flicker in you, be encouraged and struggle on, that the Sun of Righteousness, Christ, may give your soul his true righteousness and light, as he himself has promised in his holy Word. I'm thinking of a trip out there but I can't say exactly when.

Goodbye for now.

Paavo Ruotsalainen

To Peter John Ikonen, June 30, 1832

I received your letter. It was good of you to let me know that also in your area God through his Spirit has awakened people to see how terrible it is to be indifferent toward sin. Such indifference one finds in congregations all over Finland. You say in your letter that we don't let people pray on their knees, but that's not true; on the contrary, it's a lie of Satan, the spirit of lies. I've read the Bible a little and have noticed that Christ says, "One must always pray, and not tire" (Luke 18:1), and how in another place he forbids prayer after the manner of Pharisees. It's into the error of the Pharisees that the awakened fall so often, when they venture to pray to an unknown Savior, even though their hearts are still far from him. Whoever wants to pray to God in the proper order must first come to Christ by inward repentance and receive his spirit and life, strength and light. In that strength he is then fit to fall down before the Lord; he is then able to pray on his knees before the Lord without committing sin, and only such prayers are acceptable to him. But even if we were on our knees day and night and troubled ourselves like the priests of Baal in the time of Elijah, but did it outside this order, such prayers without inward knowledge of God would not be what the Savior commanded. We must all be ashamed before his great majesty; through inward sorrow and yearning we must receive from him life and spirit, before we venture to fall on our knees before him. For if we venture to fall down before him in our own name and our own spirit, it's all deception and hypocrisy, and with all such prayers the heart and mind remain unchanged. This is how we have understood the teaching of Christ; this the partially awakened take to mean that we forbid prayer, putting into our mouth the lie that we forbid all kneeling prayer. I've never forbidden it.

Now if you feel like falling on your knees in prayer before the Lord, remind yourself first: I'm a great sinner, all-seeing Savior, I'm hardly fit to fall down before you. If from that you get from the Lord the desire and the urge to do so, then go ahead and fall down and let nothing stop you. But, on the other hand, if your heart and soul know nothing about such conversation with the Savior, (it would not help) if you were on your knees day and night, for only a heart changed through inward afflictions and sorrows is fit to fall down in worship before the Lord. Doesn't the Lord himself say, "When you spread forth your hands, I will hide my eyes from you; even though you make many prayers, I will not listen" (Isa 1:15)? And what does the Apostle Paul write about it? "Whatever does not proceed from faith is sin" (Rom 14:23). True faith is nothing but the reconciliation with the Savior through true repentance that has the witness of the Holy Spirit, about which the Bible says, "Anyone who does not have the spirit of Christ does not belong to him" (Rom 8:9). But today there are many lost and erring souls who think they have the Spirit of Christ, even though they don't yet know what the Spirit of Christ is and what the effects of the Spirit might be. This error has its source in the awakening from the sleep of sin. It happens like this: they think they are already converted, even though they are unchanged in heart; that they begin to pray long prayers on their knees and do it often, thinking that in this way they can earn God's grace and mercy.

Paavo Ruotsalainen

To J. F. Bergh: September 6, 1838

Greetings to you, dear friend in the Lord:

I want to thank you for the dear fellowship I enjoyed with you last winter. I would have been glad to come to the wedding, but it just wasn't possible during the summer, partly because of my health and partly because of duties and chores here at home. Now I've decided, if it works out, to make a trip there next winter, preferably during the Christmas holidays, if you're at home then. It's been a real joy to see from the *Hengelliset Sanomat*, whose editor you are, that you have such great hidden wisdom that you understand the simple (Christian) way so clearly. But in this connection you must pay close attention to the Savior's own words. When he asked if they understood these things, namely, the hidden ways of his kingdom, and some answered that they did, the Savior said, "If you know these things, blessed are you if you do them" (John 13:17).

It's a danger among the awakened that they often stop with spiritual knowledge and rest lazily upon the hidden wisdom, with the result that the sleep of lukewarmness gives them a great deal of trouble. Dear friend, look carefully into this matter as it pertains to yourself, and don't take offense at this weak warning, but give the glory to the Savior to whom it belongs and thank God for the grace that opened your eyes to understand the secret of his kingdom. So look into and pay close heed to what the Apostle Paul, endowed with the Spirit from on high, writes: "Examine yourselves, to see whether you are holding to your faith. Test yourselves. Do you not realize that Jesus Christ is in you?—unless indeed you fail to meet the test" (2 Cor 13:5). You've got much work in your calling, so you must be on guard so that the knowledge of the living faith that you possess doesn't under the cover of an unfruitful life replace that faith itself. For living faith will not keep its power unless it is engaged in inward striving and watching.

Give my greetings to your brother and to (Stenbäck). Admonish them to be watchful and to strive for an inward knowledge of the living God. Have compassion on other weak souls, whether they are members of the higher or lower classes. Then you'll be a true soldier of Christ. I've been tempted and troubled in many ways, which I need not mention, but it's all been necessary for me. I've already been summoned to appear before the court in Kalajoki[2] because of my trips out there, but I haven't gone as yet.

Paavo Ruotsalainen

2. In 1838–39, Ruotsalainen and a number of pastors and laypeople active in the revivals were brought to trial at Kalajoki for violating the 1726 Conventicle Act, which forbade many kinds of religious gatherings outside the sponsorship of the Church. They were convicted and fined.

Addressee Unknown: 1844

Greetings to you:

First I'll let you know how things are with me. In spite of my poor health, I made a difficult trip to the fair in Kajaani, and on that trip I wrestled with death for a whole day, but the Lord in his wisdom saw fit not to cut my life's thread yet. Perhaps the Lord extended my years because before I die I must take from the philosophers their deceptive faith. Dear friend in the Lord, in that moment I wasn't any more precious in the Lord's sight than you. To you I say that you must not act like a great lord because of all your education, but feed the sheep of Christ, of which you have so many around you at this time. But if you aren't able to feed them, then the fault is your indifference. Don't be afraid, you with the one talent, so as to bury it. Give God the glory, bring out the truth on all occasions. Remember what the Bible says, "Do not fear those who kill the body but cannot kill the soul" (Matt 10:28).

Now let me tell you about another matter. For a whole day, when my old illness took over, I struggled on the brink of death, but the Savior who is rich in mercy, comforted me and kindled my faith, so that I didn't fear death. Dear friend in the Lord, don't let a single day pass from now on without asking yourself, "Do I have the right of sonship with Christ, or am I running to a stranger?"

Paavo Ruotsalainen

To Pastor F. G. Hedberg: April 10, 1844

Greetings, Honorable "Magister" Hedberg, philosopher:

Many thanks for the love and fellowship at the Venell wedding in Espoo. At that time you were like a weak lamb, and believing then that Christ justifies without the works of the law, you tricked me with your great treachery, your philosophical wisdom, into making known to you the spiritual mystery. But now afterward I see from your scoffing writings that on the hill of Espoo you were the same kind of philosopher as Judas Iscariot. When you received from me knowledge of the hidden wisdom, which philosophers can't find on their own, the devil went into you, as into Judas Iscariot, with the dipped morsel that you stole from me. How is it, philosopher, that with your sound mind you're so blind? Don't you remember the many troubles that burdened you at the time I explained to you the love of Christ? Now you've become so shameless that without any further inquiry you damn me as a preacher of the law; all the more shameful that you do it with red ink. I know the Bible as well as you do. Why did you start spoiling the Holy Bible with your philosophy, as though we peasants didn't have the light of God's Word? From this I can now see your faithlessness and spiritual pride, that you are downright ungodly, for you believe lies and state in your various letters that I cursed you during the fair in Kuopio. Yet the Bible tells even ministers not to help out the ungodly. With whose permission did you venture to fall into that error? I'm not afraid of you, nor of your threats. It is to the Lord God, who in his love has called us to himself, we must go in deepest humility after all the stumbling and falling that beset us poor things every day. But you, Mr. Philosopher, who think to drive to heaven and to Christ in a carriage "outside the proper order," know that you have a lamp but no oil and that now, dear friend, you have drawn God's curse upon yourself with your letters. You mock those who want Christ's Spirit to be their leader. How did you dare to start mocking God's people without having the witness of God's Spirit and by twisting the meaning of the Bible, as though the Lord had not granted God's Word to peasants but to philosophers only?

And now I say to you my final goodbye. Glory to God in the highest, and on earth peace, good will toward men, that in the prophets and evangelists you have revealed to us lowly people your will, so that we need not seek to understand it through philosophers! And if, good friend, you don't repent quickly, you'll be like Simon the magician. Goodbye.

Paavo Ruotsalainen

Do you think it's the right kind of book that you had published in Finnish at Turku?[3] With that book you want to confuse the order of salvation for us weak peasants, for in your spiritual blindness you demand faith from us before we have even asked for it from Christ, the giver of faith. You, Mr. Philosopher, acquire faith without real struggle and outside the proper order of salvation; and all your philosophy would indeed be in vain, if at least one philosopher couldn't make some headway with his head faith. But I recall the words of the apostle in the Finnish Bible: "Not many wise, not many of noble birth" (1 Cor 1:26) understand the hidden wisdom, only we poor and weak peasants. How did you dare to slander us as fanatics against the Holy Bible, you who right now are blinded by false light? May the freedom that you with your head faith confess as your God reward you as you have deserved. If our congregation goes before the Lord, you'll not escape your reward any more than Ananias in Peter's time, unless you repent for all the mockery and slander you've gathered from the Bible. The Lord is the Savior of us weaklings; I know that as well as the philosophers. If it pleases you, answer this letter; but if your pharisaic piety prevents it, don't answer. Goodbye.

Paavo Ruotsalainen

Old friend, let's go to the mountain to test our offerings, whether the Lord gives fire to my offering or yours; and to whose offering the Lord gives fire, let him be our God whom we must serve. These offerings must be for ten years from now, and only then will it be known to whom the Lord will turn.

3. Here Ruotsalainen is referring to the second edition of Hedberg's *The Doctrine of Faith unto Salvation* (original *Uskon oppi autuuteen*, 1843), in which Ruotsalainen thought Hedberg was attacking him.

Apparently Addressed to Pastor J. I. Bergh: November 13, 1847

Greetings, dear friends in Finland, both among the high and low classes:

As this New Year breaks upon us, I come to you, dear friends, with a complaint. The gracious czar, whom the Lord at this time has given us as our ruler, has shown good will toward us from the day we became his subjects. And his highly honored senate has been very active in carrying out his commands. Now comes the question, Where did the grave doctrinal errors in Christendom originate against the will of our pious and Christian czar? I want to point out the chief source of error, a certain minister in Sortavala by the name of Henrik Renqvist. Already as a boy in school he was awakened through the law, and to works of the law he has clung all his life, and in that way he has blinded numerous souls in many parishes. He has lost one of the articles of Christian doctrine, the one in the creed that says that the ungodly man is justified without the works of the law. It's true that he chews the Bible like a cud, but he doesn't know the passage in which Paul says that "as many as are of the works of the law are under the curse" (Gal 3:10). Doesn't he show by his actions that he is under the curse? Don't his publications show how he slanders true Christianity with his fanaticism, using in all this the Bible as his ladder? In this way he wants to use the Bible to blind the government and to call its wrath upon us humble people. Now, beloved church in Finland, there is a certain minister by the name of Hedberg,[4] the son of the sheriff of Raahe. Well, beloved Finland, in your thoughts you ask, what kind is his error? This error is different. It's like this. He had been awakened by the law and the Lord then revealed to him that the grace of the gospel is for sinners, and so he appropriated for himself a whole armful of Christ's gospel but he did it with

4. Here Ruotsalainen referes to Pastor Fredrik G. Hedberg, to whom he addressed the previous letters.

an unchanged heart. With his publications he now sows this doctrine all over Finland and even in Sweden.

Now comes the question, Why does Christ allow false doctrine to be spread within true Christendom? The chief reason is our disobedience and failure to love the truth for our salvation. For this reason the Lord himself said he would send punishment in the form of blind and foolish shepherds, and that is what is taking place right now. In the country of Finland the Spirit of the Lord has been working for over fifty years, but all the awakened have not set out wholeheartedly on the way of life. Because of them the Lord is sending blind teachers with the spirit of error, for those who go astray are those who in the beginning do not enter the way of life through the narrow gate. But why does the Lord permit this to happen to them, for don't they have immortal souls? Because the Lord has mercy on us weaklings and doesn't make us serve these people in their hypocrisy. For this reason the Lord has had mercy on us who are weak, sparing us from serving hypocrites. Dear friend, Mr. Teacher, if this letter doesn't please you, ignore it. Goodbye.

(No signature)

To Pastor Julius I. Bergh: October 27, 1848

Greetings, dear friend in the Lord, Teacher Bergh:

Just recently I received your letter in which you complain that the way of salvation is hard to follow. I'd like to ask, Why is it so hard for you? And I venture to say, as the nature of the case demands, that when the wisdom of reason is most highly developed it is Christ's worst enemy. Why, good friend, have you ventured against the Bible to block that simple way by philosophical wisdom? Don't you remember the Kuopio fair some time ago? I was then rather worthless in my own mind, even more so in the minds of the highly learned. The seed of wisdom that was in you then has been left to grow in your heart and it blinds you to the childlike simplicity in which alone we are saved. Dear friend, read once more the Holy Bible where it's written, "If any one among you thinks that he through doctrine is wise in this age, let him become a fool that he may become wise" (1 Cor 3:18). The Lord revealed to you, dear friend, during your illness how your acquired wisdom has led you into many unnecessary things that are quite worthless in regard to your faith and Christianity. But if you want to heed the Lord's discipline of which you wrote to me, then return to inward seeking after the right of sonship for which you yearn, as you say in your letter; but be careful that you don't do it with head faith. You want to ask me how head faith works. It works like this: through the Holy Spirit's illumination you've received great wisdom in your mind and understanding. By this head knowledge you then push the inward wish and desire before the Lord and then pretend to say, Let the Lord do what he wants. But to such striving the Lord pays no attention. You must, as the Apostle Paul writes to his disciples, "fight the good fight of faith" (1 Tim 6:12). But how are we to understand these words, "good fight of faith"? The good fight of faith means that when your knowledge and ability produce no peace of soul, you set the fact that your Savior sees everything before the eyes of your understanding by means of inward longing and don't give up this fighting until you receive from the Savior the hidden and quiet inward peace; now I dare to accept Christ as my helper.

Paavo Ruotsalainen

If this advice doesn't please you, kindly point out my error to me. But that error you must prove with the words of the Holy Bible, otherwise I won't obey.

Printed in Oulu in 1863, Said to Have Been Written by Paavo Ruotsalainen

You say that there is no spiritual life at all, only death. How can life be found where Christ who is life itself is not first received? For only after he has been received does life begin, and with it the doing of works of life. Because you permit something to stand in the way, whether it be knowledge of sin or hatred of sin or lack of knowledge of sin, piety or wickedness, or anything else that you seek first or from which you would be freed first before as a beggar you begin to thirst for pure grace, therefore Christ is kept from you and with Christ also life. Learn then as a sinner and as a saint, as indifferent and as awakened, as repentant and as unrepentant, to look to the almighty Christ, and take your place before, near, beside Christ until you're aware that life flows from him. Don't conclude from a few feelings that you've received Christ, for feelings and stirrings of the Holy Spirit are but the handshake of God by which the soul is prepared for Christ and for turning to him, but Christ himself is something else, in whom the sinner must trust with or without feelings.

How little as yet you hate your self-righteousness, or your own heart that hungers for self-righteousness, is something you must consider more closely according to the Word. Doctrinally you indeed follow the proper order, but practically you listen to and follow your heart that hungers prematurely for godliness and piety. It's true that godliness and the practice of piety are proper in their place, and that God can't be seen without godliness. But first one must reach that state of affairs in which godliness can be practiced and this happens when life in Christ is found. And life in Christ can be found only by learning as a sinner, as cursed, as a saint, and as a scoundrel, to ask and hunger for grace, that is, as the Apostle says, without works to believe on him who justifies the ungodly (Rom 5).

If the unbelief of the unlearned and the peasant is bad and leads under the wrath of God, much more terrible is the unbelief of the learned and the lords that deprives a man of the natural, simple ability to fall down before the Lord just as one is and to consider everything, whether it be good or bad, as sin and refuse. Learn to believe what the Word says about God and remember that Christ came as helper to the ruined, thoroughly ruined, children of Adam, to restore what original sin and actual sin had ruined in them. Keep faithfully at the cultivation of the Word, no matter how cold you may feel about it, for from there the hidden light will dawn to him who yearns for light. But don't substitute the cultivation of the Word for the practice of holiness and godly life. Look upon the Word solely as the chief means of illumination and as Christ speaking to you, and then you will cultivate it properly. The Word awakens in you a longing for Christ, the longing kindles in your heart a sighing and a yearning for the fountain of life you hope for, and before you realize, the life of Christ is awakened in you. But know that Rome wasn't built in a day; you won't grow into a Christian in a day or a few weeks, as you'd like to. Learn to be content with God's delay, in such a way, however, that you don't permit indifference to overcome your yearning, which—namely, yearning after Christ—is a part of your daily task in which you need to be encouraged with or without the Word. You have Björkqvist, Nohrborg, and Luther.[5] With them, and especially with the Bible, you know how to take care of the problem of hunger.

A Letter of Complaint to the Bishop in Behalf of the Awakened: No Date[6]

We would come to you in deepest humility, subjection, and simplicity with our feeble prayers if we would dare and if you would find it possible to receive this petition of us poor people, for at present we are living in the world in good peace under the fatherly love and protection of our most gracious czar; both temporally and spiritually he has granted us here in Finland the freedom to worship God after the teaching of Luther, as it is based on the prophets and the writings of the apostles. But contrary to this freedom granted us by our high

5. Anders Nohrborg (1725–67) was a Swedish Lutheran pastor and royal chaplain who wrote a very popular devotional book, *The Way of Salvation for Fallen Man*. Anders Björkqvist (1741–1809) was a Finnish Lutheran pastor and devotional writer.
6. It has not been possible to identify the bishop to whom this letter is addressed.

sovereign there has now arisen a terrible controversy between the indifferent and the awakened. Nearly thirty years ago God's grace began to awaken people from the sleep of sin and indifference in such places as the parishes of Nilsiä and Iisalmi and in the chapel parish of Pielavesi. And the awakenings have continued to this day. In these areas there has been no open persecution, even though there has been ridicule and slander, to which the awakened have paid no attention. But this year actual persecution on the part of the authorities like the preachers and the sheriffs has broken out. They have started proceedings against us in district and provincial courts, and heavy fines have been levied against a number of people. Now the intention is to bring everyone to court; unless serious worship of God is given up, everyone will be fined and outlawed from among the people. But we are determined to give up our lives rather than our living faith that the Lord has created in us. We are in great despair and many souls are in danger, for the weak and the newly awakened are alarmed by these terrible threats and they see no escape except to submit to our former indifferent authorities. Therefore we pray most humbly that you would have mercy upon our miserable spiritual state. Most honorable professor and noble sir, would it be possible for you to see to it that the awakened are permitted to worship God in freedom according to the Holy Bible? Our persecutors have made a big issue of the fact that the awakened admonish one another, because the newly awakened are quite helpless unless there are older Christians to counsel them. We have always lived responsibly and have never gone against the law or regulations..., nor have we...opposed even the unkind ministers, even though they have often slandered us from the pulpit and on other preaching occasions as though we were the greatest criminals. The indifferent have used these occasions to persecute us all the more with their mockery and slander that we suffer gladly for Christ's sake. But we would ask you, should you find it possible, to grant us freedom from being falsely accused before the law. If you, beloved in the

Lord, have any doubts about this our complaint, you could possibly send some awakened minister to investigate and to examine us, but all these complaints that we have laid before you are the absolute truth. We have, it is true, our laws and courts, both spiritual and temporal, but being the poor and despised people that we are, we have no way of making use of them. You, highly learned and gracious sir, know and understand this very well. This is the wish of us poor people that the Lord may grant you his grace and light that the souls of us poor and weak people would continue to be precious in your sight and that we may have the freedom in our Christian doctrine that the highly honorable and gracious czar has granted us out of his fatherly love. It has meant a great deal in awakening people that our high sovereign has sent us here in the far north many devotional books, especially Bibles, which have already borne much fruit, for example, in Karelia and in the parish of Pielisjärvi, where through the Lord's grace people have been...enlightened.

Written in Nilsiä on behalf of the awakened.

Paavo Ruotsalainen
Anders Pykö

FREDRIK HEDBERG (1811–1893)

The leader of the "Evangelical" movement in Finland, a strain of Finnish piety that differed from that represented by Pavvo Ruotsalainen, Fredrik Hedberg was a Lutheran pastor in Finland, and closer to the official church of his day than some other leaders of the awakening. Hedberg wrote The Doctrine of Faith unto Salvation, *a devotional commentary on the Letter to the Ephesians, after a spiritual awakening in 1842. In this book he sets forth his new Evangelical understanding of the Christian life and explores the proper understanding of the way of salvation.*

The Doctrine of Faith unto Salvation

Ephesians 1:6: *To the praise of the glory of His grace, wherein He hath made us accepted in the Beloved.*

Saint Paul praises only the good will of God the Father and the glory of his grace and not at all his own merit and worthiness or that of the Ephesians. He does not mention them with even half a word when talking about receiving grace and becoming a child of God. This has been written also to teach and encourage us. It is as if the Apostle were shouting with a loud voice to all who search for salvation throughout the world, "Listen souls, listen to what I am saying! If you want God to bless you with every kind of spiritual blessing in heavenly places and be counted as his chosen children, do not search for it on the basis of your own works, preparation or merit. That would be useless (Isa 55:1). Instead, all this is given to you freely and without merit by the good will of God for the sake of his dear Son, Jesus Christ, in whom he has made us acceptable." All the prophets, evangelists, and apostles, with one voice, have preached this same teaching. Now this beautiful and saving message of the gospel is circulating around the world through writings and preaching as a general call of grace by God to the wedding of the Lamb. Now the sound goes out to the sinners of the world: Come, for everything is ready! The Father has delivered up his only and dear Son. The Son has finished the entire work of redemption. He has given his blood and life on the cross to pay for the whole world's sins. He has won the victory over death, hell, and the devil, and has brought us eternal life, righteousness, and immortality in heaven by his glorious resurrection.

This briefly is the content of the doctrine of the gospel. Its nature is entirely different from that of the law. The law threatens and frightens. It demands works and merit, whereas the gospel promises and freely gives worthless sinners all the treasures of salvation, without merit, for Christ's sake. The treasures of salvation are for all who receive him and believe in his name. This doctrine requires only faith or acceptance. All that applies here is, "Open thy mouth wide, and I will fill it" (Ps 81:10).

The world, however, is full of unbelief, and this is the biggest reason for the eternal death of sinners, for without unbelief, not even sin could injure them. Christ says, "He that believeth not shall be damned" (Mark 16:16). Indeed, the unrepentant in Christendom pass themselves off as believers, especially the hypocritical self-righteous, who can often babble a great deal and beautifully about Christ and grace. Nevertheless, their shining faith is not founded on the unmerited grace of God in Christ, but is of this nature: "I thank you, God, that I am not like other people, robbers, crooks, adulterers; for I do this much good and I pray this often and this long, and I honor you and speak about you so beautifully and with a devout heart. Therefore, you, good God, must be merciful toward me and reward me with your eternal salvation." Look; this is the foundation and pillar of their faith!—And although the unrepentant sinners do not have as much to brag about as the hypocrites and work righteous, they have this idea: "There are worse people in the world than me. I have not committed any great sins, thank God! I even go to church sometimes and attend the Lord's Supper, and now and again I read and sing hymns. Surely God will forgive my sins, and therefore I hope to be saved."

This type of faith is possessed by many even in Christendom. With their mouth and tongue, they can speak about God's grace and the merit of Christ, but their heart, at least secretly or without them realizing it, trusts in their own virtue or merit, however little they have, even in the eyes of others. This deception becomes especially apparent when the law of God, at some point in their lives or at the time of death, slightly pricks their conscience and shows them how numerous and terrible their sins are. Then the game changes! Then there is no longer the least bit of knowledge or talk about God's grace. Only then does it become apparent that they have known nothing about Christ, no more than the stones and stumps in a field. Rather, they have had a false faith and a shadow Christ covering their self-trust. Now, when their foundations collapse as their conscience awakens, their faith and their Christ also give way. The only question remaining is, How can we still put together some good in order to appease God? It can best be seen from an awakened soul how much faith and knowledge of Christ a person has and how easy it is, as the unrepentant and hypocrites imagine, to have faith in God's Son.

Nevertheless, if the law of God has thus brought down your support and security and you feel yourself to be a great and damned sinner, do not throw yourself into that bottomless pit of unbelief that lives deeply and vastly in your corrupt heart of Adam. Rather, open your ears to hear the gospel. It is the voice of Christ. Read what the Lord's prophets and apostles have written in the Holy Scriptures. Read and understand! Pray as David did: "Open Thou mine eyes, that I may behold wondrous things out of Thy Law" (Ps 119:18).

Indeed, wondrous things are found in Christ's gospel, wondrous things that are so great that no heart and no one's faith can fully comprehend them (Phil 3:12)! For what can be a greater wonder than this: the holy and just God loves the sinful and godless world? And he does not love it just moderately, but with such a great and fervent love that he gives his one dear Son into shame, derision, suffering, intense agony, and death on a cross for the redemption and salvation of the sinners of the world! Through this dear Son whom he has raised from the dead and set at his right hand in heaven, he desires to bless, pardon, adopt as his children, and save us who are slaves of sin, death, and Satan, from all our sins, "that we being delivered out of the hand of our enemies might serve him without fear, in holiness and righteousness before him, all the days of our life" (Luke 1:74, 75), as the saint, Zacharias, sings.

God does this without the least bit of merit on our part, as the Apostle says. It is simply "according to the good pleasure of His will, to the praise of the glory of His grace." Whoever believes this, is truly a partaker of it. He has already received the forgiveness of all his sins.

He is a chosen child of God in Christ Jesus, chosen to be his own before the foundation of the world. He therefore rejoices with the apostle and all believers over the sheer grace of God, and in simplicity of heart, sings the new song: "Blessed be the God and Father of our Lord Jesus Christ, who hath blessed us with all spiritual blessings in heavenly places in Christ...having predestinated us unto the adoption of children by Jesus Christ to Himself, according to the good pleasure of his will, to the praise of the glory of his grace" and so on—Thus faith, and only faith, makes us rich in Christ with the riches of salvation and totally translates us onto a heavenly course into genuine participation of God's merciful and fatherly love. It loosens our tight lips and ignites our cold hearts to give praise and thanks to God for his good works, and as Luther says, "Makes altogether different men, in heart and spirit and mind and powers, and it brings with it the Holy Ghost."

Look again then, dear soul! Look very closely at these very comforting words of the Apostle that the Holy Spirit, through him, has spoken to you and to me, saying, "Wherein (in the glory of his grace) he hath made us accepted in the Beloved." There now, you hear that God has made you too acceptable to himself and his dear pardoned child. Indeed, this has not occurred because you or I, any less than other sinners, have merited this with any good work or slightest worthiness. Rather, it is clearly seen here that by his glorious and eternally exalted grace, he has made us acceptable to himself, and not only us, but all those who have faith in Christ. If this happened according to merit, neither you nor I would have any part in it, nor would Saint Paul (read 1 Cor 15:9, 10; 1 Tim 1:13, 15, 16) nor any of Adam's children (see Rom 3:12; Eph 2:8). The situation is different, however, now that we are made acceptable by God's grace, for this grace is not meager, useless, and to be looked down on. It is, as the Apostle says, glorious or great and powerful as God himself. Now, God has, as we know, created everything from nothing and can do whatever he desires. The reason his grace is so glorious, noble, and powerful is that it does even greater miracles in heaven and on earth than his omnipotence ever does. Indeed, the great miracles that the grace of God accomplishes makes sinful children of death and damnation blessed of God and accepted and dear to him, not for the sake of any goodness residing in them, poured upon them, or that works in them—for then grace would no longer be grace—but, as worthless sinners having no merit, solely by this glorious and undeserved grace of God. You who are tempted and burdened by sin, do you now understand this matter? Do you understand and believe what this entails? Frankly and unquestionably, it means that God will by no means abandon you or cast you away, even if your sins were a thousand times greater and more numerous. On the contrary, because of his great grace, he wants to accept you, as unworthy and filthy as you are in yourself, and he counts you as entirely acceptable to himself. Furthermore, he chooses you to be his dear child for all eternity. Now, if you believe this to be true, even as it is true from God's perspective, it has surely happened to you and has already been fulfilled in you.

A frightened conscience nevertheless shudders at such great grace, and reason considers it utterly impossible, saying, "How is it possible that I, such a filthy, sinful maggot, subject to death and damnation, could still be acceptable before the holy God, and be counted as his child?"

Saint Paul recognized full well this craftiness of reason and the depth of unbelief that is in us. Therefore, he immediately shows us the strong and trustworthy reason and foundation for this glorious grace of God toward us. He says that God has made us accepted in the Beloved.

Who do you suppose is this dear one or the Beloved whom God loves so deeply and holds in such high esteem that for his sake or in him, as the Apostle says, he lets the riches of his grace pour down as a flood on us sinners and unworthy children of Adam?

This Beloved of the Father and our Mediator is the Lord Jesus Christ himself, God's only Son of whom His Father testified from heaven, "This is my beloved Son, in whom I am well pleased" (Matt 3:17). You see then that God has good reason to pardon us, although we are completely unworthy in ourselves. You see, we have a Mediator or Advocate who is with the Father, Jesus Christ the righteous (1 John 2:1) who is ever acceptable to his Father although, we are unworthy. He also merits all of the Father's love by his perfect obedience, even if we have deserved and still do deserve God's wrath and curse for our sins. Since this only and eternally beloved Son of God, Jesus Christ, has taken up our cause and undertaken to be our

Mediator and Advocate at the Father's right hand, God the Father can only, and wants only, to pardon us by grace. He accepts us as his children, not because of us, but "in the Beloved" or for the sake of his one dear and most acceptable Son in whose name we are baptized, called, and betrothed to believe in him.

The very purpose for which the Apostle speaks so beautifully here of the riches of God's grace and how God has made us acceptable in that beloved Son of his, is that we would finally believe it to be true also for us and thus be saved. Indeed, whoever believes this is a partaker of it. Nothing else is required. Whoever does not believe, however, makes God's Word a lie, looks down on his glorious grace, and makes the most precious merit of Christ useless to himself. He is himself the reason for his damnation (John 3:36).

Ephesians 1:15–16: *Wherefore, I also, after I heard of your faith in the Lord Jesus, and love unto all the saints, cease not to give thanks for you, making mention of you in my prayers.*

...The most important thing is faith in the Lord Jesus. That is the core and power of Christianity, its spirit and life. But what kind of faith? A dead knowledge of an unknown Savior? An empty confession of the mouth, "I believe," confessions of which the world has more than enough? Not at all! Here, we are talking about a faith that is God's gift and that the Holy Spirit works in us through the gospel. We are talking about a faith, I say, that truly accepts as its own the Lord Jesus with all his treasures of grace. Indeed, even the hypocrites can speak about this, but they put all their trust in themselves and beautify their own "righteousness" with the name of Christ. But blessed are they who refuse to trust in themselves and put their trust in Christ's Word alone! O, what hidden blessedness this is! How unknown to flesh and blood! How hidden from all human wisdom! How the religious sects look down on it and curse it! How Satan hates and oppresses it!—Lord Jesus, you alone can open our eyes blind as we are to understand by faith the blessed mystery of your reconciling death! You alone by your Holy Spirit can enlighten our dark, unbelieving hearts to believe the unspeakable riches of grace and salvation found in you and that are offered through the gospel to all creatures. O, dear Jesus, ignite with a spark of faith the hearts of Finland's pietists who yet in throngs lie in the thick darkness of unbelief and under the heavy burden of the law, so that more and more of them would grasp this simple way that you Lord Jesus are: the Way, the Truth, and the Life forever and ever! Amen.

I am lowly dust and a newborn in the life of faith, but this I know to be true, and I wish to live and die in it, that man's whole salvation and eternal life is in these few words: "Believe on the Lord Jesus Christ" (Acts 16:31).

However poor we are, however miserable, sinful, and unworthy, this cannot harm us, if we, despite all this, believe in the Lord Jesus Christ, truly believe that he is our soul's wealth, purification, and salvation from all evil, our reconciliation with the Father, the hope of our salvation and our shield, rock, and fortress in which we are hidden and protected from destroying wrath, death, and damnation. Yes indeed, this faith alone gives us power to become children of God and makes us heirs of the heavenly kingdom through Christ. On the other hand, without this simple faith, we are truly children of wrath and death and hell's own, though we may perhaps picture ourselves as having the holiness of Paul and Peter, though we may have all knowledge and wisdom and though we may perform miracles and speak with the tongues of angels. Everything that is in the children of Adam, however, is cursed if they do not know their Redeemer, Jesus Christ and if they, as sinners, do not believe in his Word and receive from him alone God's righteousness as a gift and grace by pure grace! It is true that many pursue this in their feelings under the pull and coaxing of God's grace that precedes all. The coaxings of grace will become less frequent, however, and feelings will cease. When one's own corruption is felt and, despite all that is seen and felt, one should practice faith in the Word of grace that says that we sinners who are subject to cursing and damnation have eternal grace and righteousness in Christ, most run away and wrap themselves in their own filthy mire, constantly looking at their own sins in unbelief. The more they look at them, the more they sink....They listen only to the accusations of the law in their conscience and do not notice the merciful voice of Christ in the gospel. They listen to the judgments of other people and the decrees and reason-based regulations of leaders puffed up with their own spirituality. Thus they sink deeper and deeper into the depths of their natural unbelief or go away in despair, forsaking the living God to serve dead mammon. In this way, they finally become lost and condemned. O you poor souls! Why do you not hear the voice of your merciful Savior calling you through the gospel? Why do you prefer to believe your cursed, unbelieving heart and that Satan brain instead of your Blood Bridegroom and Savior? What need is there to go to damnation when we have a merciful Savior who receives sinners, even the greatest of sinners? Oh, come to him, come for the sake of his own invitation, all you miserable and troubled sinners! Come to the Savior just as you are! Come, in spite of anything you may lack, even if it seems that you do not yet have the right kind of repentance, and not even a sign of having turned from sin nor the least bit of spirit or life, but only sin and pure wretchedness. In this altogether lost state, believe, nevertheless, in this Lord of life who makes the dead alive and binds up the broken hearted and heals all their wounds!

The Ephesians had been taught this trusting faith in Jesus Christ and had practiced it. With childlike faith, they simply placed all their faults and shortcomings on the shoulders of their merciful Lord, and freely accepted out of his fullness all that they needed for life and salvation. The harder Satan attacked them with his fearful threats, the tighter they clung to Jesus by faith and took refuge in his Word of grace like frightened chicks under the shelter of their mother's wings. This is how they always managed to overcome all temptations and trials. These only made them more skilled in their fight of faith and brought them closer to the Bridegroom of their souls. It is true that they always felt deficiencies, faults, sins, and unworthiness within themselves, but at the same time, they knew their Advocate with the Father, Jesus Christ, who is the propitiation for our sins and himself the Lord, our Righteousness. Him they knew, and they knew the way to him, for they kept his Word and regarded it as completely true no matter how much Satan roared. They had learned this road of faith through the gospel by the Holy Spirit. That was their only victory and advantage over sin, the world, death, and Satan.

Now, do you think that this faith is ever without fruits? What does Jesus say? "He that abideth in me, and I in him, the same bringeth forth much fruit" (John 15:5). What kind of fruit? Such as the Lord of the vineyard desires and considers good: "This is my commandment, that ye love one another, as I have loved you" (John

15:12). This brotherly love and unity among believers is the best fruit of faith and the most acceptable offering of praise to the Lord for his grace.

Just as the Ephesians had faith in the Lord Jesus, so they also had this brotherly love and Christian unity among themselves, so that they did not allow any dissenters to break their unity. They remained firm in the pure doctrine of the gospel and by it of one mind and Spirit, in Christ serving one another in love and simplicity of heart according to their own gifts and strength. The Apostle had received this kind of report about them and he rejoiced greatly over it, thanking God for them. If Christians remain in faith and mutual love, their situation is good and God abundantly blesses them. As David very beautifully chants, "Behold, how good and how pleasant it is for brethren to dwell together in unity!," and he immediately declares that the heavenly Father abundantly pours out a spiritual blessing on such as these who are of one mind in their faith in Christ. He says, "It is like the precious ointment upon the head, that ran down upon the beard, even Aaron's beard: that went down to the skirts of his garments." Note, however, that this refers to the true high priest, Jesus Christ, who is the head of the church and the source of all blessing. "As the dew of Hermon, and as the dew that descended upon the mountains of Zion: for there the Lord commanded the blessing, even life for evermore" (Ps 133). Look how the Lord himself promises to dwell always and eternally with his full blessing in that congregation of believers who endeavors to "keep the unity of the Spirit in the bond of peace" (Eph 4:3).

Let us also notice, however, that this true spiritual unity is impossible without faith in Jesus. You see, as long as people seek salvation in works, they do not have and cannot retain unity of mind and spirit, but before long, there will surely arise one sect here and another one there. Each one will observe a different form of holiness and cling to different kinds of works regarding its own way to be the best. This was formerly the situation in the Roman Church with the rise, one after another, of many different orders of monks. One praised its brand of righteousness by works, while another praised its own brand until someone else introduced an even stranger and more bizarre form of worship. It is evident even today whenever the work righteous gather that they are not in agreement for long, for when seeking salvation by works, they do not know which work would best earn it. One group commands that prayers be made on one's knees three times a day, another says five times or more, if one wants to be saved. One group argues that prayer must be made on one's knees, while another says on one's face. One group wears a long beard, another wears the Körtti clothing,[1] and each believes to have found the best way to salvation. That is why I say, as long as people cling to works, they do not have any understanding of what the unity of spirit is. Only those who have been enlightened to believe in Jesus Christ and have chosen him as their all in all know and recognize from experience what this unity of spirit is that always accompanies faith. In them is still realized, albeit imperfectly because of weakness of faith, that which is said of the first Christians: "And the multitude of them that believed were of one heart and of one soul" (Acts 4:32).

This unity of spirit among believers is followed by a true brotherly love that is not forced but spontaneous, as we notice from the example of the Ephesians, for the Apostle praises their love "unto all the saints." By "saints," he means, both here and elsewhere, those who are sanctified by faith in Christ and not those who set up their own holiness without Christ but who, in spite of their gleam of holiness, are filthy and spotted in the sight of God (Isa 64:6). Those who are sanctified in Christ by faith and are counted holy by God for his sake and who have received the Holy Spirit, remain in unity of spirit among themselves, for they have "one Lord, one faith, one baptism, one God and Father of all" (Eph 4:5, 6). For that reason, they love and serve each other as members of the same spiritual body, the head of which is Christ.

If you wish to become better acquainted with the value and nature of this true Christian love, read the thirteenth chapter of Paul's First Letter to the Corinthians, where Saint Paul has remarkably explained and presented this matter. Let me just point out that the love we're talking about is not nice words or charming conduct, for even the hypocrites can imitate these and are quite the experts at

1. Traditionally, adherents of the movement have observed a strict code of conduct that discourages colorful clothes as well as dancing and other entertainment. One of the Finnish names of the movement, *körttiläisyys*, apparently derives from the typical black clothing of the adherents, *körttipuku*. By dressing in simple black clothes, adherents sought to emphasize their freedom from the dictates of fashion, although the wearing of this typical clothing has declined.

it. We, on the contrary, are talking about the love that is in spirit, deed, and truth. It does not pursue outward splendor nor seek praise from people and does not conform to the attitudes of flesh and blood, but rather to the Spirit. This true and sincere love coming straight from the heart is not found in our natural abilities, nor is it the hypocritical pretense of the work righteous. Rather, it is the fruit of a living faith, produced through having the forgiveness of sins in Christ's blood. In vain, therefore, you practice love with outward deeds and conduct thinking you have grasped it. Even if you handed out all your possessions to help feed the poor and gave your body to be burned for others, but did not have love, it would not be of any benefit to you (1 Cor 13:3). Indeed, people would thank you and soon praise you as a great saint, but before God, you, as an unbeliever would have the part of the hypocrites and liars, about which we may read in Revelation 21:8.

Therefore, before you go imitating Christian works, look carefully that you first have the Spirit of Christ. Otherwise you will be numbered among those who run uncertainly and fight "as one that beateth the air" (1 Cor. 9:26). The Spirit of Christ is not your own spirit and is not in your high imaginings and gloating religious glow. He is the Spirit of grace and truth whom we receive from Christ as a gift together with true faith. He teaches us to deny all "ungodliness and worldly lusts" and "live soberly, righteously, and godly, in this present world" (Tit 2:12) and to love our neighbor in truth.

If you, therefore, wish not only to know but also experience what this true Christian love is, learn first to believe that Christ is your own, so that he would then teach you, as his own disciple, the content and fulfilment of that "new commandment" of which he speaks in John 13:34. It is necessary, therefore, that you first be grafted into the true vine. In this way, you will surely not remain fruitless, for Jesus lives and reigns. Learn to accept the Lord Jesus Christ by faith, just as God has made him to be wisdom, righteousness, sanctification, and redemption for you. Learn to strengthen your heart against the accusations of Satan with Christ's Word and to nourish your poor soul with the milk of the gospel, and so, the Lord will train you to do all that is good and lead you to do his will.

The Apostle himself extols first the faith of the Ephesians in the Lord Jesus. From this faith then came the fruit of love toward all the saints. Saint Paul greatly rejoices that they, in one mind and spirit, had remained up to the present time in this health-giving and saving faith, loving one another. He does not cease to give thanks to God for them.

Saint Paul adds one more significant phrase: "Making mention of you in my prayers." Why did the Apostle still need to pray for the Ephesians? Someone may think, Was it not enough to thank God for that great grace that had come to them? He deemed it necessary, however, not to pray for them just a few times, but to continually remember them in his prayers. You see, true Christians are always in great danger. That is why Saint Paul says elsewhere, "Let him that thinketh he standeth take heed lest he fall" (1 Cor 10:12). Although one has owned Christ by faith and been declared righteous by God and received the fruits of the Spirit, he has not yet finished the race, but has only taken the first steps on the road of salvation. Indeed, having attained justification, many deviate entirely from the true road of salvation having a seemingly good purpose.

Although they, unlike many others, do not fall into fleshly impenitence or disgusting sins, they fall away from faith in Christ's grace and begin to set up their own righteousness without the atoning grace of Christ. This happens in many different ways. Some engage in inner struggles and seek to own Christ through feelings, without faith in the testimony of Christ given in the Word. Others begin to practice external holiness with great zeal, deciding that that is walking the road of salvation, although they are a long way from believing Christ's Word. The former look for a Christ whom they can feel, while the latter trust in their own holiness. Neither one believes the Word. Observing them at a distance, they appear to be totally different, and are, in fact, constantly at odds with each other. And yet, both of them hate the pure doctrine of the gospel and are equally distant from the true faith.

We want to look more closely at both of these false paths and better define their nature.

Firstly, those who search for an "inner light" and a "Christ in feelings" without faith in the Word are the kind who, when the feelings of grace escape them, immediately conclude that they have lost the grace of God and Christ. You see, their attention is fixed on their feelings and not on the Word. They therefore now give in to the judgments of the law thundering in their conscience, considering this state of slavery excellent spiritual poverty. They never, in opposition to the feelings of their heart, believe the Word of grace. Indeed, they do not! They just cry out with their master, "It is not suitable to boast about the Word, you must yearn until the light comes to your heart." Now, since they have heard talk about faith, they want to portray it in some way. This is their faith and its confession: "If I am able to struggle, wait and devoutly yearn, then I will surely someday again get the inner light or grasp the appearance of Christ." This, in their opinion, is faith (!) and the true fight of faith that they think then is "that someone battles day and night, with grief, and incessantly cries out for grace, awaiting the appearance of Christ." If it were so, even the Jews would have a marvelous faith, for they yearn greatly for the appearance of Christ and await the coming Savior! They, too, do not accept the Christ of which the Word of God testifies as having already come in the flesh. It is therefore Jewish spirituality to reject the Christ declared in the Word and to yearn for the appearance of another kind of Savior.

The others, who trust in their own external righteousness by works, are diligent in their works and practices by which they force their way into heaven. They often say long prayers that are for a determined time and consider them to be an extraordinary mark and proof of faith, as if the Pharisees of Christ's day, the monks of the Roman Church, the Muslims, and even the pious among the heathen had not prayed many times more often and more diligently, both on their knees and on their faces, as they still do, believing strongly that they are holy men and the best servants of God. However, all such imitations of prayer that are made without faith in Christ cannot even be called prayers.

The same is true for every other state of holiness with which those estranged from Christ's grace try to beautify their own emptiness and unbelief. Their many works and great zeal for the law are in vain, for the very law of which they boast and shout will judge them because they did not seek nor know the one who kept the law and the one Lord, Jesus Christ, to whom alone must all glory, thanks, and praise be given and in whom alone "a man is justified by faith without the deeds of the Law" (Rom 3:28).

These people who are estranged from the life of faith and who have strayed and are lost in empty yearnings or dead works can be found in our country in large numbers just as they have always been present in Christendom during times of revival. It is for this reason that I have revealed their work in a little more detail so that awakened novices may better guard against such fanatics who often come from afar like wolves in sheep's clothing, stirring them up with resplendent holiness and preaching their legalistic "gospel" and also alluring them with their own spiritless, albeit to human eyes, attractive path. Even without enticement, man is by nature always more inclined to seek life by works and salvation by setting up his own righteousness rather than by faith accepting forgiveness and grace by the merits and righteousness of another that goes against human reason and pride. That is why this trusting in one's own righteousness and this deceptive dream of obtaining God's favor by works has throughout all periods of Christendom been Satan's best trap. With it, he has fulfilled his cunning plan of drawing many souls awakened to a sense of the truth, even by the flocks, into terrible deceit. With this plan, he attempted to bring about division even among the apostles....Even today, he has not forgotten how, with subtle cunning, to drown awakened souls using these methods or others, even in those congregations where the pure doctrine of the gospel is confessed, not to mention his urging of all the impenitent and those who are a long way from knowing Christ to shamelessly trust in their outward virtue, church attendance or some other work or quality and in addition, dream of God's mercy without Christ.

Because of all this, it is truly difficult to come to true faith at all. It is even more difficult to remain in it unto the end. The Apostle Paul knew this best of all and therefore, he did not cease to pray for the Ephesians, that God, who had begun a good work in them, would also complete it in them until the day of Jesus Christ.

LARS LEVI LAESTADIUS (1800–1861)

Lars Levi Laestadius was a Swedish Lutheran pastor who lived his life in the far north of Scandinavia, and ministered to the native Sami people (the people of Lapland) as well as to Scandinavians. After an intense conversion experience, Laestadius began a wide-ranging ministry and was influential in Norway, Sweden, and Finland. Part Sami himself, he campaigned indefatigably against the use of alcohol among his Sami congregations and in the 1840s became a teetotaler, except for the use of communion wine. Author of several works on botany, Laestadius also wrote a book Fragments of Lappish Mythology, *about the traditional religious beliefs of the Sami that were being lost due to the Christianization of the people. The manuscript was lost for some time and not published until 1997. The reflections from his periodical,* The Voice of One Crying in the Wilderness *(1852–54), represent his powerful form of Lutheran Christianity.*

From *The Voice of One Crying in The Wilderness*

John was properly the first one who cried in the wilderness. A few voices had indeed cried out before him, but either their voices were too low to be heard in the abyss, or people were then even more hard of hearing than they were at the time when John cried out. The prophets did indeed cry out with a loud voice, but the people of their time did not hear them. Our Lord and Savior's own voice was higher and more powerful than all other voices that have cried out before and after him, but his voice was not heard by any people other than those who were near him. They who were far away did not hear that heavenly voice, because they were deaf. He himself in many places lamented the deafness of those of his time, of which the prophet says, "*With hearing ears they shall hear, but not understand.*" After the Savior's death and ascension into heaven, the apostles began to cry out, and only then did the ears of some open, so that their voice was heard farther than the voice of any other man who has cried before or after them. But this hearing turned again to deafness when the persecutions ceased. The apostles' voice was heard in the abyss, but the devil and his followers could not bear this voice. The devil had to bring about terrible persecutions against both those who cried out and those who heard the cries. Starting with the time that persecution of Christians ceased, the voices of those crying out weakened, and finally the cries ceased to be heard at all. If someone dared to raise his voice in popedom, as did Waldo, Wycliffe, and Huss, such a voice was immediately stilled by fire and sword. For the devil cannot bear to have someone crying in the wilderness. He is not offended by the world crying out his name in the wilderness; but if someone dares cry out the name of Jesus, then the devil becomes furiously enraged.

Finally, Luther began to cry out in the wilderness, and his voice was heard at quite a distance, and broadly. But they who should have cried out after Luther's death were troubled with hoarseness, so that the crying out in the wilderness ceased. For Spener's cry was not heard far, whether because he had a defect in his windpipe, or because people became ever more deaf and dull of hearing, so that they could not hear one word of the voice of the crier. Now in our days mankind is more deaf than ever before, and we cannot hope that our cry can be heard farther than the portals of hell. And may God allow, that it could be heard at the portal to heaven.

If one cries out in the wilderness in calm weather, he receives an answer from the mountains and hills if the weather is hot and heavy. But these mountains and these hills do not answer to all the syllables of the crying voice. For the crier hears only the final syllables of his own words, which the mountains and hills repeat. This echo is not a reply to that which was spoken, but is only a reflected voice, which the mountains and hills cast from them. That is, the mountains and hills do not accept the words of the crying voice, but cast them away from themselves. This characteristic—that mountains and hills cast a voice away from them—was possessed by them already at the time of John the Baptist. And they still have the same characteristic—those mountains that were to be made low, as the prophet Isaiah says in the epistle text for Midsummer Day. Therefore we cannot expect that the mountains and hills would accept the words of the voice of the crier. But the air is stifling and heavy both in the church and the state. The mountains and hills themselves are oppressed by the mass of spoiled air. They are about to choke from Satan's smell and stench that rises up from the abyss. Therefore they cast back the voice in multiple syllables. They repeat the syllables, often repeating the voice of one crying, and saying, "He has a devil, he has a devil!" In this way did the mountains and hills answer to the voice of the crier at the time of the Baptist, at the time of the Savior and apostles, at Luther's time, at Spener's time: "He has a devil, he has a devil!" And so do they reply even yet: "He has a devil!" Otherwise, everyone who is of his father the devil usually becomes angry when someone dares to say that their father is the devil. He may not be called devil or Satan, but rather the *angel of light* and *Lucifer*. Then, too, there is an old saying, that "the crow calls his own name."

When now the Jews asked of the voice of one crying in the wilderness, *"Who are thou? Art thou the Christ or Elias or one of the prophets?"* he answered no. If the Jews asked, *"What sayest thou of thyself?"* he replied, *"I am the voice of one crying in the wilderness,"* and so on. But the Jews' final opinion of the voice of one crying in the wilderness will be that he has a devil, he is either a fantasyer or a Jesuit, but he is no proper spiritual teacher. This is the inner conviction of all leading Jews. But if someone should ask them if John's baptism was of God or of man, they would reply, *"We do not know."*

Although the mountains and hills cast off from themselves the voice of the crier and answer in the same tone as the crier, it has nevertheless been observed that the crier's voice makes a strange impression in the living nature in the forest. In the wild wilderness where the crier cries, the voice at first sounds strange and disagreeable in the ears of the dwellers of the wilderness. In the north, for example, curiosity is aroused in the forest dwellers; that strange voice makes some curious. In others it evokes terror and fright; others again are annoyed that their sleep is disturbed, as for example, the bear. The hare listens for a moment, but soon flees if the crier's voice comes closer to it. In other types of animals, that strange voice arouses curiosity. They come closer to the crier, as for example the ptarmigan, which comes and laughs at the crier. The crow immediately comes close to the crier and calls its own name. The owl also comes within reach, fluttering its wings around the crier. It is said that in southern lands, monkeys appear when someone cries out in the forest. Briefly said: the crier's voice is truly strange to the inhabitants of the forest, but it also awakens some sort of curiosity and desire to become better acquainted with the object from which this voice comes.

From this it follows that when someone cries out in the forest, a whole flock of crows and magpies are set in motion. The mountain ptarmigan often alights at the crier's feet and laughs. The hare listens and flees. The hawks, which have their nests and their young in the spruce grove appear, shrieking terribly. The bear growls in its den. The owl flies and flutters around the crier. Monkeys have their tricks and grimaces. All this commotion among the inhabitants of the forest is brought about by the voice of the crier. To them the voice sounds strange, but it arouses curiosity in these animals; it arouses in them a desire to see and to get to know the object whence the voice comes. And should the crier not receive any reply from any man in the wild wilderness, he will at least receive a reply from the mountains, which echo with the same tone with which the crier cries. That is, if the crier cries, *Ye generation of vipers!* The mountains answer, *Generation of vipers?* If the crier cries, *Who hath warned you,* the mountains answer, *Warned you?* If he says, *To flee from the wrath to come,* the mountains answer, *Wrath to come?* If the crier says, *The axe is now laid unto the root of the trees,* the mountains answer, *Root of the trees?* If the crier says, *Every tree which bringeth not forth good fruit is hewn down and cast into the fire,* the mountains answer, *Cast into the fire?*

Although all these replies end with a question mark, let it not be believed that the mountains fear the fire; but sooner will creatures that flutter, laugh, and shriek around the crier—sooner will they perhaps be able to fear the fire, if they come so close to it that they burn their noses and paws. A fly does indeed like to buzz around a fire, because it can be surmised that it loves light. But some flies are so impudent that they are not satisfied with merely buzzing around a fire, but fly straight into the flame. But there the fly burns its wings. It falls upon the table. There it then lies on its back, and shrieks and kicks.

Our Boast before God: Reconcilement of Romans 3:23 and 2 Corinthians 1:12

In Romans 3:23, the holy Paul writes, "*For all have sinned, and come short of the glory of God.*" In 2 Corinthians 1:12, the same

Apostle writes, *"For our rejoicing is this, the testimony of our conscience, that in simplicity and godly sincerity, not with fleshly wisdom, but by the grace of God, we have had our conversation in the world, and more abundantly toward you."*

The contradiction that seemingly exists between these scriptural passages quickly disappears if we look at them in their right light. Therefore let us set forth here what, for the purpose of explaining these passages, can be held to be the most important.

In the first passage (Rom 3:23), the Apostle indicates that God's holy law sets forth all people as fallen and debased sinners who have nothing of which to boast before God, even though it is true that the seed of the serpent and Lucifer's nature in us brings about a good feeling in our corrupted flesh in seeking and gaining praise and admiration. This boasting, which we should have but do not have before God, here means the same as the glory of God's image, seal of power, and nobility. This glory was lost and utterly and deeply corrupted through the fall into sin, although the great throng neither knows nor believes the depth of this corruption, regardless of the fact that God's word and enlightened teachers bear so much witness to it.

God's holy law, which is a manifestation of God's holiness, not only indicates how we should be and live, but also what man was like when he possessed God's image and glory before the fall into sin.

When God's Spirit can set the holy mirror of this law before our eyes, even the best of natural men become sufficiently sinful. They can experience that man by his nature is deeply debased and defiled, even though the great intellect boasts so much of the nobility of its godliness, and although dead faith so greatly trusts in its supposed piety and goodness. But God's law shows that we have a tattered nobility and piety before God, because before the holy Lord we are full of sin, unbelief, spiritual darkness, and so on, as well as being wretched children of wrath, prisoners of death, and Satan's slaves. But if God's law overthrows all our own boasting before God, how much more does God's gospel do so, which shows what our redemption has cost. For precisely the fact that such a powerful Savior, the Lord of blessedness, must himself descend to such depths and to suffer in order to lift us up, best testifies as to how deeply we have fallen, and how helpless we are. Nothing can so clearly show that we of ourselves have nothing to boast of—nothing can overthrow and nullify all our own boasting before God more than our glorious Savior's deep abasement, whereby he regained for us our lost glory, or God's image, with which he now wants to and is able to enrobe us, through the medium of grace and the Spirit of grace. Where this does not take place, it is our own fault. The lifting up from a fallen condition has taken place for the benefit of all. The lost glory, or the boasting over the likeness of God's image, can be regained by each one through faith upon Christ. Accordingly, we can obtain boasting before God, even though we do not have it of ourselves. We shall now have it of God's grace, in our Savior. Therefore the Lord says (Jer 9:24), *"Let him that glorieth glory in this, that he understandeth and knoweth me."* So does David, when in Psalm 34:2 he says, *"My soul shall make her boast in the Lord: the humble shall hear thereof, and be glad."*

When the Apostle thus writes that *we have all sinned and come short of the glory of God,* he is looking at that which we are by nature. But by this the Apostle does not support the false consolation that the natural, unconverted man takes for himself from this Bible passage, so that he can sleep soundly in the sleep of sin under the pretense that things are not worse with him than they are with others, since all have sinned and come short of the glory of God. He does not consider that although we have nothing of ourselves or our nature of which to boast before God (no glory of his image), we nevertheless can regain it through faith upon him who appeared in the flesh and yet is *the brightness of God's glory, and the express image of his person.* We thus regain this boasting through justification, when all sins are forgiven and Christ's perfect righteousness is accounted to us as our own, both in the new birth and the renewal, when we are enrobed with Christ's mind and likeness. A Christian can boast over this, that he has regained God's image by becoming united with God's Son. Yes, he can, where required, refer to his conscience before men, that after his conversion, he has sought honestly to preserve his faith in good conscience and to heed the voice of his awakened and enlightened conscience. Truly, a Christian is not thereby righteous before God, before whom he always confesses sin and shortcoming; but against Satan's and the world's hatred and accusations he nevertheless can present the good testimony of his conscience, and appeal to him who examines the hearts and judges rightly. This is what Paul did to his enemies in Corinth, and this is what is meant by our passage in 2 Corinthians 1:12: *"For our rejoicing is this, the testimony of our conscience; that in simplicity and godly sincerity, not with fleshly wisdom, but by the grace of God, we have had our conversation in the world, and more abundantly toward you."*

He sets forth the testimony of his good conscience, not against the judgment of God's law, but against the perverse judgments and accusations of the world and its prince. In this place "boasting" thus means the same thing as the consolation and joy he had over having lived honestly (or in purity). But Paul did not attribute this to his own wisdom or power, but to God's grace. For no matter how much the ungodly man boasts of his good conscience (wherein his conscience sleeps and becomes calloused), sinful man can nevertheless gain a good conscience only through God's grace in Christ, and through Jesus' blood (Heb 9:14). Therefore, when a true Christian boasts about his good conscience, he does not praise himself, but rather glorifies God's awakening, converting, and protecting grace, without which we cannot spin the tiniest thread in the garment of our righteousness.

Of Faith and Works: Reconcilement of Romans 3:28 with James 2:21

In Romans 3:28, the Apostle Paul testifies, *Therefore we conclude that a man is justified by faith without the deeds of the law.* On the contrary, we hear in James 2:21, *Was not Abraham our father justified by works, when he offered Isaac his son upon the altar?*

Both of those Bible passages speak about very important things, for they speak of how we become righteous. It is absolutely necessary for us to become righteous in order to become blessed, just as true as it is that all blessedness is in God, and that God is righteous. Righteous is the man who is such as he properly should be and lives as he properly should live, that he according to God's holy and righteous law is full of purity and love and free of all uncleanness and all indifference, free of all sins, and adorned with all virtues. But where is such a man to be found? God's holy law wants to convince us fallen sinners that no such man exists or can exist. *Who can say: I have made my heart clean, I am pure from sin?* (Prov 20:9).

For all have sinned, and come short of the glory of God (Rom 3:23). With these and many other Bible passages, to which general experience corresponds, it is testified clearly and abundantly, that not one man is of himself righteous before God. It is therefore necessary to become righteous. And so infinitely necessary and important is this matter, that one must be very much asleep if even on a single evening he can peacefully fall into natural sleep without first having with tender concern considered how one becomes righteous before God. God, who in a fatherly way has taken care of the eternal blessedness of our souls, has also in his holy word, in many places in Holy Scripture, given clear and precious teachings about this, which must be especially welcome to those souls, who in a sinful and perishing world, sigh and hunger for eternal righteousness.

But the teachings that are given in the above-mentioned passages seem at first glance to be mutually contradictory. For where Paul teaches that man becomes righteous through faith alone, without works, it appears that James teaches that faith alone does not make one righteous, but that works must also be present and helping. Which of them is right? Undoubtedly both of them for God's Spirit cannot speak against himself.

Briefly to explain this apparent contradiction, it is necessary to take note of the different context and purpose that each apostle has in the mentioned passages. Even the most hurried and superficial examination of the third chapter of the Epistle to the Romans would certainly cause the most simple reader to understand that the Apostle testifies how all people, both Jews and Gentiles, were sinners and unrighteous before God and totally in need of Christ's reconciliation and merit. Who alone can place us in righteousness before God, when we receive this reconciliation with the right faith? Here the road of faith and grace is set totally against works and one's own merit. Apostle Paul does not teach that true faith lacks works. Rather does he teach that these works are not given any consideration, and are not taken into account for justification before God?—But since it is so important that we, just as though with both hands, hold fast to this doctrine, so that we would not fall into the shackles of self-righteousness—to which our corrupted nature is so inclined and that thereby we would be imprisoned under the law's bondage and curse—it could be asked how then the Apostle James can advocate a doctrine that appears so wrong and dangerous, namely that man must (like Abraham) become justified not only by faith but also by works. Here one must take note that James writes against dead faith, which already then began to haunt the Christian congregation, though it was not so general as that which we see in our days in the great so-called Christian throng, which would be better named baptized pagans. James does not teach that works make anyone a Christian, or righteous, before God. Good works only demonstrate to people who can and want to see it that man by God's pure grace for Christ's sake through faith is seen and declared to be righteous. This faith is not only some "mouth faith" or "knowledge faith," which is worse than the faith of devils, who at least tremble before the great God, while the ungodly people, on the contrary, do not very often tremble before God, though they say they believe in him.

True faith must effect love and good intentions, thoughts, words, and deeds; otherwise faith is only a dead and dangerous supposition in the soul of the sleeping and impenitent sinner. Abraham was accounted righteous only through faith. But through obedience, he showed that his faith and justification were honest and true. Thus Paul teaches that righteousness of life, whether by believers or unbelievers, does not effect or help justification before God. Again, James teaches that this justification, even though it takes place by grace through faith alone, must be followed by righteousness in life, unless it is empty and dead supposition.

Sermons

Above all else, Laestadius was known for his powerful and unflinching sermons, with which he addressed the troubled moral climate of his day, and the need for repentance and rebirth. Though he had followers across northern Scandinavia, his most permanent influence was in Finland, where the "Apostolic" Lutherans still revere his preaching. Among some Apostolic groups, one of Laestadius's sermons is still read in worship each Sunday.

Reading Examination Sermon

> *When the Lord shall have washed away the filth of the daughters of Zion, and shall have purged the blood of Jerusalem from the midst thereof by the spirit of judgment, and by the spirit of burning.* (Isa 4:4)

God through the prophet Isaiah had threatened the children of Israel, that they should die because of their sins and disobedience, but the few souls who shall be saved shall be called holy, even every one that is written among the living. Then shall the Lord have washed away the filth of the daughters of Zion and shall have purged the blood of Jerusalem from the midst thereof by the spirit of judgment, and by the spirit of burning, which will reprove the world of sin, and of righteousness, and of judgment.

The prophecy of the prophet became fulfilled when God sent a judging and a burning spirit. Mention has been made of this in many places in the Bible, as for example in Solomon's Book of Wisdom, 12:1. The incorruptible spirit is in all, for that reason thou dost punish them with a scourge wherever they sin, that they be delivered from their wickedness and believe upon thee, O Lord. By this spirit of judgment and burning, the Lord has washed away the filth of the daughters of Zion. He laments already in Genesis 6:3 that men will not submit themselves to the chastisement of the spirit of God, as the words read: *My spirit shall not always strive with man, for he also is flesh.* If the spirit of God began to rebuke man very severely, flesh could not stand it. The sorrowless believe that the spirit of God does not rebuke them anymore, since they are flesh. All the hardened ones hope that the spirit of God would no longer rebuke them, because they are flesh; but in opposition to this we will set that which the Savior has spoken to his disciples: *When the Holy Ghost is come, he will reprove the world of sin, and of righteousness and of judgment.* No matter how the sorrowless and hardened should say, the spirit of God no longer reproves us. Verily the spirit of God has reproved the people of the former world through the sons of God, who then preached in the name of the Lord, but the ungodly people did not take heed of that preaching of repentance, and that is why God said, My spirit shall not strive with man forever; he still gave them a hundred and twenty years in which to make repentance, and as repentance did not come in that time, God destroyed them by the deluge of sin. It shall be for a sign to the sorrowless, that when God's Spirit ceases reproving the sorrowless, he has then delivered them unto Satan. So long as God's Spirit reproves the sorrowless, he is still seeking them and calling them to repentance, but when he ceases reproving them, he has then decided that it is to no avail. For the Spirit of God eventually becomes tired, when the sorrowless will not receive chastisement. For such is the heart of a Parent: he reproves and chastises the ungodly children in the hope that they might become men; but when they harden, the Parent quits chastising, because all hope of correcting them is gone. The Parent finally becomes tired of rebuking and chastising, as God says through the prophet: My spirit shall not always strive with man. Then even love has died in the Parent's heart, which is evidence that he has delivered them to Satan who rules them, that is, the devil of haughtiness, the devil of disobedience, the devil of adultery, the devil of wrath, the devil of honor, and the devil of drunkenness. What else can the Parent do to such hardened ones? He must deliver them to Satan. So he did with the people of the former world, and so he did with the children of Israel, when he said, I will not strive with you everlastingly. When he warned the Jews through John the Baptist, through the Savior, and through the apostles, and these hardened Jews did not make repentance, then he gave them up to the enemies. But the hardened children suppose the Parent has become merciful when he becomes tired of always rebuking and chastising them. So terribly has the devil deceived them that they suppose it to be grace, which in reality is an indication of the Parent having abandoned them, since all love in the Parent's heart has died out. The blind wretches suppose that the Parent has become placated since he has ceased from scolding, although he says in many passages, whom he loves, him he also chastises; all the same, the hardened children suppose that the Parent has now become very loving, since he does not scold us. The devil makes them so blind that they consider it love and mercy, when he has delivered them to Satan, and then they may live as they will.

I believe the Holy Spirit has rebuked the sorrowless of this community so much that he has become tired of rebuking, and now the spirit of God has delivered them to Satan, and now let the devil do with them as he will.

We should now speak a few words concerning those whom the spirit of God has not delivered to Satan yet. There are a few souls whom the Holy Spirit always reproves of sin because they do not believe on Christ. Luther has understood that unbelief is the greatest sin a penitent person commits against the Son of God. If we look at the condition of those who do not believe on Christ, we will find that they commit a great and abominable sin when they let the blood of the Lamb of God flow to waste on the ground. The unbelievers do not understand that they are excluded from participation in the blood of reconciliation when they let the blood of the Lamb of God flow to waste on the ground. This sin will eventually fall heavily upon those who have been awakened by the spirit of judgment and of burning, but have not received the chastisement of God with so humble and contrite heart that distress would have driven them to the Savior. These prisoners of unbelief still stand far from Jesus' cross, battling with self-righteousness and warring against the devil with their own strength, and do not flee to that great Hero, who has overcome the strong man armed and has taken away his armor. Although they war against the devil with all their might, still they do not become so freed from him as to be able to believe on Christ. Even though the Father, through the Spirit, draws them to Christ, they cannot get so near him that a few drops of the precious reconciling blood would drip on them. Do you see now, you unfortunate souls, who stand so far from the cross, that you cannot see his wounds? Come nearer! Come so near, that you could see how the blood flows out of his wounds, that sorrow might press your heart, that you must begin to weep and wail with the sorrowful disciples. By this spiritual sorrow, all vain trust in the world ceases, and by this sorrow the heart is prepared to receive joy over the resurrection of Jesus. If you do not make haste to come to the foot of Jesus' cross, dogs will come to lick up Christ's blood. The soldiers will come and trample it, the thieves of grace will come to claim it, and you will be left without. Self-righteousness finally wearies the prisoners of unbelief, so that they are not able to believe anything. Here all the thieves of grace will lift up their heads and say, We are at the foot of the cross of Jesus every day, we believe God will be merciful to us. But these awakened ones do not have faith as much as a grain of mustard seed. They are always under the law, and therefore they would always press us under the law and put us under the curse of the law. We will not depart from our faith. These thieves of grace profess to be so sincere and so in unison with the Bible that the devil himself will witness that their words are founded on the Bible and in them is the real truth. But we require true contrition of the thieves of grace, first, and the fruit of living faith. So long as these essentials of Christianity are lacking, we must say to the thief of grace, You will go to hell with that dead faith, no matter how firm your faith might be. You will not be saved with the faith that is empty in your skull. You must show your faith here. For formerly men have also believed and cursed, have believed and committed adultery, have believed and fought, have believed and been drunken, have believed and sold whiskey. All these Lutheran believers have held the Christians as wild spirits, they have hated and scorned the Christians, and even now they still hate them at heart. This hatred comes out through the mouth as often as a Christian speaks to them. The Jews were the same kind of thieves of grace, for they said, *We have a father, even God; we are not born bastards.* All the same, the heart of the Jews was filled with hatred for Jesus, and the same devil still rules in the hearts of those who have not entered into the sheepfold at the narrow gate. They are full of serpent's venom, though they claim to lie at the foot of the cross of Jesus. But they lie at the foot of the devil's cross so long as they have hatred at heart. It would indeed be pleasant for the old Adam if he were admitted into the kingdom of God with hide and hair, but that is not allowed in God's word. The thieves of grace of the present times have such a belief that these awakened ones are false prophets and wild spirits. That is why they hunt mice and see many faults in Christian's lives, as the Pharisees found fault in the Savior's life, and for that reason did not believe his doctrine to be true. The thieves of grace now require the fruits of true faith of the Christians, so we also require the fruits of true faith of the thieves of grace. The Christians have never been able to live so as to be approved by the world; for the devil has so keen eyesight that he always sees faults in the Christians' lives. For that reason, the best counsel is that the thieves of grace separate themselves from the Christians; and as the devil accuses the Christians night and day, so also let his servants accuse the Christians that they are false prophets and wild spirits. Let the owls and forest devils now live on meat of mice until judgment comes. They do not have anything else to eat except the meat of mice, which they eat uncooked, with hide and hair.

We should now behold how the Lord has washed away the filth of the daughters of Zion by his spirit of judgment and of burning. That it is a judging and burning spirit by which the Lord washes away the filth of the daughters of Zion, we have seen already in the apostolic period: and the same burning spirit is still affecting an awakening and true Christianity in some even now. Those daughters of Zion who have been washed and cleansed from their filth by this judging and burning spirit, must now confess that it was the spirit that cleansed them. Like the spiritual fire, which Jesus came to kindle on the earth, burns straw and wood, and gold is thereby refined, so are your hearts, O daughters of Zion, likewise cleansed of filth by this judging and burning spirit. The Holy Spirit has first judged you and then it has burned you, and thereby you have, as the prophet says, been cleansed from your filth. You know that the filthy and evil spirit dwells in the hearts of heathens; namely, the devil of adultery, the devil of drunkenness, the devil of contention and strife, and the devil of finery, and when this judging and burning spirit first came into the community, then this filthy evil spirit began to show its teeth. All meek harlots became wroth, all honest thieves became angered, all moderate drinkers became terrified; but the judging spirit judged them, and the burning spirit began to burn them. Amen.

Visitation Sermon at Karesuando, 1852

The Apostle Paul warns those who begin in the spirit and are made perfect by the flesh that their end is death; besides he says, *For he that soweth to his flesh shall of the flesh reap corruption.*

So I also suppose it will happen if a Christian who has been a living Christian in the beginning, goes into a dead state, and thereafter founds the hope of his salvation on the former state, thinking that the former living state of soul will suffice him henceforth also, this leaves in him a dead or assumed faith. The servant who owed his master ten thousand talents received forgiveness for his sins indeed when he prayed in distress of soul. But that grace no longer helped him after he was merciless to his fellow servant. This servant most certainly had living faith, when his debt of sin was wiped away; but he could not have remained in that living state of soul very long, for when he met his fellow servant, he shows by his works that living faith was already gone.

I fear that it has so happened with many now also, as with the mentioned servant, that many have begun in the spirit and have ended in the flesh. World's love has stolen the hearts of many, and the Savior must stand on the outside, as he says in the Revelation: *I stand at the door, and knock: if any man open the door, I will come to him, and will sup with him.* How will the Savior come in, when world's love stands like a lord in the middle of the heart and preaches exclusively of faith and love, although he has neither; no faith, since not many will now believe what a living Christian says; no love, since the Christians no more fit into the same house of prayer. I fear that spiritual death is coming upon this congregation, in which there were living people before. It has come to pass as the Savior has said: *The first have become last.*

Therefore, I must remind you of your former condition, how you were as children when I was still with you, but now you have grown up. Now if this strong Christianity indicates that you have now become men and fathers in the Christianity, I no longer need to admonish you; you have become so wise and understanding, that no one need say to you, *Know the Lord.* But if this strong Christianity indicates that the vessel has become warped, that the new wine has leaked out, that the old vessel has been repaired, that the old wine is sweeter than the new, then I am afraid that the Savior's sufferings will be in vain, and that his tears in your behalf will be shed in vain, and his blood will flow to the ground in vain, and dogs will lick up his blood; but you will derive no benefit from those precious drops of blood. And I, according to the grace given me, have prayed the heavenly Father that the great cross bearer and thorn-crowned King, whose tears you have scorned in your blindness and trampled his blood under foot, would still reveal himself to you. According to the poor understanding that has been given me, I have watched in your behalf and have labored thereupon that you might be led from darkness into light, and from under Satan's rule to God. My conscience bears witness that the crucified and thorn-crowned King has not spared a single drop of blood that he has not let flow off his holy body. My conscience also bears witness that I have not spared time nor trouble in laboring among you to the end that you be taught and led to the foot of the cross of our Lord Jesus Christ, into the garden and to Golgotha. Now I fear that the sufferings of the Savior will have been in vain and also that my labor will have been in vain, since you have become so big and fathers in the Christianity, that you will no longer receive any one's admonition but what your own intellect gathers, that you believe and hold as godly wisdom.

I speak not of you all in this wise, but that the Scripture be fulfilled: *He that eateth bread with me hath lifted up his heel against me: and ye are clean, but not all.* I am afraid that if your Christianity will mature in the direction in which it has matured the past two years, it may so happen, that you, who beforetimes were like children in simplicity of faith, will become hundred-year-old hags next year, and will eventually die a spiritual death, and not a single child will weep on your grave. Where is Mary Magdalene now, who weeps upon the grave of the heavenly Parent? Where is John now, who stands at the place of the cross, and beholds how the soldiers drive the spear into the heavenly Parent's heart? They may be at the sepulchre handling the linens; Joseph and Nicodemus are laying his body into the grave of dead faith, and who knows whether he will rise again, since his children are no longer weeping and wailing; Mary Magdalene is no longer weeping tears of longing at the brink of the grave, Salome and John are not seen coming with sweet smelling spices to anoint Jesus' body. There are no longer any such orphan children who would weep and wail upon the Parent's grave. Doubtless they have become grown men and fathers in the Christianity that they need no longer weep and sigh for the Parent. Indeed, how would the children still weep, since the Parent has died long ago, and they themselves have become men and fathers in the Christianity, so that they no longer need the Parent's care. Alas, alas! How soon these grown children have forgotten the Parent's love; how soon they have forgotten with what great suffering and shedding of blood the Parent has borne them and with what anxious care the Parent has fed and brought them up. To be sure, the young of the martin are able to fly by now; but who knows how long they will fly? I have seen some young martins drop down on the dunghill when they begin to trust in their own strength too soon, and fly away from their nest before their wings can carry them; and when they drop on to the dunghill, then will come snowstorms, tempests, chill, and famine. And as they do not have strength to fly up into the Parent's nest, they must die of cold and hunger on the dunghill.

Woe, woe, unto you! You unfortunate young martin, who began to trust in your own strength too soon; why did you leave the Parent's nest before your wings could carry you? The Parent now beholds you with pity as you lie in the snowstorm and tempest on this earth; but he cannot lift you up from the ground, and carry you back into the nest, since you have become so big and so heavy that he can no longer lift and carry you. Yet you are so helpless and strengthless that by yourselves you cannot fly up into the air, and now you unfortunate weaklings may be left to die in this cold weather, while the other young martins that have stayed in their nests until they became strong will fly away into a warm climate, which is on the other side of the earth, where the sun shines directly overhead without ever setting; but you will be left to die in this cold climate, where there is neither food nor drink during zero weather. It will happen thus to the young martin that leave the parent's nest too soon, or before their wings will carry them.

Let those few souls who are still living, in whose hearts there still is the spirit of life, who have not yet become blind, who still see, where the way leads to heaven, step up to mount Sion and behold the bones of the dead that lie scattered about. Who will give life to them who lie thus scattered in the world's field? They are the children of the world who have died in sin under the great firmament, the children to whom the heavenly Parent has once given birth on his knees, in the bloodbath, with much pain and shedding of blood. But the devil has slain them, and great sorrow has come to the Parent over those children, who die so young. Now he must sit upon the grave of those children, and weep as did Rachel, who would not be comforted. Although it would be more fitting for the children to sit upon the Parent's grave and weep, longing for his merciful presence. But the Parent must now mourn for the children who have died so young. It is likely that he will no more see the children who have sunk into the grave of dead faith; there they will decay and nothing but the bones will remain.

What should we say about the children who have died so young? That great sorrow comes to the Parent over them that he longs and still calls their names after their death. O my Son! cried David, after the death of his son. O my son Absalom! But what do the dead children know about it, no matter how much the sorrowful Parent should cry, O my Son! Dead children no longer hear the loving Parent's cry, and though the Parent sheds bitter tears upon their grave, they know nothing of them. Being that there are not many children living anymore who call on his name and call him Father, I pity the children who have died so young, and it is pitiful for me to behold what great sorrow has come to the Parent. But I cannot comfort him, neither can I resurrect those dead ones, but I must say to the few souls who are still living that they beware of traveling dangerous paths, where the enemy is watching, screaming, and roaring as a bear or a lion that comes out of its den. Amen.

5

19TH-CENTURY SCANDINAVIAN HYMNODY

The hymns of the Scandinavian awakening movements were perhaps the single greatest source of their strength, and many of these hymns remain powerful and beloved up to this day. Borrowing vivid and subjective imagery from Lutheran and Moravian piety and from examples of Anglo-American gospel hymnody, these hymns express deeply personal elements of faith and hope. Women were prominent hymn writers, contributing in this manner when other forms of religious expression were not always open to them.

CAROLINA SANDELL-BERG (1832–1903)

"Children of the Heavenly Father"

Children of the Heav'nly Father safely in his bosom
gather;
Nestling bird nor star in heaven such a refugee e'er was
given.

God his own doth tend and nourish, in his holy courts
they flourish.
From all evil things he spares them, in his mighty arms
he bares them.

Neither life nor death shall ever from the Lord his
children sever;
Unto them his grace he showeth, and their sorrows all he
knoweth.

Though he giveth or he taketh, God his children ne'er
forsaketh;
His the loving purpose solely to preserve them pure and
holy.

(Trans. Ernst W. Olson, 1870–1958)

SUNG TO: "Tryggare kan ingen vara," Swedish folk tune

"Day by Day"

Day by day, your mercies, Lord, attend me, bringing
comfort to my anxious soul.
Day by day, the blessings, Lord, you send me draw me
nearer to my heav'nly goal.
Love divine, beyond all mortal measure, brings to naught
the burdens of my quest;
Savior lead me to the home I treasure, where at last I'll
find eternal rest.

Day by day, I know you will provide me strength to serve
and wisdom to obey;
I will seek your loving will to guide me o'er the paths I
struggle day by day.
I will fear not evil of the morrow, I will trust in your
enduring grace.
Savior help me bear life's pain and sorrow till in glory I
behold your face.

Oh, what joy to know that you are near me when my
burdens grow too great to bear;
Oh, what joy to know that you will hear me when I
come, O Lord, to you in prayer.
Day by day, no matter what betide me, you will hold me
ever in your hand.
Savior with your presence here to guide me, I will reach
at least the promised land.

(Trans. Robert Leaf, 1936–2005)
SUNG TO: "Blott en dag," Oskar Ahnfelt, 1813–82

CARL OLOF ROSENIUS (1816–1868)

"With God as Our Friend"

With God as our friend, with his Spirit and Word,
All sharing together the feast of the Lord,

We face with assurance the dawn of each day
And follow the Shepherd; and follow the Shepherd,
Whose voice we have heard and whose will we obey.

In perilous days, filled with storms and with fright,
A band marches on through thick gloom toward the
light.
Not many, nor mighty, disowned by the world,
They follow their leader; they follow their leader,
In confident faith, with their banners unfurled.

O Shepherd, abide with us, care for us still,
And lead us and guide us and teach us your will,
Until in your heavenly fold we shall sing
Our thanks and our praises; our thanks and our praises,
To God and the Lamb, our Redeemer and king.

(Trans. *Lutheran Book of Worship*, 1978)
SUNG TO: "Ack, saliga stunder," Oskar Ahnfelt, 1813–82

CARL BOBERG (1850–1940)

"O Mighty God, When I Behold the Wonder" ("How Great Thou Art")

O mighty God, when I behold the wonder
Of nature's beauty, wrought by words of thine,
And how thou leadest all from realms up yonder,
Sustaining earthly life with love benign,

(*Refrain*) With rapture filled, my soul thy name would
laud, O mighty God! O mighty God!
With rapture filled, my soul thy name would laud, O
mighty God! O mighty God!

When I behold the heavens in their vastness,
Where golden ships in azure issue forth,
Where sun and moon keep watch upon the fastness
Of changing seasons and of time on earth, *(refrain)*

And when I hear the roar of storm and thunder,
When lightning cleaves the heavy sky in twain,
And rainbow fair, the sign of promise tender,
Reveals itself when end refreshing rain, *(refrain)*

And when I see, in Holy Scripture reading,
Thy deeds, O God, on earth since birth of man,
Thy grace and wisdom that is shown in leading
Thy people ever safe across life's span, *(refrain)*

When I behold thy Son to earth descending,
To heal and save and teach distressed mankind,
When evil flees and death is seen recoiling
Before the glory of the Lord divine, *(refrain)*

And when at last the mists of time have vanished
And I in truth my faith confirmed shall see,
Upon the shores where earthly ills are banished
I'll enter, Lord, to dwell in peace with thee. *(refrain)*

(Trans. E. Gustav Johnson, 1893–1974)
SUNG TO: "O store Gud," Swedish folk tune

NIKOLAI F. S. GRUNDTVIG (1783–1872)

"Built on a Rock"

Built on a rock the church shall stand, even when
steeples are falling;
Crumbled have spires in ev'ry land, bells still are
chiming and calling—

Calling the young and old to rest, calling the souls of
those distressed,
Longing for life everlasting.

Surely, in temples made with hands God the Most High
is not dwelling—
High in the heav'ns his temple stands, all earthly temples
excelling.
Yet God who dwells in heav'n above deigns to abide with
us in love,
Making our bodies his temple.

Christ builds a house of living stones: we are his own
habitation;
He fills our hearts, his humble thrones, granting us life
and salvation.
Where two or three will seek his face, he in their midst
will show his grace,
Blessings on them bestowing.

Yet in this house, an earthly frame, Jesus the children is
blessing;
Hither we come to praise his name, faith in our Savior
confessing.
Jesus to us his Spirit sent, making with us his
covenant,
Granting his children the kingdom.

Through all the passing years, O Lord, grant that, when
church bells are ringing,
Many may come to hear your Word, who here this
promise is bringing,
"I know my own, my own know me; you, not the world,
my face shall see;
My peace I leave with you. Amen."

(Trans. Carl Doving, adapted)

SUNG TO: "Kirken den er et gammelt hus," Ludvig Lindeman, 1812–87

"O Day Full of Grace"

O day full of grace which we behold, now gently to view ascending,
Thou over the earth thy reign unfold, good cheer to all mortals lending,
That children of light of every clime may prove that the night is ending.

How blest was that gracious morning hour, when God in our flesh was given;
Then flushed the dawn with light and power, that spread through the darkened heaven;
Then rose o'er the world that sun divine, which gloom from our hearts has driven.

Yea, were every tree endowed with speech, and every leaflet singing,
They never with praise his worth could reach, though earth with their praises were ringing,
Who fully could praise the light of life, who light to our souls is bringing.

As birds in the morning sing God's praise, his fatherly love we cherish,
For giving to us this day of grace, for life that shall never perish,
His church he has kept these thousand years, and hungering souls did nourish.

We journey into our fatherland, where day is not frail or fleeting,
We vision a mansion, fair and grand, where joyously friends are meeting,
This life we shall share eternally, its dawn we are always greeting.

(Trans. Carl Doving)

SUNG TO: "Den signede dag," Christoph E. F. Weyse, 1774–1842

VILHELM S. P. BIRKEDAL (1809–1892)

"I Saw Him in Childhood"

I saw him in childhood with eyes brightly
  beaming,
In rays of the rainbow on mountaintops
  gleaming;
He fondly embraced me, my fancy befriending,
But veiled by the verdure the cross was
  impending.

I saw him in youth when all life was adorning
The flights of my spirit in glorious morning.
He beckoned my soul as the glow of his portal
Shed radiance and rapture on all that was mortal.

I saw him in midlife, in holy decorum;
The sinner surrendered in judgment before him;
And, trembling my heart in contrition was
  burning,
As death terror closed o'er my spirit in yearning.

'Twas then I beheld him as merciful Savior
Whose cross lost offense and restored me to
  favor
Embracing my burden I found a reunion;
The Savior and sinner once more in
  communion.

Again I shall see him when evening comes
  o'er me.
When daylight shall silently cadence before me.
And death o'er my vision dim shadows is casting,
O then I shall greet him in joy everlasting.

(Trans. Oscar Overby)

SUNG TO: "Jeg så ham som barn," Norwegian folk tune

JOHAN LUDVIG RUNEBERG (1804–1877)

"I Lift My Eyes unto Heaven Above"

I lift my eyes unto heaven above, and fold my hands to
draw near thee;
For thou, dear Lord, dost thy children love, and thou
hast promised to hear me.

How sweet to bless thee and praise the Name, for thou,
O Christ, art my Savior;
Kind Shepherd, guard me from sin and shame, and let
me love thee forever.

A little flower in thy garden fair, my life to thee has been
given;
O Savior, keep me in thy dear care, and bring me safely
to heaven.

Dear Lord, I thank thee for all thy love and gifts divine
beyond measure;
A sweeter song I will raise above to thee, my heart's
dearest treasure.

(Trans. Aino Lilja Kantonen-Halkola)
SUNG TO: "I lift my eyes," Rudolph Lagi, 1823–68

WILHELMI MALMIVAARA (1854–1922)

"Lord, as a Pilgrim"

Lord, as a pilgrim through life I go; each day your loving
presence I know.
Travel beside me, strengthen and guide me, Shepherd
divine!

Friends have forsaken; you have stood fast; you have
been faithful, true to the last;
Much I offended, yet you extended friendship divine!

You are my refuge; grant me, I pray, strength for each
burden, light for each day,
Comfort in sorrow, grace for tomorrow, Savior divine!

Lord let your presence brighten the night till the last
sunrise; then in your might,
Pardon and spare me, summon and bear me homeward
at last.

(Trans. Gilbert E. Doan)

SUNG TO: "Oi Herra, jos mä matkamies mann," Mikael Nyberg, 1871–1940

VALDIMAR BRIEM (1848–1930)

"How Marvelous God's Greatness"

How marvelous God's greatness, how glorious his might,
To this the world bears witness in wonders day and night.
In form of flower and snowflake, in morn's resplendent
birth,
In afterglow at even, in sky and sea and earth.

Each tiny floweret whispers the great Lifegiver's name;
The mighty mountain masses his majesty proclaim;
The hollow vales are hymning God's shelter for his own;
The snow-capped peaks are pointing to God's almighty
throne.

The ocean's vast abysses in one grand psalm record
The deep mysterious counsels and mercies of the Lord;
The icy waves of winter are thundering on the strand;
E'en grief's chill stream is guided by God's all-gracious
hand.

The starry hosts are singing through all the light strewn
sky
Of God's majestic temple and palace courts on high;
When in these outer chambers, such glory gilds the
night,
What the transcendent brightness of God's eternal light!

(Trans. Charles Venn Pilcher)
SUNG TO: "Blomstertid," Swedish *Koralbok*, 1697

WILHELM A. WEXELS (1797–1866)

"Oh, Happy Day When We Shall Stand"

Oh, happy day when we shall stand amid the heav'nly
throng;
And sing with hosts from ev'ry land the new celestial song,
The new celestial song.

Oh, blessed day when Christ shall come and show
himself as Lord,
And thousands meet in their new home which Jesus has
prepared,
Which Jesus has prepared.

Oh, what a mighty rushing flood of joy and love and peace
Will roll down over us with good and blessedness and
grace,
And blessedness and grace.

O Lord, your grace is ev'rything; your love has made us
free
To stand among the saints and sing the glory that we see,
The glory that we see.

(Trans. composite, *Lutheran Book of Worship*)
SUNG TO: "Lobt Gott, Ihr Christen," Nikolaus Herrman, 1480–1561

MAGNUS B. LANDSTAD (1802–1880)

"I Know of a Sleep in Jesus' Name"

I know of a sleep in Jesus' name, a rest from all toil and
sorrow;
Earth folds in its arms my weary frame and shelters it till
the morrow;
With God I am safe until that day when sorrow is gone
forever.

I know of a blessed eventide, and when I am faint and weary,
At times with the journey sorely tried through hours that
are long and dreary,
Then often I yearn to lay me down and sink into
peaceful slumber.

I know of a morning bright and fair when tidings of joy
shall wake us,
When songs from on high shall fill the air and God to
his glory take us,
When Jesus shall bid us rise from sleep; how joyous that
hour of waking!

(Trans. Carl Doving)

SUNG TO: "Den signede dag," Christoph E. F. Weyse, 1774–1842

LARS OFTEDAL (1836–1900)

"My Heart Is Longing to Praise My Savior"

My heart is longing to praise my Savior and glorify his
name in song and prayer;
For he has shown me his wondrous favor and offered me
all heav'n with him to share.

O blessed Jesus, what you have given, through dying on the cross in bitter pain,
Has filled my heart with the peace of heaven; my winter's gone, and spring is mine again.

O Christian friends, let our song ascending give honor, praise to him who set us free!
Our tribulations may seem unending; but soon with him we shall forever be.

Soon we are home and shall stand before him; what matter then that we have suffered here?
Then he shall crown us, while we adore him; so death and all our pains will disappear.

(Trans. Peter Andrew Sveegen, 1881–1959)
SUNG TO: "Å, at jeg kunne," Norwegian folk tune

BERTHE CANUTTE AARFLOT (1795–1859)

"Come Friends and Stand Beside My Gravestone"

Come, friends, and stand beside my gravestone, where I am hidden in the dust.
Let my example be your warning to think about your coming death.
And take to heart each one of you and use the time that you have left.

Our days are quickly disappearing which you must rightly realize.
Too many think their days are many then suddenly are in their graves.
O take this time of grace today to kill your sin with your own might.

O do not grieve for me, my loved ones, be joyful in the
will of God.
Think only that we are but pilgrims, our dwelling place,
it is not here.
Farewell, go forth, review your life, do not forget your
final strife!

(Trans. Gracia Grindal, 1943–)
SUNG TO: "Wer nur den lieben Gott," George Neumark 1621–81

MARIE WEXELSEN (1832–1911)

"I Am so Glad Each Christmas Eve"

I am so glad each Christmas Eve, the night of Jesus'
birth!
Then like the sun the star shone forth, and angels sang
on earth.

The little child in Bethlehem, he was a king indeed!
For he came down from heav'n above to help a world in
need.

He dwells again in heaven's realm, the Son of God
today;
And still he loves his little ones and hears them when
they pray.

I am so glad each Christmas Eve! His praises then I sing;
He opens now for ev'ry child the palace of the King.

And so I love each Christmas Eve, and I love
Jesus too;
And that he loves me every day I know so well is true.

(Trans. Peter Sveegen, 1881–1959)
SUNG TO: "Jeg er så glad," Peder Knudsen, 1819–63

NILS FRYKMAN (1842–1911)

"I Have a Friend Who Loveth Me"

I have a friend who loveth me, he gave his life
  on Calvary;
Upon the cross my sins he bore, and I am saved
  forevermore.

(*Refrain*) O hallelujah, he's my friend! He guides me to
  the journey's end;
He walks beside me all the way and will bestow a crown
  someday.

My Savior's love, so full and free, doth light the weary
  way for me,
It fills with joy each passing day and drives my sorrow
  all away.

I have a friend, a mighty friend, upon his pow'r I may
  depend;
He reigneth over ev'ry land, o'er valley, hill, o'er sea and
  strand.

O brother, join us in our song! This friend to you would
  fain belong;
Tho far from what you'd like to be, his grace sufficient is
  for thee.

(Trans. Chester Ringdahl)

SUNG TO: "Frykman," Nils Frykman, 1842–1911

MELCHIOR FALK GJERTSEN (1847–1913)

"I Know a Way Besieged"

I know a way besieged and thronging with pain and
sorrow, steep and long;
But on that way resounds a song of testing faith and
heav'nly longing.
It is the way the Christians trod to gain the crown of life
with God.
'Mid tribulations thronging.

I know a friend who never fails me, when sore oppressed
I ply the way.
In death he is my stay, my solace when the storm assails
me;
A friend so mighty and so fair, no mortal can with him
compare;
A friend who never fails me.

I know a robe of matchless splendor in which all earthly
glories fade;
A raiment rich and heaven-made for sinners who to
Christ surrender;
A wedding robe to cover shame and shield from God the
sinner's blame;
A robe of matchless splendor.

I know a call that breaks my prison when restful rays at
evening burn;
When winter scenes no more return, but glad celestial
spring is risen;
When pending petal press the sod, and roses, blossom-
ing with God
Awake to break their prison.

I know a home of joy eternal, where all the pilgrim hosts
shall meet
In radiant light, their bliss complete around the Christ in
realms supernal,
From north and south, from east and west, they gather
there with all the blest,
At home in joy eternal.

(Trans. Oscar Overby, 1892–1964)

SUNG TO: "Eg veit ein veg så full av trengsla," Carl Israel Sandström, 1824–80

ACKNOWLEDGMENTS

The selections from the letters of Paavo Ruotsalainen are taken from Paavo Ruotsalainen, *The Inward Knowledge of Christ: Letters and Other Writings*, translated by Walter Kukkonen (Helsinki: Publications of the Luther-Agricola Society B 10, 1977), and reprinted with the permission of the original copyright holder, Luther-Agricola Society.

The selections from the works of Lars Levi Laestadius are from *The Voice of One Crying in the Wilderness* and *House Postilla Sermons*, published by the Old Apostolic Lutheran Church, Hancock, Michigan, and reprinted with their permission.

The selections from the works of Gisle Johnson are from Gisle Johnson, *An Outline of Systematic Theology*, translated by Johan Koren in "A Teacher and Two Students: Gisle Johnson and His Influence on Norwegian American Lutheranism," MDiv thesis, Association of Free Lutheran Congregations Seminary, Medicine Lake, Minnesota, 1984, and used by permission of the translator.

The texts to the hymns "Children of the Heavenly Father," "Day by Day," "With God as Our Friend," "Built on a Rock," "O Day Full of Grace," "I Lift My Eyes," "Lord as a Pilgrim," "How Marvelous God's Greatness," "O Happy Day When We Shall Stand," "I Know of a Sleep in Jesus's Name," "I Saw Him in Childhood," "My Heart Is Longing," "I Know a Way Besieged," and "I Am So Glad" are used with permission of Augsburg Fortress Press. The text to the hymn "Oh Mighty God" is used with permission of Covenant Press. The text to the hymn "Come Friends and Stand beside My Gravestone" is used with permission of W. B. Eerdmans Publishing Company.

The selections from Hans N. Hauge, *Autobiographical Writings* (translated by Joel Njus), Augsburg Publishing House, 1954;

N. F. S. Grundtvig, *Selected Writings* (translated by Johannes Knudsen), Fortress Press, 1976; and Wilhelm Beck, *Memoirs* (translated by Paul Nyholm), Fortress Press, 1965, are used with permission of Augsburg Fortress Press.

The selections from C. O. Rosenius, *Romans: A Devotional Commentary* (translated by Royal Peterson), Covenant Press, 1978, are used with permission of Covenant Press.

The selections from P. P. Waldenström, *Squire Adamsson*, are taken from Paul Peter Waldenström, *Squire Adamsson, Or, Where Do You Live? An Allegorical Tale from the Swedish Awakening*, translated from the Swedish, with commentary and notes by Mark Safstrom (Seattle: Pietisten 2013), and used by permission.

The selections from Henric Schartau, C. O. Rosenius (*The Believer Free from the Law* and *Faithful Guide to Peace with God*), P. P. Waldenström (*The Lord Is Right)*, Hans Nielsen Hauge (*Testament*), and Laache (*Book of Family Prayers*) are in the public domain.

Bibliography

19th-Century Scandinavian Piety in English

An asterisk (*) before the entry indicates a source for material published in this volume.

PRIMARY SOURCES

Vilhelm Beck (1829–1901)

*Memoirs. Edited and with an introduction by Paul C. Nyholm. Translated by C. A. Stub. Philadelphia: Fortress, 1965.

Nikolai F. S. Grundtvig (1783–1872)

*The Selected Writings of N. F. S. Grundtvig. Translated by Johannes Knudsen et al. Philadelphia: Fortress Press, 1976.

Hans Nielsen Hauge (1771–1824)

*"Religious Convictions" (*Reiser*). In Shaw, *Pulpit under the Sky*, translated by Berit Ringo, 211–34. Minneapolis: Augsburg Publishing House, 1955.

*"The Story of My Life," "Religious Experiences," and "Travels (*Reiser*)." In *Autobiographical Writings of Hans Nielsen Hauge*, translated by Joel M. Njus. Minneapolis: Augsburg Publishing House, 1954.

*"Testament to His Friends." In *A Short Account of the Life and Work of Hauge*, translated by C. Brouhagh, 82–94. 1890. Also in *Pulpit under the Sky*, 201–10.

Fredrik Hedberg (1811–1893)

**The Doctrine of Faith unto Salvation*. Translated by Erick E. Erickson. Thunder Bay, ON: Finnish Evangelical Lutheran Mission, Inc., 1998.

Gisle Johnson (1822–1894)

**An Outline of Systematic Theology for Use in Lectures*. Translated by Johan Koren. MDiv. thesis Minneapolis: Association of Free Lutheran Congregations Seminary, 1983.

Nils Jakob Laache (1831–1892)

**Book of Family Prayer: Bible Lessons with Meditations for Each Day*. Translated by Peer O. Strømme. Decorah, IA: Lutheran Publishing House, 1902.

Lars Levi Laestadius (1800–1861)

The Fourth Postilla of Lars Levi Laestadius. Hancock, MI: Book Concern Printers, 1985.

**Lars Levi Laestadius' House Postilla Sermons*. N.p.: n.p., 19—. One copy in the Luther Book Stacks of the Luther Seminary Library in St. Paul, MN.

The New Postilla of Lars Levi Laestadius. Minneapolis: Anderberg-Lund Printing, 1980.

The Third Postilla of Lars Levi Laestadius. Hancock, MI: The Book Concern, 1983.

**The Voice of One Crying in the Wilderness: A Periodical Published in the Years 1852–1854*. An American translation by The Old Apostolic Lutheran Church in America. N.p.: n.p., 1988.

Carl Olof Rosenius (1816–68)

The Believer Free from the Law. Translated and introduced by Adolf Hult. Rock Island, IL: Augustana Book Concern, 1923.

Daily Meditations. Translated by J. Elmer Dahlgren and Royal F. Peterson. Minneapolis: Lutheran Colportage Service, 1973.

**A Faithful Guide to Peace with God: Being Excerpts from the Writings of C.O. Rosenius*. Arranged as Daily Meditations to Cover a Period of Two Months with the Assistance of Bishop N. J. Laache. Translated by George Taylor Rygh. Minneapolis: Augsburg, 1923.

**Romans: A Devotional Commentary*. Translated by J. Elmer Dahlgren and Royal F. Peterson. Chicago: Covenant Press, 1978.

Rosenius' Devotions. Translated by A. P. Lea. Decorah, IA: Anundsen Publishing, 1943.

Paavo Ruotsalainen (1777–1852)

**The Inward Knowledge of Christ: Letters and Other Writings*. Translated and introduced by Walter Kukkonen. "Publications of the Luther-Agricola Society, B 10." Helsinki: 1977.

Henric Schartau (1757–1825)

*"Sermons." In *Henric Schartau and the Order of Grace*, translated by S. G. Hagglund. Rock Island, IL: Augustana Book Concern, 1928.

Paul Peter Waldenström (1838–1917)

"The Biblical Teachings on Sin" (1915). In *Covenant Roots: Sources and Affirmations*, ed. Glenn Anderson, trans. Herbert E. Palmquist, 127–33. Chicago: Covenant Press, 1980.

**The Lord Is Right: Meditations on the 25th Psalm*. Translated by J. G. Princell, Chicago: John Martenson, Publisher, 1889.

The Reconciliation: Who Was to Be Reconciled. Translated by J. G. Princell. Chicago: John Martenson, Publisher, 1888.

"Sermon for the Twentieth Sunday after Trinity" (1872). In Anderson, *Covenant Roots*, 102–15.

**Squire Adamsson: Or, Where Do You Live? An Allegorical Tale from the Swedish Awakening.* Translated and introduced by Mark Safstrom. Seattle: Pietisten, 2013.

SECONDARY SOURCES

General Works on Christianity in Scandinavia

Bergendoff, Conrad. *The Church of the Lutheran Reformation: A Historical Survey of Lutheranism.* St. Louis: Concordia Publishing House, 1967.

Hunter, Leslie Stannard, ed. *Scandinavian Churches: The Development of the Churches of Denmark, Finland, Iceland, Norway, and Sweden.* Minneapolis: Augsburg Publishing House, 1965.

Österlin, Lars. *Churches of Northern Europe in Profile.* Norwich, UK: Canterbury Press, 1995.

On the 19th-Century Revival in Scandinavia and Its Leaders

Arden, G. Everett. *Four Northern Lights: Men Who Shaped Scandinavian Churches.* Minneapolis: Augsburg Publishing House, 1964.

Hale, Frederick. *Trans-Atlantic Conservative Protestantism in the Evangelical Free and Mission Covenant Traditions.* New York: Arno Press, 1979

Saarnivaara, Uuras. *They Lived in the Power of God: Lutheran Revival Leaders in Northern Europe.* Minneapolis: Ambassador Publications, 2011.

Denmark

Thaning, Kai. *N. F. S. Grundtvig*. Odense: Det Danske Selskab, 1972.
Thulstrup, Niels, and Marie Mikulova Thulstrup, eds. *Kierkegaard and the Church in Denmark*. Bibliotheca Kierkegaardiana 13. Copenhagen: C. A. Reitzels Forlag, 1984.

Finland

Foltz, Aila, and Miriam Yliniemi, eds. "A Godly Heritage: Historical View of the Laestadian Revival and Development of the Apostolic Lutheran Church in America." Self-published, 2005.
Jalkanen, Ralph, ed. *The Faith of the Finns: Historical Perspectives on the Finnish Lutheran Church in America*. East Lansing, MI: Michigan State University Press, 1972.

Norway

Aarflot, Andreas. *Hans Nielsen Hauge: His Life and Message*. Minneapolis: Augsburg Publishing House, 1979.
Molland, Einar. *Church Life in Norway, 1800–1950*. Minneapolis: Augsburg Publishing House, 1957.
Shaw, Joseph M. *Pulpit under the Sky: A Life of Hans Nielsen Hauge*. Minneapolis: Augsburg Publishing House, 1955.
Skarsten, Trygve R. "Gisle Johnson: A Study of the Interaction of Confessionalism and Pietism." PhD diss., University of Chicago Divinity School, 1968.

Sweden

Olsson, Karl. *By One Spirit*. Chicago: Covenant Press, 1962.
Stephenson, George M. *Religious Aspects of Swedish Immigration*. Minneapolis: University of Minnesota Press, 1932.

Scandinavian Hymnody

Erickson, J. Irving. *Twice-Born Hymns*. Chicago: Covenant Press, 1976.
Grindal, Gracia. *Preaching from Home: The Stories of Seven Lutheran Women Hymn Writers*. Grand Rapids: William B. Eerdmans, 2011.
Ryden, E. E. *The Story of Christian Hymnody*. Rock Island, IL: Augustana Book Concern, 1959.
Stulken, Marilynn Kay. *Hymnal Companion to the Lutheran Book of Worship*. Philadelphia: Fortress Press, 1981.

INDEX